Helldorado
Bringing the Law to the Mesquite

William M. Breakenridge

HELLDORADO

Bringing the Law to the Mesquite

By
William M. Breakenridge

Edited and with an Introduction by
Richard Maxwell Brown

University of Nebraska Press
Lincoln and London

First Bison Book printing: 1992
Most recent printing indicated by the last digit below:
10   9   8   7   6   5   4   3   2   1

Library of Congress Cataloging-in-Publication Data
Breakenridge, William M., 1846–1931.
Helldorado: bringing the law to the mesquite / by
William M. Breakenridge: edited and with an introduction
by Richard Maxwell Brown.—Bison book ed.
p.   cm.
Originally published: Boston: Houghton Mifflin, 1928.
Includes index.
ISBN 0-8032-6100-4 (pbk.)
1. Breakenridge, William M., 1846–1931. 2. Frontier and
pioneer life—Arizona. 3. Frontier and pioneer life—Ari-
zona—Tombstone. 4. Arizona—History. 5. Tombstone
(Ariz.)—History. 6. Outlaws—Arizona—History. 7. Peace
officers—Arizona—Biography. 8. Arizona—Biography.
I. Brown, Richard Maxwell. II. Title.
[F811.B82   1992]
979.1—dc20   92-15378
CIP

♾

CONTENTS

ILLUSTRATIONS

HISTORICAL INTRODUCTION

AFTER growing up in a small Wisconsin town before the Civil War, William M. Breakenridge
(1846–1931) went West where he spent the rest of
his long life. In Colorado and the Great Plains
country during the 1860s, Breakenridge took part
in the Indian wars of that decade and was on hand
as a scout and courier when John M. Chivington's
men massacred Cheyenne and Arapaho Indians on
Sand Creek in Colorado in 1864.[1] Breakenridge's
era of the 1860s and 1870s in Colorado and adjacent states and territories also coincided with the
expansion of the West's far-flung railroad network.
Billy Breakenridge (or "Breck" as he was usually
called) worked on the Union Pacific, Kansas Pacific,
Denver and Rio Grande, and Santa Fe railroads in
various capacities from brakeman to surveyor and
road grader. His railroad work carried him, finally,
to La Junta in southern Colorado, a jumping-off
place for the raw territories of New Mexico and Arizona. A job guiding a party of Eastern settlers took
Breakenridge to Arizona in 1876 where he was to

[1]In addition to those cited in the notes to Chapter III, two
leading sources on the Sand Creek episode are Harry Kelsey, "Background to Sand Creek," *Colorado Magazine*, XLV
(Fall 1968), 279–300, and Michael A. Sievers, "Sands of
Sand Creek Historiography," *ibid.*, XLIX (Spring 1972),
116–42. Among treatments of the Indian side is Donald J.
Berthrong, *The Southern Cheyennes* (Norman, 1963).

put his skills as a horseman and gunhandler to new use as an officer of the law.

After brief stints in Prescott and Phoenix, Billy Breakenridge settled down in the wild, new mining boom town of Tombstone. By 1881, Breakenridge was employed as a deputy sheriff in vast, violence-prone Cochise County, Arizona, of which Tombstone was the seat. It was here that Breakenridge was to know such famous Western gunfighters as Wyatt and Virgil Earp, Doc Holliday, Bat Masterson, Luke Short, and Buckskin Frank Leslie. He also encountered the celebrated bad men, Curly Bill Brocius and John Ringo, and others. Breck had a talent for making arrests without violence, but he could take care of himself as he did in 1882 when he killed one outlaw and wounded another in a blazing pre-dawn shootout.

With the waning of Tombstone's silver bonanza, Breakenridge moved on to a series of jobs including those in which he served as deputy United States marshal and as special officer and, later, claim agent for the Southern Pacific Railroad. By the 1920s, Colonel Billy—as many then referred to him—had settled into an easy, reminiscent retirement in Tucson where he was not far from the scenes of violence in Tombstone and Cochise County that he had known so well in the 1880s. Colonel Billy loved to tell stories of the old days in Colorado, in Tombstone, and on the trail of train robbers as a Southern Pacific officer. Having mastered the typewriter as he had earlier mastered the saddle and the six-shooter, Breakenridge made the transition from making history to writing it. He became active in the Arizona Pioneers Historical Society and was elected president of that organization—to which he dedicated *Helldorado*—in 1927. Earlier, in 1924, Breakenridge wrote a series of newspaper articles on "Early Days in Tombstone" which became the germ for *Helldorado*.[2] The latter was issued during 1928 by a leading Eastern publishing company, Houghton Mifflin. The book was an immediate success. Distinguished by a plain-spoken authenticity, *Helldorado* earned praise for being "as clean-cut as the whiz of a bullet to its target" with a "most direct narrative style" "packing action into every line" with "no time for moralizing or romancing."[3]

The publishing of the regionally and nationally acclaimed *Helldorado* in 1928 inspired William H. Kelly, publisher of the *Tombstone Epitaph*, to sponsor in the town that was "too tough to die" the first annual "Helldorado" celebration in 1929. The four-day event included the October 26th anniversary of the 1881 gunfight near the O. K. Corral.[4]

Colonel Billy was a featured participant in the celebration, and the experience may have whetted his appetite to do another book—one that was to be

[2]William M. Breakenridge clipping file (Arizona Historical Society, Tucson).

[3]*Arizona Daily Star* (Tucson), October 28, 1928.

[4]Helldorado, 1929, manuscript collection (Special Collections, University of Arizona Library, Tucson).

written in conjunction with his friend, the Western writer, Eugene Cunningham. But the new book was not to be, for late in 1930 Colonel Billy was stricken with appendicitis. He survived the appendectomy, but five weeks later at the age of eighty-five he passed away in his quarters at the Old Pueblo Club in downtown Tucson on January 31, 1931.[5]

Breakenridge was not forgotten after his death. Lengthy, laudatory obituaries appeared in Arizona and Los Angeles and were topped by a prominently headlined notice in the prestigious New York *Herald Tribune*.[6] The old, former deputy sheriff who had helped bring the law to the mesquite of Cochise County had grown gracefully from the blue-eyed youth who was described as "stocky, powerful," and "quick-tempered, yet quick to smile" to the mellow old-timer who died, in Eugene Cunningham's words, "a modest, forthright soul, whose sense of humor was gentle, if keen, whose memory was like a filing cabinet, whose opinions were reasoned and tempered with kindliness."[7]

William M. Breakenridge was one of the thousand or more professional gunhandlers on the frontier. Myth and inaccuracy have often clustered around the real deeds and misdeeds of these men, but what has

[5]William M. Breakenridge biographical file (Arizona Historical Society, Tucson).

[6]Breakenridge clipping file. New York *Herald Tribune*, February 2, 1931.

[7]Eugene Cunningham, *Triggernometry: A Gallery of Gunfighters* (Caldwell, Idaho, 1941), pp. 90–91, 127–28.

been overlooked is that, while they emerged from the conditions of life in the pioneer West, the gun-fighting exploits of these heroes and villains were associated, also, with a profound change in American social and legal values in regard to homicide.

In traditional English common law as imported to America by the colonists, one could successfully plead justifiable homicide in self-defense only if it could be proven in court that one had obeyed the legal *duty to retreat* before killing in self-defense. Under this legal doctrine, one's first responsibility was to flee from the scene, in which case no killing could occur. But there were situations in which flight from a man bent on doing harm was impossible. Yet, even in such dire cases, the old common law used down to the time of Coke and Blackstone did not allow one, without penalty, to stand one's ground and fight and to kill one's assailant in self-defense. Instead, the common law held that one was obligated to retreat as far as possible—"to the wall at one's back" was the legal concept. Only when the wall was reached would the law allow one to turn and kill in self-defense.

In the United States during the nineteenth century, the duty to retreat was replaced with a new, typically American doctrine: that one had *no* duty to retreat but, instead, could *stand one's ground*, fight back, and legally kill in self-defense without first retreating or fleeing. State supreme courts of the Western regions upheld the stand-one's-ground doctrine and proclaimed, in effect, that the concept of duty to retreat was inappropriate to American society. These courts held that to flee or retreat from a homicidal situation was a cowardly act in keeping with neither the American character nor American conditions.[8]

Of thousands of Western gunfights, one of the most stunning and one that became a part of the legend of the West was the shootout in Tombstone to which Breakenridge devotes all of Chapter XI. This was known as the gunfight near the O.K. Corral in which Wyatt, Virgil, and Morgan Earp and Doc Holliday faced Ike and Billy Clanton and Tom and Frank McLaury with a resulting exchange of bullets that was fatal to Billy Clanton and the McLaury brothers. A month-long inquest after the event produced a finding by magistrate Wells Spicer that the Earps and Holliday were innocent of murder in the three deaths but had acted in self-defense in their capacity as peace officers. The decision was a controversial one, but Spicer's ruling was squarely in the context of the new Americanized law of homicide which allowed one to stand one's ground and kill in self-defense.

The spirit of the new American legal doctrine of stand-one's-ground and the distaste for the idea of retreat was summed up a century later in a story

[8]I have treated the duty-to-retreat and stand-one's-ground doctrines in the *Vanderbilt Law Review*, XXXII (January 1979), 232–50.

told by President Dwight D. Eisenhower in 1953 to
a Washington, D. C., audience. As quoted by Kent
L. Steckmesser,[9] the President paid tribute to the
face-to-face gunfight of the West:

> I was raised in a little town of which many of you may
> never have heard. But out in the west it is a famous place.
> It is called Abilene, Kansas. We had as our Marshal a
> man named Wild Bill Hickok. Now that town had a code,
> and I was raised as a boy to prize that code.
>
> It was: meet anyone face-to-face with whom you dis-
> agree. You could not sneak up on him from behind, or do
> any damage to him, without suffering the penalty of an
> enraged citizenry. If you met him face-to-face and took
> the same risks as he did, you could get away with almost
> anything, as long as the bullet was in front.

President Eisenhower could just as easily have
been speaking of Wyatt Earp or Billy Breakenridge,
for, as Eisenhower revealed, the Code of the West—
epitomized by gunhandlers like Hickok, Earp, and
Breakenridge—was to him, and to a great many
other Americans, the American code.

The transition from the social and legal doctrine
of the duty to retreat to that of stand-one's-ground
was a major influence on all Westerners and was a
principal reason why they were so often predis-
posed to commit violence in situations of conflict
and confrontation. Yet, as he undertook his duties
as a deputy sheriff of Cochise County during 1881,
Breakenridge found himself in a matrix of specific
local factors which made the county and its seat,

[9] *The Western Hero* . . . (Norman, 1965), p. 158.

Tombstone, a seething cauldron of strife and no-duty-to-retreat gunplay. Social, economic, and political tensions in Cochise County and Tombstone produced alignments and a clash in value systems leading to a series of violent events—all described here by Breakenridge—that are among the most sensational and significant in Western history.[10]

Cochise County, Arizona, was an arena of sharp political conflict in which Democrats were arrayed against Republicans in a way that was quite typical of late-nineteenth-century politics in America. The closing decades within the nineteenth century comprised the period in our nation's political history when the spirit of partisanship was most active, when the Democratic and Republican Parties were strongest, and when the percentage of voting by the enfranchised was highest. Arizona reflected the national pattern: there was hot competition between the Democrats and the Republicans at all three levels of government—the territorial, the county, and the municipal. Cochise County was characterized by a front of Republican Tombstone against the Democratically-inclined remainder of the county.

[10]The following discussion of Tombstone, Cochise County, and the Earp brothers is, in addition to Breakenridge's account, based on the sources cited in the notes to Chapters VII–XIV and on the following works: Howard R. Lamar, ed., *The Reader's Encyclopedia of the American West* (New York, 1977), pp. 327–29. Glenn G. Boyer, *Suppressed Murder of Wyatt Earp* (San Antonio, 1967). Alford E. Turner, ed., *The Earps Talk* (College Station, 1980).

The mine and mill managers and supervisors of Tombstone and its three satellite towns of Charleston, Contention, and Fairbank, as well as the business and professional men of these communities, tended to be Republicans. The Republican Party in Cochise County was, thus, an urban group whose members were often Northern in background as exemplified by the mayor, John P. Clum; mine owner and manager E. B. Gage; mine partner, banker, and diarist George W. Parsons; magistrate and attorney Wells Spicer; and Tombstone's chief marshal, Virgil Earp, and his brother Wyatt.

The rural/Democratic-urban/Republican split in Cochise County was sharpened by the economic dichotomy of the county which found the Republican Party clustering around the mining and milling industry which dominated Tombstone and its satellite mill towns while the Democratic Party focused on the pastoral occupation of cattle ranching. The value system of mining-oriented Tombstone placed a heavy emphasis on law and order as the basis for social stability and economic progress. Business and professional men in Tombstone were heavily dependent upon the vigor of the mining industry for their prosperity, and the mining industry was, in turn, heavily dependent upon the investments of outside capitalists, especially those of the eastern United States and California. Such investors were repelled by violence and lawlessness verging on anarchy which threatened their outlays of capital.

The value system that was predominant in the rural reaches of Cochise County was far different. Out in the county there was an emphasis on highly traditional values. Loyalty to family, individual self-reliance, and self-redress of wrongs were among the values most highly regarded. In reflection of a free-and-easy attitude toward rustling and outlaws that was often found throughout the rural West, there was little esteem for law and order as such. Although horse theft was strongly condemned, the rustling of cattle did not result in social stigma provided it was not directed against closely neighboring herds. There was general recognition that many respectable ranching estates had, in their early days, been built up with the assistance of rustling. Outlaw activity was widely tolerated as long as the culprits observed the universal customs of personal courtesy and respect for others.

As cowboys, many of the young men of Cochise County often took part in both legitimate ranching and the illicit activity of rustling. A host of the cowboys were from Texas or the South, and their more law-abiding fellow Texans and Southerners tended to excuse their brash young compatriots. Around the northern margins of Cochise County, the cattle king, Henry Clay Hooker, a New Englander in origin, was an indignant victim of rustling, but most of the rustlers of Cochise County concentrated their cattle thefts across the border in Mexico or against more distant neighbors like Hooker. As exemplified by Newman H. (Old Man) Clanton, not all of the rustlers were youngsters, but so many were that the term "cowboy" became a generic label for the rural outlaw faction of Cochise County which ran in a spectrum from full-time ranchers like the Clantons and the McLaurys, who actively dealt on the side in stolen cattle, to the professional outlaws and gunfighters like John Ringo and Curly Bill Brocius who had Texas cowboy backgrounds.

Yet, the alignment of the rural cowboy faction of outlaws against the urbanites from Tombstone was embedded in a deeper antagonism than even that of the lawless against the law abiding. The two factions represented, respectively, a cowboy pastoral culture *versus* an urban capitalistic culture. For the cowboys out in Cochise County who periodically made trips to Tombstone, the object was often a good time through drinking, gambling, and fornication. The tendency of the cowboys to enshrine Tombstone as a place of pleasure contrasted with the austere goal of the economically ascendant mine managers of Tombstone. The mining executives and their allies among the business and professional men saw young, booming Tombstone as a big-time mining center of the West which featured capital-intensive industry and technologically advanced hard-rock deep mining in the interest of steady capitalistic profit. In this image of the economic development of Tombstone there was hardly a place for violence-prone cowboys attracted by Tombstone's

faro layouts, dance halls, and loose women after
weeks of dusty toil out on the range. The conflicting
aims of pleasure-minded cowboys and profit-minded
capitalists created an insoluble mixture of opposing
tendencies that periodically exploded in violence.[11]

Headed by Wyatt and Virgil, the five Earp brothers formed a crucial bloc among the contending
forces. Wyatt Earp had served as a lawman in
Dodge City and elsewhere in Kansas, but in Tombstone Wyatt and his brothers wished to forsake the
Dodge City model and reverse the pattern of their
lives. The Earps were men-on-the-make attracted to
the possibilities of gain in fast-growing Tombstone
and the flourishing mines of Cochise County. The
Earps desired to be respected as successful businessmen, and they went in heavily for speculative investments in mineral properties and real estate.
They stood in well with such members of the social,
economic, and political elite of Tombstone as E. B.
Gage and John P. Clum, men who were also leaders
of the Republican Party in the boom town. Yet, the
Earps could not completely transcend the Dodge

[11]In its aspect as an attraction for gunplaying cowboys,
Tombstone resembled raucous Dodge City and other Kansas
cattle towns as treated by Robert R. Dykstra, *The Cattle
Towns* (New York, 1968), and Nyle H. Miller and Joseph
W. Snell, *Great Gunfighters of the Kansas Cowtowns, 1867–
1886* (Lincoln, 1963). In its aspect as a mining center dominated by aggressive capitalists, Tombstone resembled the
silver metropolis, Virginia City, Nevada, as treated by Rod-
man W. Paul, *Mining Frontiers of the Far West, 1848–1880*
(New York, 1963), chapter 4.

City pattern, for the habits of saloon life, gambling, and enforcing the law against cowboys as in Dodge City were what they knew best. Moreover, there was an interest in the gunhandling talents of the "fighting Earps." Tombstone mining and milling executives and business and professional men organized themselves in a vigilante movement known as the Citizens Safety Committee. In so doing they wished to stabilize life in Tombstone and convince actual and potential Eastern and California investors that Tombstone was an orderly city into which capital could be poured with a heady expectation of profits. The vigilante movement was unwieldy and never went into action. For day-to-day preservation of order, the Tombstone elite felt the need for the skills of Virgil and Wyatt Earp who had a knack for knocking cowboys on their heads and were never afraid to draw their six-guns against the outlaws or the unruly. As good Republicans, the Earps were more than acceptable to those who comprised the town establishment of Tombstone.

During 1881, a feud had developed between the Earps and Doc Holliday on one side and the cowboy faction on the other. In effect, the Earps and Holliday were violent point-men for the social and economic values represented by urban, industrial, capitalistic Tombstone while the Clantons and the McLaurys (supported by their outlaw allies, John Ringo and Curly Bill Brocius) were equally violent protagonists within the rural cowboy coalition of

Cochise County.[12] The festering conflict erupted in violence on October 26, 1881, in the prototypical Western gunfight of all time: the fatal encounter near the O. K. Corral. As noted earlier, the Earps and Doc Holliday were found, justifiably, to have slain their antagonists, Billy Clanton and Tom and Frank McLaury, in the enforcement of the law and in self-defense. Yet, the anti-Earp historian, Ed Bartholomew, joined by other but by no means all authorities, branded the episode as simply one of barefaced murder on the part of the Earps and Holliday.[13] The controversy is now more than a century old, and it will probably never be settled definitively. Whether the Clantons and the McLaurys presented a mortal threat to the Earps and Holliday as the

---

[12]In the factional fighting between the county cowboy element and the urban capitalistic elite of Tombstone, the numerous miners of Tombstone seem to have been neutral, probably because there were no issues in the feud involving their own wages and working conditions. In 1884, however, a pay cut caused the miners to go out on strike.

[13]Ed Bartholomew, *Wyatt Earp, 1879 to 1882: The Man and the Myth* (Toyahvale, Texas, 1964), p. 223 and *passim*. Among those agreeing with Bartholomew are Frank Waters and Odie B. Faulk. Strong disagreement with the anti-Earp interpretation has been registered by Josephine Sarah Marcus Earp, John Myers Myers, Glenn G. Boyer, and Alford E. Turner. The works of these pro- and anti-Earp authorities are cited in the notes to this book. Two earlier pro-Earp works—Walter Noble Burns, *Tombstone: An Iliad of the Southwest* (Garden City, 1929), and Stuart N. Lake, *Wyatt Earp: Frontier Marshal* (Boston, 1931)—are now rejected by both pro- and anti-Earp authorities as being badly flawed by exaggeration, inaccuracy, and mythology.

Earps claimed, or whether the Earps provoked their opponents and then, with Holliday, murdered them as others have claimed, the fact is that on the afternoon of the shootout, Wyatt and Virgil Earp and Doc Holliday were older, much more experienced gunfighters and were more determined and better prepared for a showdown than were the Clantons and the McLaurys. The Earp party also had an edge in that the first shots were fired, as the Earp family tradition maintained, by Doc Holliday and Morgan Earp. With the circumstances in favor of the Earps and Holliday, it is not surprising that the gunbattle ended with their triumph.

In *Helldorado*, Breakenridge declared that Tombstone was relatively safe for the peaceably inclined and that the spectacular shootings involved, principally, the lawless. Tombstone's image "as a wild and wicked city, with a man for breakfast every morning" was, as he wrote, "all a mistake." Yet, Breakenridge's point that the violent reputation of Tombstone was unjustified is belied by the large number of homicides that occurred in the town. The early-1880s Tombstone diarist, George W. Parsons,[14] demonstrated that Tombstone's negative image was highly accurate. Tombstone in the era of Breakenridge and the Earps does, indeed, conform to a pattern of two other comparably violent mining

[14]George Whitwell Parsons, *The Private Journal* . . . (Phoenix, 1939), pp. 92, 131, 142, 151, 177, 178, 186–87, 199, 209, 213–15, 270, 282–83, 286, 290, 296–300, 313.

towns in California: Bodie and Aurora. In studying
Bodie and Aurora, historian Roger McGrath found
that the homicide rate in these two towns was about
six times higher than in the most murder-prone
American cities of the 1970s. But McGrath noted a
significant difference, too: that, in contrast to many
American cities of our own time, robbery and rape
seldom occurred in Bodie and Aurora.[15] Such was
the case with Tombstone and many other cities of
the Old West. In Tombstone, therefore, homicide
was frequent, but, as Breakenridge emphasized, robbery was scarce and there were no reported cases of
rape. Violence like that found in Bodie, Aurora, and
Tombstone adhered, thus, to the image of the Wild
West which stressed the prevalence of face-to-face
shooting encounters.

Exemplified by the gunfight between the Earps
and Holliday and their Clanton/McLaury opponents, much of the violence in Tombstone and Cochise County was part of a struggle for power between
two well-armed, violence-prone factions. This was
a pattern throughout the West. Although Western
violence became a source of escape entertainment
for modern-day Americans who absorbed its images
through fiction and film, the men of the Western
frontier—entangled in the social and legal doctrine
of no duty to retreat—killed each other not for the

[15]Roger McGrath, "Frontier Violence in the Trans-Sierra
West" (Ph. D. dissertation, University of California, Los
Angeles, 1978).

fun of it, but for deadly serious purposes related to
the contest for social, economic, and political power.
Within this framework of violence, the personal
styles of behavior of the individuals involved could
vary considerably from the aggressive gun-play of
the likes of the Earp brothers and Wild Bill Hickok
to that of Billy Breakenridge. In Cochise County,
Sheriff John H. Behan had given his deputy, Breakenridge, the particular assignment of enforcing the
law against such dangerous outlaws as Curly Bill
Brocius and John Ringo. In the challenging task of
collecting taxes from the desperadoes and, when
necessary, arresting them, Breakenridge was highly
successful. His grasp of the psychology of the cowboy and the outlaw stood him in good stead. He
was a Northerner from Wisconsin, but William M.
Breakenridge got along well with the cowboy brig-
ands out of Texas such as Curly Bill and Ringo—
perhaps because, like the Texans, Breakenridge was
a Democrat in his politics. On the other hand, the
members of the cowboy-outlaw element respected
Breakenridge's manly talents as a plainsman, a trailer of Indians and bad men, and a handler of guns.
To boot, Breakenridge had a strong sense of Western humor with considerable emphasis on paradox,
exaggeration, and irony. It was a clever strategy of
Breakenridge to reverse tension-packed encounters
with outlaws into occasions of good-natured byplay.
Instead of taking offense at Breakenridge's request to
him to assist in collecting taxes in the outlaw center

of Galeyville, Curly Bill saw the irony and the humor in the plea and yielded to it. The theme, therefore, of Breakenridge's career as a deputy sheriff in Cochise County was his ability to enforce the law in the most dangerous circumstances without resort to violence. Only once did violence occur, and Breakenridge, although fatally wounding wild and young Billy Grounds, felt that if he had been allowed to handle the situation alone, he could have brought in both Grounds and his outlaw sidekick, Zwing Hunt, without injury to anyone.

Breakenridge was not directly involved in the feud between the Earps and Holliday and the cowboy faction, but, in a sense, he was in the middle between the two opposing social forces, for Breakenridge had an affinity for both sides: impersonally for the urban, industrial, capitalistic alignment as represented by the Tombstone-based Earp brothers and personally for the rural cowboys. Blending personal preferences with impersonal duty, Breakenridge operated on a theory of law enforcement that, despite his highly-valued proficiency with guns, played down violence. Breakenridge's great hero and model as a peace officer was not, for example, Wild Bill Hickok, who was famous for his killings as town marshal of Abilene, but Hickok's predecessor, Tom Smith, who effectively enforced the law without recourse to firearms. Thus, Breakenridge saw his mission, literally, as taming the bad men: cajoling them into obeying the law or accepting the consequence of arrest. In contrast to Hickok or the Earps, Breakenridge's mode was to handle things in such a way as to avoid the stand-one's-ground, no-duty-to-retreat confrontations that so often resulted in death to one or both participants.

Despite his ability to get along well with cowboys and outlaws and, thus, carry out the law in their midst, Breakenridge's life-long career in the West was resolutely spent on the side of authority. Aside from his many years as an officer of the law, Breakenridge was often in the employ of the West's greatest corporations and in contact with some of its most eminent capitalists and corporate executives. In his younger days on the Great Plains, Breakenridge had worked for the Union Pacific and Kansas Pacific Railroads, and in the same period of his life he worked directly for General William J. Palmer, the brilliant entrepreneur who built the Denver and Rio Grande Railroad. In spite of his friendship with desperadoes like Curly Bill and John Ringo, Breakenridge never made the switch (as did the Arizona peace officers, Burt Alvord and Billy Stiles) from the side of the law to a life of crime. After his terms as deputy sheriff of Maricopa and Cochise Counties and as deputy United States marshal, it was easy for Breakenridge to make the transition from his role as a public enforcer of the law to private employment as a special officer for the Southern Pacific, which he served in the years when that railroad was the greatest industrial corporation in the West. While working for the Southern Pacific, Breakenridge got to know the hard-bitten but aristocratic Virginian, Epes Randolph, who headed extensive operations of the railroad in the Southwest and Mexico. Great men of authority like Palmer and Randolph were fond of Breakenridge, and he served them loyally.

Although Breakenridge was a superb plainsman and gunhandler of the Old West, he tied his own career firmly to the railroad: the supreme modernizing force in the West that was outmoding the gunfighting exploits of the Earps and others. *Helldorado* is a personal record of one man's mastery of two contrasting dimensions of the frontier West: the traditional Western reality of the Indian fight and the gunfight and the growing Western reality of industrialization and corporate development. William M. Breakenridge flourished in the pioneer era of the gunfight and survived its dangers to grow old and successful in the modern West that greeted his own story, *Helldorado*, with nostalgia and a sigh for the old times that its author knew and loved best.

EDITOR'S FOREWORD
AND ACKNOWLEDGMENTS

THE TEXT as reprinted here contains occasional errors of fact. Because the author wrote about events that in most cases occurred forty to seventy years earlier, there are more than a few examples of misspelled names or incorrect dates. Whenever possible, I have corrected these and other errors by the use of footnotes throughout the text. Thus, when a discrepancy occurs between the text and a note, it should be assumed that the discrepancy is not the result of a typographical error, but rather of my use of a footnote to correct a mistake by the author.

The reader should note, too, that brief chapter titles have been substituted for Breakenridge's old-fashioned practice of providing only an outline of the contents of each chapter in lieu of a chapter title. Following the editorial policy of the *Lakeside Classic* editions, William MacLeod Raine's brief introduction to the original 1928 edition of *Helldorado* has been replaced by the present editor's Historical Introduction. Some of the illustrations in the original edition have been dropped in favor of other pictures in order to illustrate better the contents of the book. Also provided exclusively for this edition of *Helldorado* are the maps and the index.

I HAVE benefited from the generous assistance and encouragement of a number of fine individuals and organizations located in Tucson, Arizona: Margaret Bret Harte, Susan Peters, and C. L. Sonnichsen of the Arizona Historical Society; Harwood P. Hinton and Bruce J. Dinges of the University of Arizona; Lonnie E. Underhill; and the Special Collections division of the University of Arizona Library. Indispensable has been the aid of the staff of the University of Oregon Library.

RICHARD MAXWELL BROWN

July 26, 1982

NOTE TO THE BISON BOOK EDITION

Readers of *Helldorado* may notice William M. Break-enridge's insensitivity to ethnic and racial minorities. His use, for example, of the epithet *redskins* was typical in his time and is only now fading away in ours. What Breakenridge saw as a cavalry action or "fight" at Sand Creek (chapter III) others—even at the time and certainly since then—saw as a massacre of Indians by white troops. The best study of the episode is now Gary L. Roberts, "Sand Creek: Tragedy and Symbol" (Ph.D. dissertation, University of Oklahoma, 1984). The best book on the 1881 Tombstone gunfight near the O. K. Corral (chapters XI–XII) is now Paula Mitchell Marks, *And Die in the West: The Story of the O. K. Corral Gunfight* (New York: William Morrow, 1989). In *No Duty to Retreat: Violence and Values in American History and Society* (New York: Oxford University Press, 1991), chapters 1–2, I have expanded my own treatment of the doctrine of no duty to retreat, western gunfighters, the Tombstone troubles of 1881, and the career of Wyatt Earp that appears here in my 1982 introduction to *Helldorado*. For preparation of the 1982 edition I most gratefully acknowledge the aid, encouragement, and friendship of Frank H. Hoell. As the dynamic managing editor over many years for the Lakeside Classics published annually by R. R. Donnelley & Sons Company, Mr. Hoell has played a vital role in preserving for modern readers such enduring examples of Americana as *Helldorado*.

Richard Maxwell Brown
March 26, 1992

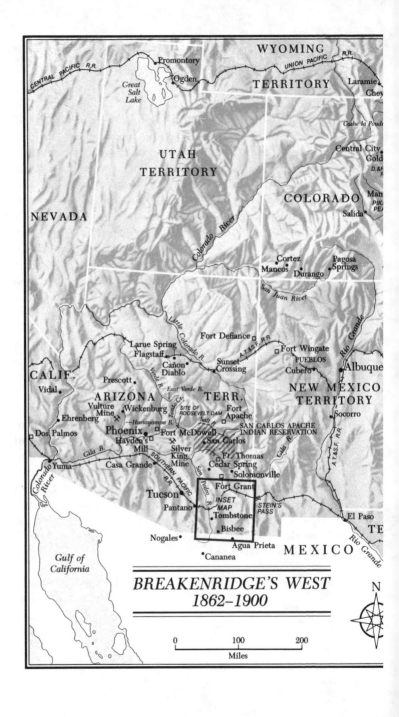

BREAKENRIDGE'S WEST
1862–1900

| 0 | 100 | 200 |
Miles

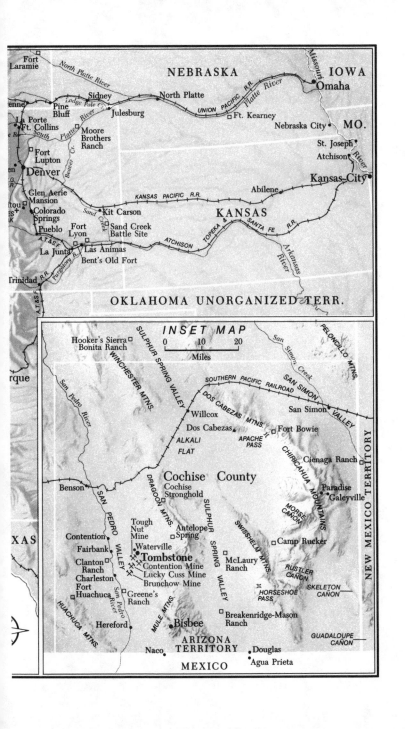

Helldorado
Bringing the Law to the Mesquite

I

Boyhood Days

SOME of my friends say that my life has been eventful enough to make interesting reading, and since a good deal of it was spent in helping to tame the Indians and bad men in Colorado and Arizona, maybe they are right.

When I was first urged to tell my story, I did not take the suggestion seriously, because I could recall old acquaintances—some on the right side of the law and some on the wrong—who could have told much better stories than mine. Their stories, however, never will be told, because every one of those old fellows is dead.

As I have already lived ten years beyond the allotted threescore and ten, it can't be long until I'll be travelling the same trail, but before I go I am going to tell some of the things I know about the West as it was before it was a misdemeanor to carry a gun, and before Geronimo became a Sunday School superintendent.

Talking about yourself always seemed to me to be a pretty poor kind of indoor sport. I never did much of it, and wouldn't do it now, except a few of my friends have been telling me how wrong it would be for me to die and carry off stories that

3

nobody else can tell, simply because there is nobody else left to tell them; if the idea of telling
these stories is wrong, blame my friends; if the idea
is good but the stories bad, blame me. So I will
begin at the beginning and tell my early history.

The first episode in my life was my birth; I was
born in Watertown, Wisconsin, December 25, 1846.[1]
Grandfather Breakenridge moved from Massachusetts in 1826 to Quebec, Canada, when father was
just a small lad, and raised his family there. When
father was old enough to set up for himself, he married a Scotch girl named Elizabeth Ross. There
were four children in our family; George, Nancy,
William, and Celeste. They arrived in that order.

Father was in the logging business in Canada, and
I often heard him tell, while talking with some of
his old companions, of the hardships and dangers
they incurred while bringing their rafts of logs

[1]Founded ten years before Breakenridge's birth, the village of Johnson's Rapids on the Rock River became the
small city of Watertown. By 1860 when Breakenridge was
fourteen years old, Watertown was the seventh largest city
in the state with a population of 5,302 composed of New
Englanders, Irish, and a large bloc of Germans. In its first
two decades Watertown had been the headquarters of horse
thieves and counterfeiters. Politically, Watertown was
strongly loyal to the Democratic Party. Although it contributed three companies to the Union Army during the Civil
War, Watertown was a center of Copperhead sentiment.
William F. Whyte, "Chronicles of Early Watertown," *Wisconsin Magazine of History*, IV (1920–21), 287–314. Writers'
Program of the Work Projects Administration, *Wisconsin: A
Guide to the Badger State* (New York, 1941), pp. 518–19.

down the St. Lawrence River, and of the fierce
fights at the river towns between the rival lumbermen who were driving the rafts. Quite a few of the
lumbermen of that time were French Canadians.

Grandfather and all of his children with their
families moved to Wisconsin, and until the Milwaukee and Western Railroad reached Watertown, father supported his family by hauling freight from
Milwaukee to Watertown. The road was a plank
toll road, about forty-five miles long, and he made a
trip once a week. In winter we had so much snow
he did his hauling on bob sleds. While I was still a
small boy he frequently let me go with him on his
trips, and I soon learned how to hitch up and handle his team.

As soon as I was old enough I attended the district school, which was the proverbial 'little red
schoolhouse,' situated in a large grove of maple
trees and about a quarter of a mile from the river,
where we had the usual old swimming hole. The
scholars were of all ages from the little tots learning
their A, B, C's, to the grown boys and girls who
worked on the farm during the summer and attended the school during the winter. As I remember it
we had no school during the summer.

My earliest recollection is of the Christmas when
I was four years old. My oldest sister, Nancy, took
me by the hand and led me through the snow to the
house of an old German woodchopper who gave me
a black waterspaniel puppy for a Christmas present.

I remember it was a bright sunshiny day and I carried the puppy partway home. We raised him and he became as one of the family. I named him Dick. He died soon after I left home.

My boyhood days were spent with my playmates in the usual ways of country children. The woods around our village were full of all kinds of wild fruit and nuts. In the fall we used to gather large quantities of butternuts, hickorynuts, and hazelnuts, and after shucking and drying them filled up the attic with them for winter use. In the meadows and hills were plenty of wild strawberries, raspberries, blackberries, and plums. We used to make a little pocket money gathering them and selling them to the housewives, besides furnishing our own mothers with plenty to put up in preserves, jellies, and jams.

In the spring of 1858, when I was eleven years old, my brother George hired out to a fellow townsman named Tom Smith, to go to Denver, Colorado. They started with a four-horse team loaded with provisions, and Smith intended to buy a freighting outfit at either St. Joe or Nebraska City, and go freighting across the plains to Colorado or some other of the Western Territories. At St. Joe, Smith bought a twenty-wagon train with four mules to each wagon, and he and my brother went through with a load of freight bound for Denver. When they reached Denver, Smith went into partnership with John Martin, an Englishman, and started a grocery store and a livery stable, and kept George on the

Platte route as wagon-master with the teams between Denver and the Missouri River. I remember
the whole episode very well because at that time the
spirit of adventure was strong within me, and I was
disappointed because they would not take me along.

I attended school until I was fourteen years of
age, and then I got a job as newsboy on the Milwaukee and Western Railroad.[2] I made very good wages
because, on account of the Civil War, newspapers
were in great demand. I bought them for a cent and
sold them for five cents and frequently sold over a
hundred on a trip. Small change was so scarce that
postage stamps were legal tender, but they soon got
spoiled and worn out. I wanted to enlist for the war,
but was too young, and could not get my parents'
consent.

About this time Hub Atkins, a conductor on the
railroad, who had enlisted as a lieutenant at the
beginning of the war, was wounded and discharged.
He returned to Watertown as a captain, bringing
with him a fine black horse and a Negro servant.
That was the first Negro I had ever seen, and, as he
used to let me ride the horse to exercise him, we
became friends, and he told me many interesting
stories about the South and the war. He used to go
swimming with us boys in the 'ole swimmin' hole,'

[2]The Milwaukee and Watertown Railroad (called the Milwaukee and Western by Breakenridge) was incorporated in
1851. It eventually formed a link in the present main line of
the Milwaukee Road from Chicago and Milwaukee to the
Twin Cities.

and we all liked him and made quite a hero of him.

In the winter of 1862, a Government agent came through the country hiring men and boys to work in the Quartermaster's Department. I left my job as newsboy in Milwaukee, ran away from home, and hired out with a lot of others. All the baggage I had was a small grip I carried on the train in which was a clean shirt and a comb and brush. I had on a fairly good suit of clothes and an overcoat. We were two days and nights on the train in the day coach, and on our arrival at Rolla, Missouri, at midnight we had to march three miles out to camp.[3] We had no blankets, but took shelter in a large tent with a big campfire in front of it, and slept huddled up to each other on the ground. As I had always had a warm, soft bed to sleep in, and mother always came in to see that I was tucked in carefully, I thought at the time I was being used rather rough.

The next morning we were given breakfast and taken to the Quartermaster, where we were sworn in for six months, given clothing and blankets, and parceled out to the different jobs. I was turned over to Mr. McNeil, a wagon-master who was fitting out a mule train to haul supplies to Springfield, Missouri. He was a fine man, and evidently had boys of his

[3]Located in southern Missouri, Rolla was an important railhead for the military operations of the Union Army and was the place to which the defeated Union forces retreated after the disastrous Battle of Wilson's Creek in September, 1861. Jay Monaghan, *Civil War on the Western Border, 1854–1865* (Boston, 1955), pp. 160, 164, 182.

own, for as I was rather young and small for my age he took me under his own care and had me sleep in the tent with him and the assistant wagon-master. When I told him my story he made me write to my parents and tell them where I was.

The day after our arrival we were sent to the corral to catch up the stock, and each man was told to catch up six mules. Most of the teamsters were clumsy farmhands and they caught up the gentlest ones first. McNeil told me to wait until they got through and he would help me pick out a team. The result was that I got six young active mules that were only just broken, and did not need the whip to keep them at work as the older, slower and gentler ones did. I remember that I had to stand on a water bucket to put their collars on, but I was naturally fond of stock, and had handled horses from the time I was big enough to help father hitch up his team, so I got along finely with the assistance of my friend the wagon-master. I took great pride in keeping my team in good shape, and saw that they were well fed even if at times I had to steal grain for them from the corral boss. Greasing my wagon was the hardest work, but the teamsters used to help each other.

My first trouble was with the teamster who drove the team ahead of me. He was a surly, grumpy fellow, and was always the last one to have his team ready. I always got up a lot earlier than the rest of the teamsters and was generally the first to have my team hitched and ready to travel, and that seemed to give him a particular grudge against me.

We used to corral our teams on each side of the road in a semicircle, with the wagons rather close to each other, and one morning after I had my team hitched up, my leaders swung around into his mules while he was hitching up their traces. They did no damage, but he lost his temper and struck one of them with his whip and began to curse me. My mules got scared and nearly broke the tongue out of the wagon before I could get them straightened out again. He was still calling me names. I jumped over the leaders' chain and came up to him as he was hooking his wheelers' traces, struck him over the head with the butt of my whip, and knocked him under the wagon. He was pulled out by some of the other drivers and came to just as McNeil came up. McNeil read the riot act to him and told him I had done just right, and that if he ever offered to abuse me again he would chain him to the hind end of a wagon and make him walk the rest of the way. I had no more trouble with him.

There had been a great deal of rain and snow, and the roads were soft. The lead wagons usually pulled through all right, but the road would soon become so badly cut up that the rear teams would have a hard time to make it. By yelling and throwing clods of mud at the mules, I went through with a rush and seldom got stuck or had to have help.

On account of bad roads and heavy loads, we

made slow progress, but at last we reached Springfield, where we unloaded our wagons, and then got everything ready to make the back trip to Rolla.

Jack, the assistant wagon-master, was taken sick and had to be sent to the hospital, and when we were ready to start back, McNeil told me to get Jack's horse and come with him. We rode into the corral and McNeil called the teamsters together and told them that as Jack was unable to return with us he had appointed me as assistant in Jack's place; that whatever I told them to do would be the same as coming from him, and for them to obey my orders just the same as they had Jack's. Our grouchy teamster was transferred to another outfit. The rest of the men were a good natured lot and seemed to like me, so I had no trouble. We were going back with our wagons empty, and made good time, but I was kept busy seeing that the men greased their wagons, cleaned their mules' collars, and kept their outfit in good shape.

When we got to Rolla, McNeil went to the Quartermaster, told him I was too young for the hard work of a teamster, and asked him to make a place for me in the store department. The Quartermaster did this, but I would rather have been with the teams.

When my parents got my letter which told them where I was, they tried to get me to come home. But when they found that I did not want to go back, they wrote to my brother George in Denver to try to get me with him. Mother wrote asking me to go to him, and soon afterward I received a letter from George telling me that, if I would meet him in St. Joe about the last of February, he would take me across the plains to Denver. I showed the letter to the Quartermaster and when he asked me if I wanted to go, I told him 'yes.' He gave me a permit to leave, paid me off, and after I had bid McNeil good-bye, I took the first train for St. Joe.

On my arrival there I went to the Bull's Head corral and livery stable, where Smith's teams always put-up, and learned that George had not arrived yet. The proprietor told me that I might sleep in the office, and if I wanted to work until George got there I could have a job driving carriages for him, but that I would have to keep my clothes clean and my shoes shined.

In about two weeks Smith, the owner of the out-fit, came in with the freight teams, instead of my brother. He had left George in Denver in charge of his livery stable, and I was to return with the teams and join my brother.

II

Off to the West

THE FALL before, the Ford Brothers, who ran a large gambling house in Denver, had left a fast trotting horse, which had been taken sick at St. Joe, in charge of the liveryman I was working for. They asked Smith to bring it out with him on his return trip. The horse was put in my charge to take care of on the trip. So with the horse hitched to a road cart, I followed the teams, and was proud to have a race horse to drive. Most of my time while we were in camp was put in rubbing down this horse. He was well taken care of.

We passed many camps of Indians on the Platte River, but as they were not very well armed at that time they professed friendship, and came into our camp begging and looking for something to steal, or a strayed animal that they could run off. They had to be watched carefully.

One day while we were in camp for noon, two mules got out of the herd and started up the road. They were about a half mile away when they were seen, and Smith told me to get on his horse and bring them back. There were several renegades in that vicinity who made a living by stealing strayed stock from freighters and then selling them to other outfits. I started after the stock and had nearly come up to them when two shots were fired from the hills close by and ticked up the dust in the road between me and the mules. Instead of turning back, I put my horse on a run and soon got ahead of the stampeded mules and turned them back. Smith heard the shots and realized what was up. He and his men took their guns and came running after me, and met me coming back with the mules. I was in luck, however, for the lay of the land was such that if the mules had got a quarter of a mile farther around a point of a hill the thieves could have got them easily.

When we reached Jack Morrow's ranch at the mouth of the North Platte River, I saw Bill Cody, or 'Buffalo Bill,' for the first time. I thought he was the handsomest man I had ever seen.

One of the very interesting sights to me during the trip was the Ben Holliday Overland Mail Stage, which carried the mail and passengers between the Missouri River and Denver.[1] Holliday had four- and six-horse teams, and bought the best horses that could be obtained. They made the trip of six hundred miles in six days. The stage stations were from eight to twelve miles apart, and the horses came

[1] Hard-bitten and often dishonest, Ben Holladay (1819–1887) organized his Overland Stage Line in 1862, absorbing Russell, Majors, and Waddell in the process. In 1866 Holladay sold out to Wells, Fargo & Co. and began building a spectacular but ill-fated career as a steamship and railroad promoter in the Pacific Northwest. James V. Frederick, *Ben Holladay, The Stagecoach King* . . . (Glendale, 1940).

into the stations and out again on a run. The stock-
tenders had the outgoing horses all ready to hitch to
the stage, and the driver never left his seat while
they made a lightning change. Then away on a run
for the next station! The freight wagons usually
stopped when they saw the stage coming, and the
stage would pull out around them.

There was no more excitement on the trip that I
remember, and after making a very successful trip of
it we arrived in Denver in good time, where I met
my brother and was certainly glad to see him. Billy
Ford gave me fifty dollars for taking such good care
of his horse, and I at once spent it for clothes.

At this time there were about twelve thousand
people in Denver.[2] It was a floating population.
Emigrants would stay over a few days to rest, and
would then move on either to the mining camps in
the vicinity of Denver or to some of the other Western Territories, while the teamsters would return to
the States for more freight and supplies. The streets
were crowded with people as the business section
was confined to a few blocks. On Blake Street, from
Sixteenth Street to Cherry Creek, a distance of two

[2]Springing up on Cherry Creek and benefiting from the
Colorado Gold Rush of 1859, Denver, incorporated in 1861
and boosted by developer William Larimer and editor William N. Byers, quickly gained permanent status as the state
metropolis. The city was named after General James W.
Denver, the governor of Kansas Territory. Lyle W. Dorsett,
The Queen City: A History of Denver (Boulder, 1977),
chapters 1–2. Gunther Barth, *Instant Cities: Urbanization
and the Rise of San Francisco and Denver* (New York, 1975).

blocks, were the wholesale houses, auction houses, corrals, and gambling houses. Fifteenth Street for the same distance, from Blake to Laramie Street, was full of retail houses, banks and restaurants, and on Laramie Street were the drygoods houses, but there were saloons on all the streets. There were three hotels—Sargent's, the Broadway Hotel and The Planters'.[3] Several large corrals and livery stables did an enormous business. The residence part of the town was built close to the business section, so that the town was very compact. This was true in the summer of 1863, but the place grew very rapidly from that time on.

I did not want to work under my brother, so I loafed for a few days and then got a job as a day herder with a cattle train that was returning to the Missouri River for freight. They had six-yoke of oxen to each team of two wagons, and there were twenty teams.

When the teamsters made camp they drove half the wagons on each side of the road in a semicircle. On the right hand side they drove so that the front

[3]Of these hotels, the Planter's House was not universally praised; its bar reminded an aristocratic English visitor in Denver of a "cockroach corral." By 1865 booming Denver had twenty-five hotels including the three mentioned by Breakenridge. Richard A. Van Orman, *A Room for the Night: Hotels of the Old West* (Bloomington, Ind., 1966), pp. 64–67. In referring to the Broadway Hotel, Breakenridge apparently had in mind what was in reality The Broadwell House of the 1860's whose proprietor, Broadwell, Breakenridge later mentions as Mr. Broadway.

Leading Denver hotels in the 1860's —
The Planter's House, 16th and Blake Streets, and
The Broadwell House, 16th and Larimer Streets.

left hand wheel of the rear wagon locked with the hind right hand wheel of the wagon ahead of it, and vice versa on the left hand side of the road, leaving the road open for other teams. This made a tight corral to hold stock with the exception of the ends, and the herders watched those openings.

In the morning the night herder would bring in the cattle to the corral of wagons as soon as it was light enough to see to yoke them. The train would then drive until about nine or ten o'clock when they would stop and make camp, turn the cattle out to graze in care of the day herder, and lie there throughout the heat of the day until three or four o'clock in the afternoon, and then drive until dark.

When we arrived in Nebraska City, we learned we should have to wait for a boat to bring freight up the river, so the cattle were turned out to pasture. While we were in camp two cattle thieves saw a small boy herding stock near the creek. They coaxed him into some willows out of sight, murdered him, and sank his body in the creek. Then they took the cattle into town and sold them. But the crime was discovered sooner than they expected, and they were arrested just as they were leaving town. A vigilance committee was formed and they were taken to the public park for trial. They were found guilty, and were hanged within three hours after they had committed the crime.

While waiting for the freight boat to come, I got a chance to hire out to a man named Saunders to go with him through Iowa as far as Ottumwa, which was by then the end of the railroad, buying cattle and shipping them from Ottumwa East. There were three of us in the party—Saunders, another cowboy, and myself. Saunders bought cattle wherever he could find them for sale and all three of us drove the herd. We drove slowly, and, as we didn't have a chuck wagon, we would stop any time during the afternoon that we struck a town.

We had covered about half the trip when a very curious thing happened. We had had a long monotonous drive, and we were mighty glad when, toward the end of the afternoon, we came to a little village where we could put our herd of fifty head into a corral, and all of us get a good night's sleep. Next morning we turned the cattle out to graze, and while Saunders and I got breakfast in the hotel the other man looked after the herd. As soon as I was through breakfast, I went out to the herd and the other man went in to his breakfast. I saw that a thunderstorm was coming up, so I bunched the cattle just as it began to rain, and started toward a schoolhouse nearby for shelter. I had hardly got away from the herd when lightning struck them and killed five head. There must have been five prongs of lightning struck, for the dead cattle were lying in the shape of a horseshoe, and about fifteen feet apart. My horse fell on his knees and I was thrown over his head, but I soon got up and reached the schoolhouse and shelter.

The storm didn't last very long, and we were soon on our way. But before we left, Saunders sold the dead animals to a local butcher for a small amount. I never could understand why he didn't get full price, as the meat wasn't hurt any more by being killed by lightning than if the beeves had been hit in the head with an axe. At Ottumwa, Saunders went East on the train with the cattle, and the other man and I returned to Nebraska City.

Here I got another job as a day herder for an outfit loaded for Denver. On this trip there was another boy two years older than I, who was working as an extra hand. He was in mischief all the time and as he could run very fast, they called him 'Antelope.' There was also a green Irishman, a driver, and whenever we met any teams he hailed them with, 'Hello, b'yes, how's times in Dinver?' One day while we were in camp he went to sleep under a wagon. Antelope, who chewed tobacco, crawled up and hit him in the eye with a quid of tobacco and ran, and was out of sight before Pat got his eyes open. When Pat realized what had happened, he crawled out from under the wagon, stood up, and said scornfully, 'I can lick any man that's mean enough to spit in another man's eye when he's down.'

Pat was afraid of snakes, and the men took delight in telling him snake stories. One day when the rest of the men were all asleep under the wagons, Antelope killed a bullsnake, which is harmless. He took a horseshoe nail and drove it through its head, and, bending the nail into a hook, fastened it to Pat's trousers. Then jabbing him with a pin, he yelled, 'Snakes! Snakes!'

Pat jumped up and seeing the snake fast to him, and feeling the prick of the pin, started running up the road holloing, 'Snake bit! Snake bit!' He nearly ran himself to death getting to a camp some three hundred yards from us.

When we got to Fort Lupton, the wagon-master went into camp in order to give the cattle, which were badly run down, about a week's rest. He then rode on into Denver to see the owners of the stock. About four miles from our camp was a place on the Platte called Frémont's Orchard. Instead of being actually an orchard, it was nothing more than a cottonwood grove. The teamsters, however, filled Pat up about the fine fruit down there, so the next morning he started afoot with a gunny sack to get some apples in Frémont's Orchard. He returned that night a sadder but wiser man, but he was still asking everyone we met, 'How's times in Dinver?' He got tired of lying in camp, so he started out for Denver afoot. It was about thirty miles from where we were camped. When the wagon-master returned, he moved the teams into Denver, and the very first thing we saw was Pat working in the chain gang. The men all hailed him with, 'Hello, Pat, how's times in Dinver?'

It seemed to me that I was always broke. I no sooner earned any money than I hurried to spend it. We had not been paid off, but I couldn't wait, so, as soon as I got my camp work done, I hurried off to my brother George, to get some of the clean clothes I had left with him and to borrow some money. He gave me some money and told me to go and have my hair cut, get a bath and supper, and come back to him, and I could sleep with him that night and not have to return to camp.

I had my hair cut, and got the bath and supper—and a mighty good supper it was, too—and I was on my way back to George when I heard a woman singing in a gambling saloon. Up until this time I had never been inside a gambling house, but I could not resist the singing and music, and I sneaked in, keeping close to the wall for fear someone who knew me might see me.

I worked my way close to the music stand, and after listening to several songs started to go out. Joe Frye, a gambler who knew George, and had seen me with him on my previous trip, jokingly said, 'Why, Billy, you are not going away without paying for that music, are you?'

I answered, 'No, sir; who shall I pay?'

He then explained that I should make a bet at his game, which was monte. I laid down a dollar and started out when he called me back and told me I had won. I moved it to another card and won again, and in trying to lose it so that I could get away, I won everytime, and left there with eighty dollars!

I hurried back to my brother with my hat full of

money and told him what I had done. He lectured me for going into a gambling saloon; but it did no good, I am sorry to say, for that first bit of luck has cost me many a dollar since.

Brother George wanted me to stay and work with him, but I didn't want him for a boss, so he got me a place in Sargent's hotel as night clerk. I quit teaming for a while, but I longed for the open outdoor life on the plains, and I soon left my work as night clerk and again went as horse wrangler with another train headed for the river for freight. As I had a remarkably good pair of eyes, I learned to be a good trailer, and frequently, when on a dark or stormy night some of the stock would stray away from the main herd in spite of the night herder, I would be sent out to find their trail and follow them up.

When I was just a little codger, my grandfather, who lived about two miles from Watertown on a farm, taught me to shoot squirrels out of the high maple and hickory trees with his squirrel rifle. I wasn't big enough to hold it steady without resting it on a stump or rail fence, yet I got so that I rarely missed one even in the top of a tall tree, and generally hit him through the head.

There was plenty of game on the plains; buffalo roamed in countless thousands, and antelope were nearly always in sight. At times when buffalo were crossing the road in large herds, the freight teams were compelled to camp, as the stock was afraid of the buffalo and was more than likely to stampede.

Occasionally when we made our noonday camp, I used to go hunting, and never went very far before I got a buffalo or antelope, so we generally had fresh meat. There was no timber on the plains for wood, and we had to use buffalo chips for fuel.

The first thing the men would do, as soon as camp was made, would be to take a gunny sack and start picking up dried buffalo chips for the cook to get our meals with. Because there was no timber, and the tall wavy grass would become wet with dew, the prairie chickens would come out and roost in the road. Frequently I would start at daylight ahead of the teams, and by sunup have bagged enough of them to feed the whole crew. And when they were cooked in the Dutch oven with strips of bacon, they certainly made a delicious meal.

The Indians were beginning to get restless and commit depredations. On our return trip we came across one camp where they had killed several men, run off the stock, and burned the wagons. The Indian agents were in partnership with the Indian traders, and the redskins were becoming well armed, as they would pay outrageous prices in buffalo robes and ponies for guns and ammunition. At Fort Kearny we were stopped by the post commander, and held there until we had one hundred men well armed in the party. This did not take too long, as there were a lot of emigrants going West. As soon as we reached our quota we selected a captain, who took charge of all the men and teams, and moved on.

Our captain had been an old Government wagon-master, and as soon as we got away from the fort we drove in the formation I have already described. Most of the emigrant wagons were lightly loaded, and could make better time than the heavily loaded freight teams. So they went ahead, but we generally camped close together.

The captain kept the stock under close herd and put out plenty of guards, and we got along all right until we came to the Jack Morrow Ranch. Some of the emigrant teams that were loaded light had gone ahead as usual, and when they reached that place, which had a shady reputation, drove down close to the river to camp. When the main part of the train got there, we made camp as usual on each side of the wagon road, and about a half mile from where the emigrants were camped. In the morning some of their mules were missing. The captain, who was an old hand in the business, put Morrow under arrest and told him that if the mules were not found within two hours he would have him hanged to the rafters in his stable. Morrow sent out his Indians, and the mules were in camp long before the two hours were up.

At Julesburg we were again held up for a short time, and for the same reason we were held up at Fort Kearny. This would not have happened but for the fact that some of the emigrant teams in our outfit were in such a hurry that they had driven around the post during the night. We did not have to wait long, however, as another train of one hundred men came along within a few days, and we went on with them toward Denver.

The Indians had driven off most of the stock belonging to the ranchers between Julesburg and Lupton, and had burned some of the ranches that had been abandoned. Between Julesburg and Fort Lupton the ranch owners had taken their families and moved on to larger ranches for protection. These ranches along the Platte River were places of supply for the immense travel that was on the road; they sold hay, grain, and provisions—mostly canned goods. The Indians, however, had driven off most of their stock, and had burned many of the abandoned ranches, so that supplies were not plentiful.

Although we frequently saw small bands of Indians on the bluffs after leaving Julesburg, and at night saw their signal fires, we had no more trouble and reached Denver without any accidents.

This time I remained in Denver for some time. My brother had gone with a mule train to Montana as a wagon-master, and all through the winter I stayed in Denver working at odd jobs. I got acquainted with a lot of the young people and enjoyed going to their dances and parties.

This was during the winter of 1863, a very cold one with many storms. Tom Smith, with whom my brother had left home in 1858, had made a great deal of money in Denver, and had decided to take a trip back East to our old home in Wisconsin. When he left, he took a man with him, drove a two-horse buggy, and led a favorite saddle horse. Smith was a hard drinker. One day a blizzard hit them, and in order to keep warm, Smith drank all the harder until he became utterly helpless. The snow became so deep that the horses could not make any headway, so his man turned the horses loose and bundled Smith onto the saddle horse, wrapped him up in blankets and buffalo robes, and then led the horse through the snowdrifts until they reached a ranch. He worked so hard trying to save Smith that he kept himself from freezing, but Smith was so badly frozen that he died soon after reaching the ranch.

During this winter the Territorial Legislature was in session at Golden City, and I got an appointment as page during the whole session.

In the spring I drove a team for a telegraph company that built a line from Denver to Central City.[4] When the line was completed I went to work as a messenger boy in the telegraph office at that place, and, as the mine managers were very generous, and always paid me well for delivering their messages promptly, I made good wages.

[4]Located about thirty-five miles west of Denver, Central City (founded in 1859) became one of Colorado's richest mining camps with the wealth from its gold mines forming the sound economic core of Colorado Territory in its early years. Writers' Program of the Work Projects Administration, *Colorado: A Guide to the Highest State* (New York, 1941), pp. 264–66.

III

Cavalry Action

DURING the fall and winter of 1863 and the spring and summer of 1864, the Indians became more and more aggressive, until hardly a day passed that they did not commit some depredation on the isolated ranches, or on emigrants coming into the country. All of the prisoners taken by the Indians were women and children.

Freight teams were pulled off on account of the raids, and provisions and necessities were getting scarce. Flour was forty-five dollars a sack, and other commodities in proportion. On account of the Civil War the Government could not spare any troops to send out West to protect the frontier, but the Secretary of War did direct Governor John Evans of Colorado[1] to enlist a regiment of volunteers for the purpose of operating in that country against the Indians. It was a one-hundred-day regiment, and was known as the Third Colorado Cavalry.[2]

At the time Governor Evans received authority

[1]Information about Dr. John Evans may be found in the Special Biographical Notes at the end of this chapter.

[2]The enlistment and organization of the Third Colorado Cavalry is described in Raymond G. Carey, "The 'Bloodless Third' Regiment, Colorado Volunteer Cavalry," *Colorado Magazine*, XXXVIII (October 1961), pp. 275–300.

to call for volunteers, the Hungate family lived at a sawmill some thirty miles up Cherry Creek from Denver. Hungate, his wife, and two children were murdered and mutilated in the most horrible manner. In order to arouse sentiment their bodies were brought to Denver and exposed on the streets, and a message was sent to Central City, and all other large mining towns, calling for volunteers to enlist in the United States Army for the purpose of going after the murderous redskins.

A meeting was called one evening by Hal Sayre at Central City and after several speeches volunteers were called for and a company of over a hundred men enlisted the same night. Boylike, I was one of the first to get my name down on the enlistment roll, and two days later we started for Denver. In my opinion exposing of the mutilated bodies of the Hungate family on the streets of Denver did not have any effect or arouse any more sentiment against the Indians than was already felt by the citizens of Central City and the adjacent mining camps where volunteers were being enlisted.

The regiment, called the Third Colorado Cavalry, was raised within a week. George H. Shoup was colonel,[3] under Colonel Chivington, who was commander of the division.[4] We were recruited for one

[3]Information about George L. Shoup may be found in the Special Biographical Notes at the end of this chapter.

[4]Information about Colonel John M. Chivington may be found in the Special Biographical Notes at the end of this chapter.

Recruiting poster for the Colorado Cavalry.
Courtesy Colorado Historical Society

hundred days' service. Our company of one hundred and one men was Company 'B.'[5]

We elected our own officers: Hal Sayre, a mining superintendent, was elected to be captain;[6] H. B. Orahood, a druggist at Central City, was elected first lieutenant;[7] and Harry Richmond, a tragedian with Languish and Atwater's theatrical troupe, second lieutenant.[8] Late that fall, just before we were ready to start from Bijou Basin, Hal Sayre was promoted to major and Orahood was made captain.

There was great difficulty in furnishing the horses and ordnance stores necessary to mount and equip the regiment, and two months had passed before we were ready to move; and then only a part of the regiment was ready for service. Our company was made up of miners, millmen, bankers, merchants, lawyers, businessmen and workmen, who had left their homes and businesses to fight the Indians and try to put a stop to their attacks. As soon as they

[5] As Carey, " 'Bloodless Third' Regiment," pp. 279–80, notes, Company B was composed of men from Central City, a town which had close contact with Denver.

[6] Information about Hal Sayre may be found in the Special Biographical Notes at the end of this chapter.

[7] Information about Harper M. Orahood may be found in the Special Biographical Notes at the end of this chapter.

[8] According to Carey, " 'Bloodless Third' Regiment," p. 284, Harry Richmond was an actor in Langrishe and Dougherty's theatrical company (not Languish and Atwater's as Breakenridge recalled). A fictionalized portrait of Richmond appears in *A Very Small Remnant* (New York, 1963), Michael Straight's novel based on the Sand Creek massacre.

were mustered in, those that wished to get it received leave of absence to return to their businesses until such time as the regiment was outfitted and ready to proceed against the Indians.

This was in August, 1864. Governor Evans received a message from a friendly half-breed named Little Geary, who lived on a ranch about seventy miles east of Denver on the South Platte. This man Geary was a great-grandson of one of the signers of the Declaration of Independence, but he had lived with the Indians for a great many years, and was married to one of them.[9] He had a Cheyenne wife and a large bunch of stock, and late one night two Cheyenne chiefs came to his ranch and advised him to get out at once. They told him that some eight hundred Indians were encamped about a hundred miles from Denver at the head of Beaver Creek. The band was composed of Cheyennes, Arapahoes, and Sioux. Their plan was to divide up into small parties, and two or three nights later to make an attack on each farmhouse or ranch all along the Platte River for a hundred miles below Denver; also on the post at Fort Lupton and from the head of Cherry Creek toward Denver, all at the same time, and kill, burn, and steal stock. Little Geary started early that same morning for Denver, arrived there that night, and at once reported to Governor Evans.

The Governor immediately put all the recruits

[9]Information about Elbridge Gerry may be found in the Special Biographical Notes at the end of this chapter.

George L. Shoup
Colonel

Hal Sayre
Captain, Co. B

Harper M. Orahood
First Lieutenant, Co. B

Several of the original officers of the
Third Colorado Cavalry.
Courtesy Colorado Historical Society

under the command of Colonel Chivington, and all that could be armed and mounted were sent out to guard and protect the settlements that were expected to be attacked. He also sent couriers to notify the settlers. A few days before this a militia company from Denver had been sent to Fort Lupton.

I was detailed to carry dispatches to Fort Lupton and the few ranches along the Platte. With the help of the corral boss I got my pick of the saddle horses, and I certainly got a good one! I believe I was the best mounted soldier in the regiment.

The Indians came in at the different points as was expected on the night designated, skulking along under the bluffs where their trails were seen the next day. They found that the settlements had been reinforced and were prepared to defend themselves, so they went back, but at the head of Cherry Creek they killed two or three persons and stole some stock, and before Little Geary could get back home they stole a few of his horses and ran them off.[10]

I was at Lupton the night they were expected to attack it, and was on picket duty about a half mile

[10] In retaliation for Elbridge Gerry's warning the settlers of the projected onslaught, Indians made heavy raids on Gerry's horse herds for which the federal government gave, in 1872, a reimbursement of $13,200 which he used to build the Gerry House hotel in the new town of Evans near Greeley. Gerry died in 1875 revered by the citizens of Greeley as the "first permanent white settler" in Weld County. Ann W. Hafen, "Elbridge Gerry," pp. 158–60, in LeRoy Hafen, ed., *The Mountain Men and the Fur Trade of the Far West: Biographical Sketches . . ., VI* (Glendale, California, 1968).

from the fort. There was no moon, but the stars were shining. I was on top of a small hill with my horse about twenty-five yards behind me under cover of the hill. I dared not get up and walk around, as I should be seen, and about two o'clock that morning I had to make a desperate effort to keep awake. It was a fearful feeling. I took powder from a paper cartridge and rubbed it in my eyes to keep awake, and when daylight came and I returned to camp I was wide awake again and did not go to sleep until afternoon. We rode out to the bluffs that morning and found where a small party of Indians had come up and then returned the same way they had come. We saw signal fires in several directions that night which must have been sent up to advise the redskins not to attack, as the fort and settlers were prepared for them. I have no doubt there would have been the most extensive massacre that night that had ever been known but for the precautions that were taken to prevent it.

About the first of September, 1864, Major E. W. Wynkoop, First Colorado Cavalry,[11] in command of Fort Lyon, received a message from Black Kettle, White Antelope, and several other prominent chiefs of the Cheyenne and Arapahoe tribes, that they wanted to make peace. The chiefs said they had some white women and children, whom they were willing to give up providing that peace was granted

[11]Information about Edward W. Wynkoop may be found in the Special Biographical Notes at the end of this chapter.

them, or whom they would exchange for two Indians who were with one of the companies of scouts.

Major Wynkoop went out to the Indian camp at Smoky Hill and reported that he found them drawn up in line of battle. He sent in an Indian he had with him to get them to hold a council instead of to fight; and he held a council in the presence of their warriors with their bows and arrows drawn. They agreed to allow Black Kettle, White Antelope, and Bull Bear of the Cheyennes,[12] and two or three Arapahoe chiefs to go with him to Denver for the purpose of making peace, and he assured them that he would see them safe back to their camp. Four white prisoners, a woman and three children, were delivered to him by Black Kettle, the head chief of the Cheyennes.

General Curtis[13] telegraphed Colonel Chivington that his terms of peace were to require all bad Indians to be given up, all stock stolen by the Indians to be returned, and hostages given by the Indians for their good conduct. The Indians would not comply with these terms. They said they had not received power to make peace on such terms. This ended their talk.

Major Wynkoop on his own authority did allow some of the Indians—a band of about six hundred,

[12]Information about these three Indian chiefs may be found in the Special Biographical Notes at the end of this chapter.

[13]Information about General Curtis may be found in the Special Biographical Notes at the end of this chapter.

together with the chiefs mentioned—to camp at or
near Fort Lyon,[14] promised them the protection of
our flag, and issued them rations as prisoners of war.
Very soon after doing this he was relieved of the
command at Fort Lyon, and Major Anthony placed
in command at that post.

Major Anthony required the Indians to comply
with General Curtis's terms. They at first promised
to do so, but did not carry out the promise. They
turned over some twenty head of stolen Government and civilian stock and a few arms, but not one
quarter of the arms that were reported to be in their
possession, and the arms they did turn in were almost useless. Major Anthony fed them for about ten
days and then told them he would feed them no
longer. He returned the few useless arms that they
had turned in and drove them from the post. This
took place on the 12th or 15th of November. Major
Anthony knew that they were not friendly and only
wanted to be fed during the winter months, and he
was afraid to have them so near the post.[15]

After the Third Colorado Cavalry was partly

[14]Fort Lyon (originally established as Fort Wise in 1860)
was a United States Army post located on the north bank of
the Arkansas River near the present town of La Junta, Colorado. It was named after Union Army General Nathaniel
Lyon who was killed in the 1861 Battle of Wilson's Creek in
Missouri. Robert W. Frazer, *Forts of the West: Military Forts
and Presidios and Posts Commonly Called Forts West of the
Mississippi River to 1898* (Norman, 1965), pp. 39-42.

[15]Information about Major Anthony may be found in the
Special Biographical Notes at the end of this chapter.

mounted and equipped, we were stationed at Bijou Basin, about sixty miles from Denver. I was detailed to carry the mail and dispatches.

We were armed with old out-of-date, muzzle-loading muskets, which were loaded with paper cartridges. We had to tear off the end of the paper cartridge with our teeth, pour the powder into the muzzle of the gun, ram the bullet and paper down on top of the powder, and then see that the nipple that held the cap was primed before putting the cap on. These guns carried plenty of powder and lead, but could not be depended on for accurate shooting except at close range, and it was slow work reloading them. However, I was fortunate enough to trade my musket for a Sharp's carbine.

As the Indians were still out on the warpath, I used to start with the mail from Bijou Basin after dark, ride all night, then stop at a ranch house that was well guarded and sleep during the day; leaving there early in the afternoon and get into Denver that evening. I returned the same way. On my last trip into Denver with the mail, it was too dark to see much of anything, and I passed a courier who was bearing dispatches to the regiment ordering them to move south toward Pueblo. On my arrival in Denver I was turned back with orders to intercept the regiment on its way south.

I left Denver in the afternoon and that evening reached a ranch where I was known, and where I stayed all night. Next morning I started early for a place called the 'Double Chimney,' a ranch house which was situated on the divide between the Platte and Arkansas Rivers, in a large forest of pine trees, where I expected to meet the regiment. This ranch had been burned by the Indians a short time before, and there was nothing left but two fireplaces with a chimney between them, and a portion of a corral. There was a small stream of water with a few young cottonwood trees.

I had an extra blanket tied on behind my saddle, with some toilet articles wrapped up in it, a small hatchet, a feed of oats for my horse, and a good lunch. On my arrival at the chimneys it was nearly dark, and I was satisfied that the troops had not passed. It had begun to snow, but it was not cold. I tied my horse to some small cottonwood trees so he could eat the bark from them, and with a piece of board I picked up in the corral cleaned the snow out of one of the fireplaces, banked it up on each side, and built a fire. Then I cut some pine boughs for a bed, spread my saddle blanket to lie on, and placed my saddle for a pillow. I had no fear of any Indians being in that vicinity, as it was snowing and after dark. I gave my horse the feed of oats, ate my lunch, lay down, pulled my overcoat and an extra blanket over me, and like a sound healthy seventeen year old boy was soon fast asleep. I slept soundly until morning, and awoke with about two inches of snow on top of my blanket.

It had stopped snowing, so after taking care of my

horse and giving him the rest of the oats, I saddled up and took the road toward Bijou Basin, and in a short time met the troops riding toward Pueblo. We camped at the 'Double Chimney' that day. From there toward Pueblo it was all downgrade and the snow soon disappeared, except where it had drifted. We made good time and soon reached Pueblo.

As I had been detailed to carry dispatches, I had no guard duty to do, and having an excellent horse I rode ahead with the scouts. They were splendid fellows and knew their duties. As I remember them they were Ed Safely, Duncan Kerr, Old Jim Beckwourth, a mulatto, Charley and Marianna Autobee,[16] and Antoine Genise. They taught me how to scout, and the ways and habits of the Indians.

My buddy, Bird Harris, a telegraph operator, was taken sick a short time before the regiment left Bijou Basin, and was sent to the hospital in Denver. He asked me to take charge of his horse, a dandy saddle horse, and as my brother had charge of the transportation teams, I got him to keep it in his train along with some extra stock he had. So while we were on the march I usually rode Bird's horse and saved my own as much as possible.

From Pueblo we traveled down the Arkansas River. The snow in the valley had nearly disappeared, but at a point among some sand hills it was

[16]Information about Jim Beckwourth and Charles Autobees may be found in the Special Biographical Notes at the end of this chapter.

still quite deep. There had been a thaw and then a freeze, so that over the snow there was a hard thin crust. Scout Kerr and I were riding along by ourselves, and when we rounded this point we saw hundreds of antelope that had come out of the hills to the river for water and were returning. As long as they traveled slow they could walk on the snow crust, but when they tried to run the bucks broke through and could not make any headway. Kerr and I rode after them, and, by riding one on each side of a buck, catching him by his horns, and lifting him up so that Kerr could cut his throat with his bowie knife, we managed to kill eleven. We could have killed a good many more, but the deep snow tired our horses. With our halter straps we hauled them down to the road, and when the teams came along we loaded up eleven dead antelope that we had killed without firing a shot.

At Booneville, about twenty miles below Pueblo, Colonel Chivington met us. From that point no one was allowed to pass us in either direction, not even the mail. So that when we reached Fort Lyon we took them by surprise. We arrived there about four o'clock in the afternoon. Old Jim Beckwourth and some of the other scouts had been sent ahead to locate the Indian camp, but they had avoided the fort. At eight o'clock that night the order came to 'boot and saddle' and we started northeast for the Indian camp at Sand Creek, about thirty-five or forty miles from Fort Lyon. Colonel Chivington had

*James P. Beckwourth, one of the scouts
with the Third Colorado Cavalry.*

Courtesy Colorado Historical Society

part of two companies of the First Colorado Cavalry with him, numbering about a hundred and twenty-five men, and at Fort Lyon we were joined by Major Anthony with a hundred and twenty-five men and two pieces of artillery. Our regiment had about five hundred men, as, when we got orders to move, a lot of the soldiers were home on leave of absence and were not notified in time to join us.

All the time we were on the road or in camp, the general topic of conversation was that when we got to where the Indians were, we were not to take any prisoners; that the only way to put fear into them was to fight them their own way and scalp every one of them. I had been told that the commanding officer had given orders to take no prisoners. As usual I was ahead with the scouts, and I remember I slept about half the night in the saddle. About three o'clock in the morning we came upon a large band of Indian horses grazing on the mesa. I was sent back to the command to inform Colonel Chivington, while the scouts quietly rounded up the herd. The troops were only a short distance behind us and Colonel Chivington sent part of a company of Mexicans to drive the horses quietly back to Fort Lyon. He then appointed me courier for the day between himself and Colonel Shoup.

This was on the 29th of November, 1864. At that season of the year three o'clock in the morning is still dark. When the command came to where I had left the scouts, I heard Jim Beckwourth tell Colonel

Chivington in the presence of the other scouts that
the Indians were in camp about six miles from there
and that there were one hundred and thirty lodges
of Cheyennes and eight lodges of Arapahoes, and
that the Arapahoes were there on a visit, and were
all warriors. This was the same tribe of Indians of
which Black Kettle was the head chief.

We had six miles to go to reach Sand Creek and
the Indian village,[17] and, as soon as the Mexican
troops had got the band of horses started toward
Fort Lyon, we kept on and reached the bank of the
creek just as day began to break.

We had been traveling over a rather level rolling
mesa. And as we came to the creek we saw a wide
valley with brush and bunch grass growing in it.
The Indian camp was on the bank of the creek,
which had a small stream of running water in it. A
few horses were grazing not far from the camp, not
over twenty-five or thirty head, I think, and we saw
smoke coming out of the tops of some of the tepees.
It is rather hard to express the sensation I felt as we
came in sight of the battlefield. While I had been
close to several Indian skirmishes I had never been
in a real fight with them, but my feeling of antipa-
thy toward the Indians was so strong that I forgot
all fear and was only anxious to get into a fight with

[17]The Indian camp was on the east side of Sand Creek
about ten miles north of present Chivington, Colorado—
named after Colonel Chivington—on state highway 96.
Writers' Program, *Colorado*, p. 273.

them. The idea that I might get hurt never entered my head. I had no conscientious scruples in regard to killing an Indian, but I did draw the line at scalping or mutilating them after they were dead.[18]

There were a hundred and twenty-five men of the First Colorado Cavalry with us, and because they had been in several battles with the Indians and Confederates, they were known as 'The Bloody First,' while our regiment, which had never been in a battle of any kind, was called 'The Bloodless Third.' We stopped to strip our saddles of blankets, food, and everything else we should not need in the fight, and while we were thus engaged the word came back among our boys that the First should go ahead and clean up the village. This meant that we would not get into it at all, and we would still be known as 'The Bloodless Third.' So when the order came to charge the camp everybody broke ranks and it was a stampede through the Indian village.

The attack was made about sunrise. The Indians were surprised, but they were much better armed

[18]The officers of Breakenridge's Company B were not as squeamish about scalping Indians as Breakenridge. Major Hal Sayre (the original commander) took an Indian scalp which remained a family heirloom; Sayre seems to have used his pistol to blow off the top of the head of a wounded Indian boy. The Thespian, Lieutenant Harry Richmond of Company B, killed and scalped eight Indian prisoners. Robert M. Utley, *Frontiersmen in Blue: The United States Army and the Indian 1848–1865* (New York, 1967), pp. 295–96. Robert H. Sayre, "Hal Sayre—Fifty Niner," *Colorado Magazine*, XXXIX (July 1962) pp. 161–77.

than the soldiers and they put-up a desperate fight.

The Indians had excavated trenches under the bank of Sand Creek for several miles, and they took shelter in these trenches as soon as the attack was made.[19] Although they put-up a stubborn resistance and contested every inch of the ground, they were slowly driven back from one position to another for about four miles, and finally about two o'clock in the afternoon they dispersed in all directions and were pursued by the troops until night. In my opinion if any escaped it was women and children who fled while the Indians were making such a desperate fight, as I saw very few squaws and no children.

Shortly before the Indians scattered, Colonel Chivington sent a few men back to burn the village, but as an afterthought he sent me to the village to tell them to save some of the largest tepees for hospital use for our wounded men.

In going to the village I kept down the creek over the ground we had been fighting over, and saw a good many dead Indians, all of them scalped. About a mile from the village an Indian arose from behind a tuft of bunch grass, when I was about thirty feet from him and shot at me with an arrow; he

[19]Utley has concluded that the "excavated trenches" to which Breakenridge refers were "scooped depressions in the sand"—not prepared in advance of the attack—behind a natural bank and that only about thirty warriors took advantage of this protected position to put up a resistance during the morning of November 29th before escaping from the scene. *Frontiersmen in Blue*, pp. 294–95.

*An artist's conception of the cavalry action at Sand Creek.
The First and Third Colorado Cavalry are shown
attacking the Cheyennes and Arapahoes.*

*Colonel John M. Chivington, who led
the Colorado Cavalry at Sand Creek.*
Courtesy Colorado Historical Society

missed me but slightly wounded my horse on the rump. I was riding with my Sharp's carbine across my lap, and before the Indian could dodge I fired and hit him. I was so close I knew I had killed him, and I did not stop, but kept on to camp.

The chief surgeon picked out the tepees he wanted to use and had them cleaned out. The ambulance was kept going bringing in the wounded. In the camp was a large quantity of supplies, buffalo robes, and dried buffalo meat known as 'jerky.' There was also plenty of flour, bacon, and other food and in several of the tepees was found wearing apparel that had been taken from ranches that the Indians had looted and burned and from wagon trains that they had destroyed.

Colonel Chivington reported that nineteen scalps of white persons were found in the camp, and that the surgeon told him that one of them had been taken from the victim's head not more than four days previously.[20]

The soldiers had been told by Governor Evans's proclamation that they could have for their own use all property that actually belonged to the Indians that they might capture, and they got quite a lot of buffalo robes and other trophies before the camp was burned.

The scouts and others guessed about five persons to a tepee, which would make six hundred and fifty

[20]Others staunchly denied Chivington's contention that white scalps were found in the Indian camp.

Cheyennes and forty Arapahoes in the village at the time we attacked it, and I cannot see for the life of me how very many of them could have got away, as we were right on top of them all the time. Colonel Chivington in his report stated that he had seven men killed, forty-seven wounded, and one missing; and he judged that there were five hundred or six hundred Indians killed; that he passed over a large portion of the battlefield and saw but one woman that had been killed, and no children. He stated that eight Indians were captured by the troops and that they were sent to Fort Lyon. I did not see any captured Indians.

While the Indians claimed this as their hunting camp, their main camp was at Smoky Hill where Major Wynkoop went to recover the four white captives. These Indians had been getting Government rations up to within a few days before we attacked them. Between ration days they would make raids from their camp and kill and rob emigrants and burn ranches, but they always returned in time to receive their next ration of supplies from the Indian agent.

On December 1, 1864, Major Scott Anthony in his report to his commanding officer said that there were eleven hundred Indians in the camp we attacked, but in Washington, on March 14, 1865, after he had fallen out with Colonel Chivington, he stated that he did not think there were more than from seventy-five to a hundred Indians in the fight. All the officers that were on the ground estimated the Indians to number from seven hundred to one thousand, while the Indian agents, who were nowhere near there, stated they had been told that about a hundred were killed, and that three-fourths of them were women and children. They claimed the inspector told them so, but there is no report made by any inspector.[21]

There were a lot of scalps of white men and women, some very fresh, found in the tepees; but so far as scalps went, our boys had the best of it, for every dead Indian was scalped once, and some of them two or three times. About the first Indian killed was the head chief, White Antelope. Duncan Kerr, the scout, killed him. Lieutenant Colonel Bowen was told that White Antelope's body was down by the creek and he had better go down and get his scalp. He went down and found that the

[21] Utley's careful estimate of the numbers of participants and casualties at Sand Creek is that about 500 Cheyennes (along with a few Arapahoes)—about two-thirds of whom were women and children—were encamped in about 100 lodges comprising Black Kettle's village. Chivington attacked with nearly 700 men, a force which included all of Shoup's Third Colorado Volunteer Cavalry Regiment and more than half of the First Colorado Volunteer Cavalry Regiment. Twenty-four hours later some 200 Indians (about two-thirds of whom were women and children)—nearly half of Black Kettle's camp—lay dead on the field of Sand Creek. Only nine of the attacking soldiers were killed. *Frontiersmen in Blue*, pp. 292–97. The most complete treatment of the episode is Stan Hoig, *The Sand Creek Massacre* (Norman, 1961).

dead Indian had been scalped so often that there was no hair left, so he cut off his ears for pocket pieces. A long time afterward he was treated to free drinks if he would show the ears.

Our supply teams came up that night with my brother in charge of them, and we remained in camp all the next day attending to the wounded and resting our horses. I got hold of a bale of buffalo robes, used some of them for a bed, placed the rest in one of the wagons, and my brother took them to Denver. They were already cured and tanned, and at that time could be bought from the Indians for a very few dollars. The day we were in camp, while I was out scouting for Indians, I found two hobbled horses about three miles from camp in a little nook on the creek. They were of good size and in fine condition, and evidently the favorite horses of some Indian, and hobbled to keep them close to camp. I caught them and brought them into camp, and when we got ready to leave, I had them led behind the wagons to Denver, where I sold them for a hundred dollars.

I did not want to scalp an Indian, but I wanted a scalp, so I traded a buffalo robe with one of the boys for two scalps. Shortly after I was mustered out, my sister wrote asking for some of my hair to use in some kind of fancy work she was doing; I answered that I had had my hair cut short to prevent being scalped, but that I was sending her two Indian scalps. I guess they did not take very well at home, for I got a letter from mother giving me a good dressing down for sending such horrid things to my sister.

Major Bent had come West in the employ of the Hudson's Bay Company and built a fort at the mouth of the Purgatory River, where Las Animas now stands. He traded with the trappers and Indians, married a Cheyenne squaw, and raised several children.[22] He had two boys that he sent to St. Louis to school. While there they lived at the Planters' Hotel. Old Jim Bridger, a noted scout, who came West about the time Bent did, and had never gone back, decided to make a visit to St. Louis. While there he called on the Bent boys at their hotel, and on his return to the West, when telling about it, said, 'A guide showed me their tepee, but when I started to come away I got lost in the canyons' (too many halls). The Bent boys, after finishing their education, returned to the Indian tribe. They were both killed in the Sand Creek fight.[23]

On December 1st, having sent the dead and wounded to Fort Lyon, Colonel Chivington started with us down the creek toward where it emptied into the Arkansas River. On the way we gathered up about a hundred head of horses and mules, most of which were Government stock, or belonged to

[22]Information about Major William Bent may be found in the Special Biographical Notes at the end of this chapter.

[23]Information about George and Charles Bent may be found in the Special Biographical Notes at the end of this chapter.

private citizens, that were stolen by Indians.[24]
When we reached the Arkansas River he directed me
to carry a dispatch to Denver, then to go with a few
men and drive the stolen stock to Lyon, and turn
it over to the commanding officer at that post.

The Colonel then continued on down toward
Smoky Hill in hope of overtaking a large encamp-
ment of Arapahoes and Cheyennes, under Little
Raven, but on account of the worn out condition of
the horses he could not catch them. On December
5th, the stock being exhausted, and the time of the
Third Regiment being nearly out, he determined to
relinquish the pursuit for the time, and started on
the return trip to Denver.

I had been riding Bird Harris's horse, but as soon
as I reached Fort Lyon, and had turned over the
herd, I got my own saddle horse that my brother
had taken to Lyon with the wounded soldiers, and
started with my brother for Denver.

At Sand Creek, where we stripped our saddles of
everything we should not need in the fight, I had
left a good overcoat, but when I went to get it I
found it had been stolen and an old ragged thing

[24]The news of Chivington's conquest at Sand Creek was
joyfully celebrated in Colorado, but elsewhere the episode
of November 29th soon came to be perceived much more as
a brutal massacre of surprised and friendly Indians (most of
whom were women and children) than as a true battle, an
interpretation adopted by three official investigations that
took place in 1865 and one that remains the consensus of
modern scholars.

little better than nothing had been left in its place. I managed to keep warm, however, on the ride back to Denver by spreading over the saddle and the head of the horse a buffalo robe with the hair side out, climbing into the saddle and then folding the robe back over my legs and up over my chest, fastening it there with a strap over my shoulders. Thus in my ride over the divide between Pueblo and Denver, where it was very cold, I managed to keep comfortable. I did not know at the time that the robe was full of lice, but it didn't take me very long to find it out, and when I got to Denver everything I had, including myself, had to be deloused.

Unfortunately Colonel Chivington had made a lot of enemies among the army officers. They were apparently jealous of him because of his activity and the fact that Major General S. R. Curtis was urging him to go ahead as fast as possible. Through influences at Washington, after the Third Colorado Cavalry had been honorably discharged, their time of service having expired, Colonel Chivington was retired. He was relieved by Colonel Moonlight.[25]

[25]Information about Colonel Moonlight may be found in the Special Biographical Notes at the end of this chapter.

SPECIAL BIOGRAPHICAL NOTES

In order to properly provide background information on the main characters in *Helldorado* but without lengthy footnotes appearing in the text, the following is provided:

MAJOR ANTHONY. General Curtis sent Major Scott J. Anthony from Kansas to replace Wynkoop at Fort Lyon. Anthony, having previously served under Chivington in the First Colorado Volunteer Cavalry Regiment, was, as Breakenridge suggests, out of sympathy with his predecessor Wynkoop's peaceful policy toward the Indians. Utley, *Frontiersmen in Blue*, pp. 289, 292–96. In Kansas before the Civil War, Anthony had been an antislavery merchant who helped the Leavenworth Rangers fight off proslavery raiders from Missouri. Anthony joined the Colorado gold rush in 1860 and resumed his mercantile career in the settlement that eventually became the town of Leadville. He was a cousin of Susan B. Anthony who was in the forefront of the late-nineteenth-century national campaign for woman suffrage. Hoig, *Sand Creek Massacre*, pp. 94–95.

CHARLES AUTOBEES. Born of French-Canadian descent in St. Louis in 1812, Charles Autobees became a Mountain Man in 1828 and was in the northern Rockies until his 1835–1853 stint as a Taos, New Mexico, trader. Thereafter, Autobees established himself as one of the pioneer settlers of southeast Colorado by settling down on a ranch on the Huerfano River twenty miles east of the present city of Pueblo where he resided until his death in 1882. In 1837, Mariano Autobees was born in Taos to the union of Charles Autobees and Serafina Avila whose marriage was not solemnized until 1842. Janet Lecompte,

"Charles Autobees," pp. 21–37, in LeRoy R. Hafen, ed., *The Mountain Men and the Fur Trade of the Far West: Biographical Sketches* . . ., IV (Glendale, Calif., 1966). Mariano Autobees was a second lieutenant in Company H of the Third Regiment at Sand Creek. Carey, " 'Bloodless Third' Regiment," p. 283.

JIM BECKWOURTH. One of the most interesting men in the history of the Old West, James Pierson Beckwourth (1798–1866), also known as Beckwith, was the son of a white Virginia overseer and a mulatto slave woman. Freed from slavery in Missouri by his father, Beckwourth moved into the Rocky Mountain country in 1824 and in 1828 was adopted into the tribe of Crow Indians with whom he eventually became a chief before leaving them to go on to California and then Colorado. Delmont R. Oswald, "James P. Beckwourth," pp. 37–60, in Hafen, ed., *Mountain Men*, VI.

GEORGE and CHARLES BENT. Breakenridge is speaking of the half brothers, George and Charles Bent whose mothers were, respectively, Owl Woman and her sister, Yellow Woman, whom William Bent married after Owl Woman died. The Bent brothers were educated at Westport, Missouri, where they were in charge of Colonel Albert G. Boone, the grandson of Daniel Boone. George and Charles Bent survived the Sand Creek massacre, but Charles died in arms against the whites in 1868. After being reconciled to peace with white people, George Bent wrote valuable accounts of the turbulent decades of the 1850s and 1860s and lived until 1918. George E. Hyde, *A Life of George Bent Written from His Letters*, ed. Savoie Lottinville (Norman, 1967).

WILLIAM BENT (1809–1869) built his fort—known first as Fort William and then as Bent's Old Fort—in 1833 on the upper Arkansas River not far above the inflow of the Purgatoire near present Las Animas, Colorado. The impressively walled fort was a trading post rather than a military bastion, and it enabled Bent and his partners to dominate the Indian and white economy of a large area until Bent closed it down in 1849 and moved his business, eventually, thirty-eight miles down the river to Bent's New Fort near where Fort Lyon would later be built. David Lavender, *Bent's Fort* (Garden City, 1954).

BLACK KETTLE. Probably born in 1812, Black Kettle was the Cheyennes' principal chief by 1860. He had an imposing command presence, but because the Cheyennes' chieftainship system had no mechanism to enforce discipline, Black Kettle and other peace-minded chiefs had great difficulty controlling the hostility of young warriors toward the whites. Black Kettle was accurately described by a contemporary white as "a mild, peaceable, pleasant, good man," but many pioneers, not directly acquainted with Black Kettle and unaware of his peaceful influence among the Cheyennes, viewed him as the evil genius behind Indian attacks on settlers. Stan Hoig, *The Peace Chiefs of the Cheyennes* (Norman, 1980), chapter 8.

BULL BEAR. Although a chief of a bellicose faction, Bull Bear joined Black Kettle and White Antelope in attempting to soften relations between Indians and whites during the 1860s. By the 1880s Bull Bear had settled down on the reservation and had a son who attended the Carlisle Indian School in Pennsylvania and took the name of Richard Davis. Hoig, *Peace Chiefs*, chapter 7.

COLONEL JOHN M. CHIVINGTON. The Reverend John M. Chivington (1821–1894), a Methodist minister known in Colorado as "the Fighting Parson," moved steadily westward from his Ohio birthplace and arrived in

Denver in 1860. With the outbreak of the Civil War, Chivington traded the Bible for bullets, and, as an officer at Glorieta Pass in 1862, played a decisive role in repelling the Confederate invasion of New Mexico. Now a hero back in Colorado and fired by political ambitions in 1864, Chivington spearheaded the attack on the Cheyennes and Arapahoes at Sand Creek described later by Breakenridge. The leading historian of the United States Army in the West, Robert M. Utley, wrote that Chivington's role in the Sand Creek episode earned him the characterization "of a crazy preacher" who thought he was Napoleon. Utley, *Frontiersmen in Blue,* pp. 284–85. A sympathetic treatment is Reginald S. Craig, *The Fighting Parson* (Los Angeles, 1959).

GENERAL CURTIS. Graduating from West Point in 1831, Samuel Ryan Curtis (1805–1866) served in the Mexican War and eventually became a two-term Republican Congressman from Iowa. With the outbreak of the Civil War, Curtis went into the Union army as a brigadier general. The high point of his military career came in April, 1862, when Curtis victoriously commanded the Union forces at Pea Ridge, Arkansas, in what was the greatest Civil War battle west of the Mississippi. Rewarded with promotion to major general, Curtis became commander of the Department of Missouri and in 1864 of the Department of Kansas. As commandant of the Department of Kansas, Curtis was handicapped by his lack of experience in dealing with Indians, and he unwarily supported the hard-line policy of Chivington and Evans against the Cheyennes and Arapahoes. *Dictionary of American Biography,* IV (New York, 1930), pp. 619–20. Utley, *Frontiersmen in Blue,* pp. 285, 287–89, 292, 297, 304–6.

DR. JOHN EVANS (1814–1897) was born in Ohio, passed through Indiana, and came to Chicago where he taught at Rush Medical College, was a very successful investor in real estate, helped found Northwestern University (located in Evanston, a town named for him), and became a leading Republican. President Abraham Lincoln appointed Evans to serve as territorial governor of Colorado (1862–65) where he remained to be a leading businessman, railroad developer, and the founder of what later became the University of Denver. Harry E. Kelsey, Jr., *Frontier Capitalist: The Life of John Evans* (Denver, 1969).

ELBRIDGE GERRY. Known in the West (to which he came in 1840) as "Little Gerry," Elbridge Gerry was born in Massachusetts in 1818 and was the great-grandson of his namesake, Elbridge Gerry (1744–1814), who not only signed the Declaration of Independence but became vice president of the United States under James Madison. Although not part Indian, Little Gerry was married to an Indian in Colorado where he became a successful trader and rancher on the South Platte River. Hafen, "Elbridge Gerry," pp. 153–60.

COLONEL MOONLIGHT. Thomas Moonlight (1833–1899) came to America as a penniless Scotch immigrant youth. His period as an enlisted man in the United States Army prepared him for entry into the Union service as a Captain in 1861. Having attained the rank of colonel, Moonlight, as Breakenridge notes, served briefly as Chivington's successor before being transferred to present Wyoming for his final months of service which were blighted by Moonlight's embarrassingly inept command of a cavalry foray against the Sioux. After the Civil War, Moonlight was such an active and successful participant in the politics of the Democratic Party in his home state of Kansas that President Grover Cleveland appointed him to be the territorial governor of Wyoming (1887–89) and later the minister to Bolivia (1894–98). *The National Cyclopaedia of American Biography*, XII (New York, 1904), p. 312. Utley, *Frontiersmen in Blue*, pp. 307n., 317–19.

HARPER M. ORAHOOD was born in Ohio in 1841, grew up in Illinois, and, going to Colorado in 1860, spent his first ten years in mercantile activity in Central City and the neighboring town of Black Hawk. In 1870, Orahood switched to the profession of law and later held public offices in Denver and Central City. *The National Cyclopaedia of American Biography*, XIII (New York, 1906), p. 59.

HAL SAYRE. Hailing from New York, Hal Sayre (1835–1926) was one of Colorado's leading pioneers. He laid out Central City in 1859 and became a leading mine owner and mining engineer, an associate of Senator Henry M. Teller, a Central City banker, and the builder of an imposing mansion in Denver. Sayre, "Hal Sayre."

GEORGE L. SHOUP. Denver merchant George L. Shoup (1836–1904) left Colorado in 1866 and eventually became Idaho's last territorial and first state governor, 1889–1890, and, subsequently, a two-term United States senator. Howard R. Lamar, ed., *The Reader's Encyclopedia of the American West* (New York, 1977), p. 1109.

WHITE ANTELOPE was, like Black Kettle, a leading Cheyenne chief who actively worked for peace between Indians and whites in Colorado and Kansas during the 1860s. Hoig, *Peace Chiefs*, p. 59 and *passim*.

EDWARD W. WYNKOOP (1836–1891) was the only leading participant to emerge with honor from the Sand Creek episode. A Pennsylvanian, Wynkoop arrived in Colorado in 1858 via Kansas and after a turbulent early career in Denver was commissioned a second lieutenant (rising to the rank of major) in the First Colorado Volunteer Regiment and served well in the successful campaign against the Confederates in New Mexico in 1862. Thinking he had pacified the Indians in the fall of 1864, Wynkoop was outraged at the Sand Creek massacre which he viewed as a brutal betrayal of trust by Chivington. After the Civil War, Wynkoop became an Indian agent and worked once again for Indian-white peace but was thwarted by General Winfield Scott Hancock and Colonel George A. Custer with the result being another massacre of the Indians in 1868 on the Washita River in present western Oklahoma by Custer's troopers of the Seventh Cavalry. Thomas D. Isern, "The Controversial Career of Edward W. Wynkoop," *Colorado Magazine*, LVI (Winter/Spring 1979), pp. 1–18, provides biographical information and explores the controversy over what was perceived to be Wynkoop's pro-Indian policy. Wynkoop is the protagonist of Michael Straight's historically authentic novel, *A Very Small Remnant* (New York, 1963).

IV

My First Business Venture

AT THE TIME I was mustered out of the army, on
December 29, 1864, I hired out to Mr. Broadway, who owned the Broadway Hotel in Denver,
to take charge of four teams and drive one of them.

During the winter the Indians had run off nearly
all the ranchers on the Platte River and destroyed
their homes. The only ranches which had been able
to fight them off between Julesburg and Fort Lupton were at Riverside Station, Moore Brothers', and
the Godfrey Ranches.

The Moore Brothers' Ranch was founded by Jim
Moore soon after the pony express was abandoned.
Jim Moore was one of the noted pony express riders.[1]
He made a record for endurance when at one time,
on arriving at the end of his scheduled ride of about
seventy miles, he found that the rider who was to

[1]Initiated in April, 1860, the Pony Express carried the
mail from St. Joseph, Missouri, to Sacramento, California,
under a contract granted to Russell, Majors, and Waddell
(and later Wells, Fargo) until in October, 1861, completion
of the transcontinental telegraph line ended the service.
Jim Moore was one of 109 known Pony Express riders and
one of the first to be hired. Raymond W. and Mary L. Settle,
Saddles and Spurs: The Pony Express Saga (Harrisburg,
1955). Roy S. Bloss, *Pony Express—The Great Gamble*
(Berkeley, 1959), pp. 148–50.

take his place had been murdered by Indians. He then continued to ride on to the next way station and when he arrived, found the return rider was sick in bed and unable to get up. Moore immediately made the return ride without rest, and rode a total of two hundred and eighty miles in about thirty hours, changing horses every eight or ten miles. After he started up the ranch, his brother Charles joined him. These ranches at this time were being guarded by soldiers, as they were also stage stations and a cavalry escort was sent out with each stage.

Indians had run off all the beef cattle on the river and the troops had to depend on buffalo meat. The Government gave a contract to Bill Cody to furnish the soldiers with buffalo meat. He was a good shot and the buffalo were plentiful, and it was here he got the name of 'Buffalo Bill.'

The Platte Valley was an immense hayfield, and the ranchers put up large amounts of hay in stacks. They built their houses and corrals out of heavy sod, cut in strips two by four feet and laid up in walls, which soon became very solid and could not burn. The houses were covered with dirt roofs, and the thick walls made a good defense to fight behind. The Indians burned a good many haystacks, but most of the houses were fireproof.

On our return from Sand Creek, my brother was appointed master of transportation at Fort Laramie for the Government, and was there and at Forts Phil Kearny and C. F. Smith for some time.

It was cold, freezing weather when I left Denver with the four teams and an escort bound for Julesburg after supplies to be delivered to the different stations along the road where troops were stationed. We passed the Godfrey Ranch just after the Indians had attacked it and had been driven off. Several ranchers near there had abandoned their homes and had gathered at Godfrey's, where they defeated the Indians. At the American Ranch, two miles from Godfrey's, we found the remains of a dead Indian who had evidently been badly burned in the same fire that had burned out all the woodwork in the building and the hay which had been stacked close to the house inside the corral.

We loaded our teams with supplies at Julesburg[2] and returned to Fort Lupton without any mishap. The Government had hauled a large lot of supplies into Julesburg to be distributed from there to the different posts in the West, and had built a large stockade out of corn in sacks. These walls were then

[2] Julesburg, Colorado, which Breakenridge frequented in the middle and late 1860s began as a stagecoach and pony express station on the overland route. The town has had four incarnations, all within six miles of each other along the South Platte River. Before its abandonment in 1867, the second town of Julesburg was the target of a destructive raid by Cheyenne Indians in early 1865. The third Julesburg (1867–1881), a railroad town, was known as "the wickedest little city east of the Rockies." After 1881, the fourth and current Julesburg has maintained a calmer status as one of the leading small cities of northeast Colorado. Writers' Program of the Work Projects Administration, *Colorado: A Guide to the Highest State* (New York, 1941), pp. 208–10.

covered with huge tarpaulins and supplies stored within them. Civilian teams were hired to haul them to Fort Laramie, Fort Phil Kearny, Fort C. F. Smith, and other points where the troops were stationed. I stayed with the teams for a year or more hauling materials from Julesburg to the different places where soldiers were stationed, and during that time we had several skirmishes with the Indians, but were always lucky in beating them off.

The Government had taken the old Springfield rifle and converted it into a breech-loading needle gun of very long range. It would carry a mile or more. I bought one from a soldier when they were first issued, and by cutting off about four inches of the barrel, I was able to retain it as a condemned piece. I resighted it with peep sights, and it would shoot right where I held it; and I was a good shot.

The Indians were in the habit of coming out on a bluff about half a mile from Julesburg and jeering at the soldiers. Soon after I had my gun fixed to suit me, I was in Julesburg after a load of supplies, and while I was in the corral they came out on the bluff as usual. I brought out my gun and taking careful aim over the top of the corral I fired at an Indian at least a half mile away, and we all saw him drop from his horse onto the ground. Two other Indians ran their ponies up to him, and, stooping from their saddles, caught him by his arms, one on each side and dragged him out of sight. They abandoned that hill after that.

After a time the Indians had been driven back farther north, and were not nearly so bad as they had been; so, as Government freighting was getting slack, I determined to start out for myself. I bought a four-mule team from Mr. Broadway, paying part cash and the rest on time. Freight rates were very high, and, if you had good luck and lost none of your stock, you could make big money freighting. On my first trip to St. Joe, I made enough to pay off almost all that I owed on the outfit. I stuck at work with the team and very soon had it paid for.

I got a chance to take a load of liquor and a saloon outfit to Pine Bluff on the line of the Union Pacific Railroad where contractors were getting out wood and ties. The end of the road was at North Platte. As the Indians had been driven back in that direction, and the Sioux were claiming the country and were very troublesome, I knew it was a hazardous trip to attempt, but I had got used to taking chances, and, as I should get at least five hundred dollars clear if I got through, I attempted it. There were three of us in the party, the man that owned the outfit, his barkeeper, and myself.

After leaving Denver we had no trouble and in due time reached the Cache la Poudre River at La Porte, and followed down the river to near Fort Collins. The road then turned northwest, and that night about dark we reached what was known as Willow Creek. It was raining slightly, and as soon as we could get supper we picketed the mules as

close to the wagon as possible, and turned into bed
under the wagon. We were awakened by a loud
yell, and soon after we heard the mules running.
We knew that our mules had been stampeded by
Indians. It was very dark, but, after ascertaining that
the mules were really gone, we took the back track
for La Porte, about thirty miles, because that was
the nearest place we could get assistance. After going
about half-way as fast as we could walk, we reached
a dry creek bed, and, as the men with me were very
tired, I told them to hide in the brush and I should
be back before night. I reached the Cache la Poudre
about daylight, and in one of the first camps I
struck I found my old friend Antoine Genise, one
of the scouts, with his Sioux wife and several children. He gave me some breakfast and then caught
up two ponies and went with me to La Porte, where
I soon got several horsemen and a man with four
mules to go back with me.

We picked-up the men I had left and got to the
wagon about dark and found nothing had been molested during our absence. Antoine said it was the
work of Indians, and we found where they had lain
in the willows watching us make camp.

I always believed it was some French renegades
that got the mules, as the Indians were never known
to make an attack in the middle of the night. They
always attacked about daylight. We were not prepared to follow them, so I traded my wagon and
harness, together with the freight money due me,

for a horse and saddle, and returned to Denver broke once more. The man I traded with took the loaded wagon through to Pine Bluff.

On my arrival in Denver I sold my horse and saddle, and the next day went to work for a man who was going to North Platte with an ox train after a load of freight. When we reached the crossing on the South Platte, the river was up and the owner could not get his oxen across, for as soon as they got into deep water where they had to swim, they turned downstream and came back to the side from which they started. He offered a dollar a head to anyone that would take them across, and I took the contract, but he and his men were to assist. I yoked up two oxen, which I drove ahead, while he was to keep the rest of the herd driven up close behind me. I had a strong stick with a brad in it, and when we came to the deep water, which was not very wide, I got right behind my two oxen, grabbed their tails, and by using the brad freely kept them going straight ahead, and the rest of the cattle followed like sheep. We ferried the wagons across and were soon camped in North Platte.

North Platte at that time was a town of about fifteen hundred people. As in all Western towns that had sprung up overnight, the people lived and transacted business in tents with board floors and sides, and the busiest people were the gamblers, saloon keepers, and painted women. Spotted Tail, a friendly Sioux chief, with a band of his Indians, was

camped a short distance from town near the forks of
the North and South Platte, and a troop of soldiers
also were stationed here. The U.S. Government
was feeding the Indians.[3]

I stayed in town for a few days and then went to
work as a freight brakeman under Conductor Moffitt. He was cross-eyed, and I was told he was a hard
man to get along with, but I found him a very pleasant man, and I liked to work under him. I was made
head brakeman. The engines were very small wood-
burners, and the freight cars were low and small,
carrying from twelve to fifteen tons. They were
equipped with hand brakes and link and pin cou-
plers. There were twenty cars to a train, and the
loads were principally rails, ties, and supplies that
were hauled to where the track was being laid.

A favorite sport of the Indians was to shoot arrows at the train at night, and, as the lantern which
each of us had to carry made a conspicuous mark, I
used to leave mine a few car lengths away from the
car on which I was riding.

Moffitt was soon promoted to be a passenger conductor, and he advised me to stay with him, as he

[3]During 1867, the Union Pacific Railroad was built west
from North Platte, Nebraska, through Julesburg, Colorado,
and Sidney, Nebraska, to Cheyenne, Wyoming. (Wyoming
was then a part of Dakota Territory.) Because of their portable collections of stores and saloons and peripatetic gamblers and fast women which moved west with the railhead,
towns such as these and Bear River City, Wyoming, were
known as "hell on wheels." Robert G. Athearn, *Union Pacific Country* (Chicago, 1971), chapter 3.

expected another promotion very soon, so I transferred to the passenger train. The railroad was being financed by the Government, and shortly after my transfer, President Grant with a special train of army officers and politicians came through on inspection. Most of them were Indian sympathizers, and one of them made a speech at North Platte taking the frontiersmen to task for their cruel treatment of the Indians. He said that if the Indians were left alone they would be peaceful. He said also that he had not seen any hostile Indians.

He was interrupted by a frontiersman, who said: 'Yes, you came through with an escort on a train that was well guarded. Now I have got two good saddle horses, and if you will come with me I will show you hostile Indians, but I will not guarantee that you will get back to tell about it.' Needless to say, his challenge was not accepted.

Shortly after this the railroad was completed to Julesburg and as all freight for the West was to be delivered there, the inhabitants of North Platte got ready to move their portable houses and fixtures to Julesburg. Within a week all the houses were moved there, and were running full blast again. Moffitt was made assistant superintendent, and went to Julesburg. I was appointed yard master at North Platte.

One night that summer, about twenty miles east of North Platte, the Indians and some white renegades pulled up two rails and stuck them in a culvert so that the ends would puncture the engine boiler when the engine ran into them. The next train along was a freight train: it was completely wrecked and all the train crew killed. As soon as the news reached North Platte, some infantry were loaded on to flat cars and ran down to the wrecked train just in time to see the Indians disappearing. Some of the Indians had tied a bolt of calico or some other goods to the horses' tails, so that when they put their horses on the run it would stream out behind them. They took what goods they could carry and left the rest on the ground. The soldiers were afoot and could not follow them.

Several of the freight crews refused to run their trains at night and they were discharged, but night service was discontinued very soon after this. Caseman, who was laying track at the front, was hiring all the men he could get, and these discharged men wanted to go there. Conductors, however, had been ordered not to haul them, an order that seemed to me to be foolish, for the men wanted work and the road wanted men. I had just been appointed conductor, and had only made a few trips when one day a lot of these men boarded my caboose and I took them to the front. Using my own judgment, however, instead of obeying orders, proved costly for I was suspended for thirty days.

The end of the track was now at a town in Nebraska named Sidney, about twenty miles east of Julesburg. It was the end of a division, and Superintendent Moffitt had moved his office there. Julesburg continued to be the shipping point for all freight billed to Colorado, and Sidney was the point from which freight for all other Territories was shipped, and it was the end of a freight division. Moore Brothers still held their ranch on the South Platte, about forty miles south of Sidney, as the stages and all freight teams passed there and there was a lot of travel. The Indians were in winter quarters and not committing any depredations: they were waiting for spring.

That fall of 1867, Charley Moore came to Sidney and started a store, saloon, hotel, and butcher shop. As I was out of a job, I hired out to him to look after his interests in his several properties.

Jim Moore remained at the ranch on the South Platte until the track had nearly reached Cheyenne that winter; then he went there and opened a large feed corral. The many saloons, gambling houses, and sporting houses remained at Julesburg until the railroad reached Cheyenne, and then nearly all of them moved to that place, but Julesburg still continued to be quite a lively town.

Sidney was a lively little frontier town,[4] and I

[4]Named for Sidney Dillon, the Union Pacific Railroad's chief construction contractor, the town of Sidney grew up around Fort Sidney, established in 1867 for the protection of the railroad construction workers. From its earliest days Sidney was one of the wildest towns of Nebraska's frontier era. Writers' Program of the Work Projects Administration, *Nebraska: A Guide to the Cornhusker State* (New York, 1974), pp. 211–18.

liked it very much. The houses were substantial and warm and comfortable, and business was very good, but I did not like the confinement of the house.

That winter Moore had sent some teams over to the ranch for hay. The ground was covered with snow and it was very cold. The teams were overdue, and he told me to try to find a man to send to the ranch and see what was the matter. Idle men were scarce, and I volunteered to go myself if he would let me. He consented, and mounted on a good horse I struck across the country for the Platte, which I reached opposite the Riverside Station, which had been abandoned. I was clothed very warmly, but the cold would penetrate.

Although the river was wide, it was not over a foot deep at any place, but there was a bed of quicksand underneath the ice. It was very slippery and although my horse was shod he had hard work crossing it. When we crossed with the ox teams we had to go ahead and cut holes through the ice, and with a shovel dig up and scatter sand over the ice, where it would instantly freeze and make good footing for the cattle.

When I got across the river and rode up to the ranch house, I got the worst scare of my life. It was very cold and I had been riding in the snow until I was partially snow-blind, so I thought I would stop and go in and build a fire in the fireplace and get warm before going to the ranch, some ten miles away. I was so cold I had left my rifle on my saddle, and had hard work to tie my horse to the hitching post. My pistols were buttoned under my overcoat as, on account of the extreme cold weather, I was not looking for Indians. They were supposed to be in winter quarters.

On account of the glare of the sun on the snow, when I got inside the door everything was black to me. I could not see a thing and had to feel my way.

Right in my face a voice said 'How.'

I knew it was an Indian, and I jumped backward out of the door into the light. Standing in the door was an Indian. He held out his hand and said 'Come.' There was nothing else for me to do, for if I turned to run he could get me in the back, and I could not reach my pistols. So I went in and he led me into the back room, where there were two more of them, and they had a horse in there. They had a small fire built in the top of an old stove, but I had got over being cold; in fact I broke into a cold sweat as soon as I saw them. I got my back against the wall, unbuttoned my overcoat and got my pistols where I could reach them. By this time my sight was getting better and I felt more comfortable. The Indians had a large white canvas on which was painted in large letters, 'Spotted Tail's band of friendly Sioux.' In case the soldiers caught them away from their camp at North Platte, they could hold it up so that it could be read at a long distance, and they would not be fired upon.

The Indian that spoke to me was Spotted Tail's

son, and they were looking for a band of ponies that had strayed away. I asked him where they were going, and he replied, 'Charley's.' I had not recovered from my sudden scare. I believe that if I had tried to spit when I first saw him I should have spit my heart out, for it was still up in my throat.

I said to him, 'Let's go,' and we got on our horses and started. The other two were afoot. We rode fast and on reaching Moore's ranch turned our horses into the haystack in the corral. The men had just finished their supper, and while the cook was making more coffee for us the two footmen came in. The Indians did not find their ponies, as old Jack, the foreman of the ranch, had found them and with some of his men had driven them to Cheyenne and sold them. They had just returned, which accounted for the delay of the hay teams. There had been a heavy snowstorm which covered up all tracks of the Indian stock, and because the Indians could find no trail of them they gave up the hunt.

Next day we started for Sidney with the hay. When we got to Riverside we made camp, and it took all the next day to sand the ice and get the wagons across. The Indians started back with us, but left us at our first camp, keeping down the river toward Julesburg.

By spring the Indians were very bad and were constantly committing depredations. They could be seen every day on the bluffs above Sidney, just out of rifle range, making insulting gestures, and the soldiers, being infantry, could not go after them.

The section men working on the railroad were all well armed, as they were likely to be attacked at any time. One day, while they were working about two miles from Sidney, two of the men took a keg and went to Lodge Pole Creek for water. It was only a little way from the railroad, and, as a keg full of water would be heavy to carry, they left their guns at the hand car. The Indians came on them at the creek, killed and scalped them, and filled their bodies full of arrows.

One day, Wilse Edmondson and Tommy Calhoun, a conductor and brakeman, borrowed my fishing tackle, to go fishing down on the creek about a half mile from town. Soon after they left, a band of six Indians ran through the edge of town close to the soldiers' barracks and attempted to cut the ropes on several horses that were picketed there. I was in the store. The men all ran out and one of them took my Springfield needle gun that was hanging on the wall near the door. The soldiers drove the Indians away from the picketed horses, and they retreated toward the creek where the men were fishing. All the men that were armed followed them up as rapidly as possible. As soon as I could lock up I started, found my rifle was gone, and had to stop to get another. It was a Spencer carbine which loaded in the stock with seven cartridges, held in by a spring. Throwing one into the barrel of the gun I mounted Moore's fast saddle horse, not

taking time to put the saddle on, and with James
Pringle, a ranchman, started for the creek after the
Indians. My horse was a bit faster than Pringle's
and when I reached the creek I saw Edmondson on
his hands and knees, with an arrow in his back. He
asked me to pull it out and to go and look after
Calhoun, who was on the other side of the creek. I
had to pull very hard to get the arrow out, and by
this time several men had come up. They returned
for a wagon to carry the wounded men to town, and
I crossed the creek to where Calhoun was. He had
been scalped and shot with several arrows, but was
still alive. The prompt action of the soldiers and
citizens in following the Indians up so closely is all
that saved their lives.

They both recovered and Calhoun had a silver
plate fitted into the top of his head to cover the
scalped place. I saw in a newspaper a few years ago
that he was still living. The Indians always scalp by
taking the scalp lock, about the size of a silver dollar, from the top of the head.

Pringle and I kept on chasing the Indians, and I
was some distance ahead of him. Soon I saw them
climbing a steep bluff out of the creek bottom.
They had to go slow, as it was very steep, and I
reached the foot of the bluff about seventy-five
yards behind them. I fired at one just as he reached
the top of the hill and saw his horse make a plunge
and disappear. I felt sure that I had hit him and
tried to throw another shell into the gun, when I

found that the spring that held the cartridges in the breech had come out and all the shells had fallen out of the gun. Fortunately, I still had my pistol in case I needed it.

Just then Pringle, who was about a quarter of a mile behind me, fired a shot to draw my attention and motioned for me to come back. I was behind a point of the bluff and could not see the town. He turned his horse toward Sidney and I rode after him. When about halfway there I overtook him. The bluffs were alive with Indians and the soldiers were firing at them. Pringle said his pony had given out, so I stopped and he got on my horse behind me. He saw me when I fired at the Indian going over the bluff, and from where he was could see the top of it. He told me he saw the Indian fall out of the saddle. We made a run for the town and got back safely. The pony followed us and the savages were driven off. Two days afterwards we learned that an Indian had been brought into Spotted Tail's camp shot through the body; then I knew that I had got him as he went over the bluff.

The Fort Phil Kearny massacre occurred about this time. A wood contractor had a camp a few miles away from the fort, but had had to abandon it on account of the Indians killing some of his men. One day a wood wagon started for the abandoned camp, but the Indians chased it back to the fort, and the driver came in with his team on a run. The Indians hung around and dared the soldiers to come after them. A small company of soldiers, with about all the civilians in camp who could get away, volunteered to go along. There were ninety men in all. They were led into ambush by an over-zealous officer. All of them were killed and most of them scalped. A hay contractor named Wheatley was among them. His body lay behind a rock, and there was a hat-full of empty shells by him. After killing him the Indians did not scalp him on account of the brave fight he made. The Indians later reported that over a hundred Indians had been killed, but they outnumbered the whites ten to one.[5]

[5]Fort Phil Kearny (named after a Union general of the Civil War) was established in July, 1866, about fifteen miles north of present Buffalo, Wyoming, as one of a chain of forts erected to protect the Bozeman Trail from Wyoming to Montana. The massacre (in which seventy-nine military and two civilians died) occurred on December 21, 1866, and the "over-zealous officer" referred to by Breakenridge was Captain William J. Fetterman who led his men into the ambush by 1500–2000 Sioux, Cheyennes, Arapahoes, and Crows under the overall leadership of the Sioux chief, Red Cloud. This was one of only two occasions in American Army history (the other was the massacre of Custer's force on the Little Big Horn in 1876) in which an entire detachment was killed by the enemy. James Wheatley, a Civil War veteran, was a civilian employee in the fort's quartermaster department. Wheatley died bravely during the massacre, but, contrary to Breakenridge's statement, he was scalped. It was the post bugler, Adolph Metzger, who, according to one report, was not scalped by the Indians in their tribute to his courageous fight against them. Dee Brown, *Fort Phil Kearny: An American Saga* (New York, 1962). J. W. Vaughn, *Indian Fights: New Facts on Seven Encounters* (Norman, 1966), chapter 2.

V

Building a Railroad

DURING the fall of 1868 the railroad had reached beyond Laramie, and the contractors were grading the roadbed in Webber Canyon. My brother, who owned several teams, had left the Government employ and received a contract from the railroad to build a certain amount of roadbed in this canyon. He wrote asking me to come and help him fill his contract. I was tired of being confined to the store and hotel at Sidney, and, as there was a chance to make more money at the front, I went up and joined him in Webber Canyon. By the time we got the work finished on his contract, the grading of the roadbed was completed through the canyon, and had reached the Salt Lake Valley beyond Ogden, Utah. The track layers were right on the heels of the graders.[1]

When there was no more railroad work for the teams, we moved-on down to Ogden, where George started-up a livery stable, and I took two six-mule teams and loaded them with freight for Bannock,

[1]The building of the Union Pacific Railroad across Wyoming and Utah, through Weber Canyon and to Promontory Point in 1868–69, is described in Robert G. Athearn, *Union Pacific Country* (Chicago, 1971), chapters 4–5.

Montana. We were gone nearly two months on this trip, and got through finely, as nothing unpleasant occurred.

Bannock had been at one time a very prosperous camp, with rich placer mines, but, at the time I arrived there with the teams, it was very quiet and dull. We were shown the worked-out placer claims, and the historic hangman's tree where many stage robbers, or, as they were called at that time, 'road agents,' were hanged by the Vigilance Committee. Sheriff Plummer and the notorious Slade were leaders of the gang of road agents, but they were all hanged or run out of the country.[2]

Shortly after we returned from Montana, the connection was made between the Central Pacific and Union Pacific Railroads at Promontory, Utah, on May 10, 1869.

Right after the Union Pacific built into Ogden, that spring, the Dan Rice Circus came there. It was the first circus ever to come to Utah. Currency was very scarce among the Mormons, and they did their marketing through barter. They would bring in

[2]In 1863–65 the vigilantes of Bannack and Virginia City, Montana, put to death thirty bad men including the nefarious sheriff, Henry Plummer, and the desperado, Joseph A. (Jack) Slade. Thomas J. Dimsdale, *The Vigilantes of Montana* . . . (Virginia City, 1866). Merrill G. Burlingame, "Montana's Righteous Hangmen: A Reconsideration," *Montana: The Magazine of Western History*, XXVIII (Autumn, 1978), 36–49, is the best of the analytical treatments by historians but is not as full a description as Hoffman Birney, *Vigilantes* (Philadelphia, 1929).

chickens, eggs, grain, or garden stuff, and exchange it at the stores for necessities wanted at their homes. They paid into the tithing house, for the benefit of the Mormon Church, one-tenth of everything they raised or accumulated.

The day of the circus I was downtown and in the pool room of the West Hotel. I got into a pool game with some of the men belonging to the circus and we played for circus tickets. I was lucky enough to win some twelve or fifteen tickets.

My brother's wife, the widow of Wheatley, who had been killed at Fort Phil Kearny,[3] had hired a Mormon girl to help her, and a lot of her friends or relatives from Paradise Valley came in to see her and the circus. On going home to dinner I saw a bunch of Mormon girls in the front yard, and, as I had won enough circus tickets to supply them all, that afternoon I took my sister-in-law and the girls to the show. They certainly seemed to enjoy the performance.

Soon after this George decided to move to Cheyenne. He took his wife on the train to Cheyenne and I brought the teams and livery stock through. The livery stock was led behind the wagons and I

[3]Breakenridge's sister-in-law was a beautiful nineteen-year-old wife when she came to Fort Phil Kearny in 1866 with her brave husband, James Wheatley. George Breaken-ridge and the former Mrs. Wheatley were married in 1868 and lived on a ranch near Fort Laramie, Wyoming, before moving west with the railroad. Dee Brown, *Fort Phil Kear-ny: An American Saga* (New York, 1962), pp. 103, 200.

drove a span of horses to a buggy and carried my bulldog Fan in the buggy with me.

While we were on the Laramie plains a hailstorm struck us and the mules could not face it. They turned at right angles to the road and went across the prairie. They were kept from stampeding only by the brakes of the wagons. We went about a mile before we got out of the storm, and the hail raised large lumps on the stock and cut through the wagon sheets on the wagons.

In passing through a short but very deep canyon my bulldog, who hated the Indians and always gave warning when they were near, began to growl, and I knew there must be Indians nearby. As it was down grade, we soon got the teams started into a lively gait. Just as we got out of the canyon, we saw about twenty Indians ride up to the edge of the canyon behind us. As we had good protection here and some high rocks to fight behind, we made camp, secured our stock, and waited. When they came too near, we covered them with our guns, and motioned for one of them to come to us. He claimed they were hunting stray stock and begged for tobacco. We gave them some and sent them away, but we did not proceed until Fan quit growling. I never knew her to bark, but when she growled, there was sure to be trouble somewhere around.

On reaching Cheyenne my brother loaded the teams with freight for Denver. From that time on I was kept busy driving between the two places. I found that Denver had improved very much in the two years I had been away. The Kansas Pacific Railroad was building very fast toward Denver. The end of the track was at Kit Carson, close to the line between Kansas and Colorado. My brother went there to try to get work for his teams.

As in the meantime the teams were idle, I took them out in the direction of Kit Carson to find grass to graze them on. When we reached Sand Creek, we found an abundance of fine feed, but the large bands of wild horses were a menace, as they were likely to run off our stock, and as small bands of Indians were in that vicinity, we had to herd our mules closely. We built a small corral of cedar posts, and there was a small pond of good drinking water right at the camp. We kept a guard on at night to watch for Indians. A short distance from the camp were two large ponds of water where the wild animals came to drink, and antelope and buffalo were plentiful. We were a little scarce of ammunition, and when we wanted meat one of us would go down to the ponds and hide in the tall rushes that grew between them and wait for antelope to come to water. We would wait until two or more were lined up at the water hole so as to get at least two at one shot. The antelope were in flocks of hundreds.

We had a wagonload of corn for the mules, and when our flour ran out, we parched the corn and ground it in a matate to make bread. One day old Charley Autobee and his son Marianna, who were out hunting, came to our camp. They were two of the scouts I was with at the Sand Creek fight. They took several antelope heads, cleaned them, roasted them in a pit in the ground, and then removed all the meat, put it in a stew pan with some vegetables and corn meal, and seasoned it with red peppers. It was a meal fit for the gods.

After our mules got acquainted with the range and had settled down, I took a light team into Kit Carson after supplies. George was there and he had formed a partnership with a man named Sam Carpenter to handle a grading subcontract. They sent me back for the teams, and as soon as we could get them there we went to work on the grade.

Kit Carson was a typical Western frontier town, principally gambling saloons and dance halls. Cowboys, buffalo hunters, teamsters, railroad men, and soldiers were there to make it lively.

The town marshal, named Tom Smith, was the bravest man I ever had the pleasure of meeting. He was about six feet in height, and weighed about two hundred pounds; a powerful, athletic man, very quick and active, always neatly dressed, and very quiet and gentlemanly. He looked like a successful business or professional man. He rarely carried a gun, but depended on his strength and agility in arresting and disarming the men he went after. He did not know what fear was. He was not a two-gun man with a lot of notches on his pistol, but he would shoot if compelled to. When the men got too

*Tom Smith, marshal of Kit Carson, Colorado
and Abilene, Kansas.*

Courtesy Dickinson County Historical Society

boisterous, he would go among them and if they did not obey, he would arrest and lock them up, knock them down if necessary and disarm them. They all respected him, for he played no favorites.

My brother's partner, Sam Carpenter, introduced me to him the first night I arrived in Kit Carson, and I saw some of his work. I took a walk with him through the saloons. In one of them was a bully trying to pick a fight with two gentlemen because they had not invited him to drink with them. Quick as a flash Smith took in the situation, grabbed the bully by the shoulders, kicked him out-of-doors, and then took him to the lockup.

It had been the custom in these frontier towns to appoint as marshal someone known to be a dead shot, quick on the draw, and with a reputation as a man killer. And I never heard of them making an arrest. Cowboys in from a long hard drive with cattle from Texas and Oklahoma proceeded to have a good time. Their chief amusement was to get half drunk, run their horses through the principal streets, and shoot off their six-shooters into the air, or maybe shoot out the lights in a saloon. These man-killing officers who went after them shot them first before trying to arrest them, and the law was behind them, as the men were shot while they had pistols in their hands. The officers had to take no chances, and it meant another notch on the gun. This kind of officer never made any arrests except dead men.

Smith had different ideas. He told me one time,

'Anyone can bring in a dead man, but to my way of thinking a good officer is one that brings them in alive.'[4]

The buffalo hunters had just begun slaughtering the buffalo for their hides, and that fall and winter they killed them off very fast. The hunters were well equipped. They were followed by the skinners, who took off the head, which they had a way of preserving, then skinned the animal, all but the hind quarters, which they wrapped in the hide. The rest of the carcass was left for the wolves. Then came the teamsters, who loaded the skins and hind quarters on their wagons. As soon as they got a load they hurried to the railroad and shipped to Kansas City and other points.

At the height of the season a single hunter could keep a large number of skinners busy, as the meat had to be handled rapidly. The men were well paid and spent their money in the saloons as fast as they got it. Taxidermists were always busy mounting the heads of the buffalo, antelope, deer and wolves. The Atchison, Topeka and Santa Fe and other Western

[4]Breakenridge's high opinion of Thomas J. Smith (1830–1870) was shared by many. After having served as a New York City policeman, Smith came west, led Union Pacific Railroad construction workers in the 1868 Bear River, Wyoming riot, and then earned an enviable reputation for keeping the peace in Kit Carson and, later, Abilene, Kansas. T. C. Henry, "Thomas James Smith of Abilene," *Kansas Historical Collections* (1905–06). Howard R. Lamar, ed., *The Reader's Encyclopedia of the American West* (New York, 1977), pp. 1124–25.

roads bought them in large quantities and placed them on the walls of their stations for both ornament and advertisement.

Kit Carson continued to be the shipping point for Texas cattle until the Chicago and Rock Island began to build from Kansas City toward El Paso. After they passed Abilene, the cattle men made this their shipping station, as it was much nearer.

Very soon a half-dozen frontier shipping stations were established along this line—all of them wild and woolly. Kit Carson was soon abandoned, and Tom Smith went to Abilene which had grown into the most lawless town of them all.

It had been impossible to get the right man to act as city marshal in Abilene until Smith arrived and accepted the office. When it was learned that he did not carry a gun, there were doubts about his lasting very long. There was a town ordinance posted prohibiting the carrying of concealed weapons inside the town limits, and all were warned to deposit their arms at the hotel or saloons. Smith enforced this by arresting everybody he saw carrying a gun, until the cowboys coming into the town usually left their arms in the custody of the saloon keeper until they were ready to return to camp. There was little shooting in the town after he became marshal.

Smith was killed about a year later while trying to arrest two murderers whom he had located in a dugout several miles from town. He took a man with him and rode out to their camp. Leaving his

man with the horses he entered the dugout and told
the men he was there to arrest them. They both
rushed him. He knocked one unconscious, and was
struggling with the other when the first one came to
and struck Smith in the back of the head with an
axe and killed him. The man he left with the horses
ran away, but he reported the affair in town and a
posse of cowboys and hunters took the trail and soon
ran them down and hanged the murderers. All the
surrounding country turned out to Smith's funeral,
and a few years ago Abilene citizens erected a monument to his memory. So perished a brave man.[5]

After Smith was murdered, the cowboys soon began to return to their old sport of shooting up the
town, and killings became frequent. All the old
time gunmen were either gamblers or connected
with gambling houses and saloons. Wild Bill Hickok was persuaded to take Smith's place as marshal.
His methods were different from Smith's. He was a
killer, but he always had the law on his side. He was
brave and fearless and never hunted trouble, and no
doubt was the best two-gun man in the West, and
could draw and shoot faster and more accurately

[5] Andrew McConnell and Moses Miles were the two home-
steaders who killed Smith on November 2, 1870, after the
latter had served only five months in Abilene. *Contra* Breakenridge, the two murderers were not lynched but were tried
and sentenced to prison. The monument to Smith in Abilene was dedicated on Memorial Day, May 30, 1904. Nyle
H. Miller and Joseph W. Snell, *Great Gunfighters of the
Kansas Cowtowns* (Lincoln, Neb., 1963), pp. 415–19.

than any other. He had killed a number of men before he came to Abilene, and while he was marshal there shot and killed several more. He was too quick on the draw for any of them. Hickok was killed in the Black Hills mining camp while he was sitting at a card table playing poker. A cowboy, Jack McCall, who had it in for him, stepped behind him and shot him through the head killing him instantly. He was so quick that he struck the floor with his six-shooter in his hand.

My brother George and his partner, Carpenter, had a good contract to take out a deep cut with a high fill on each end of it. But unfortunately there was a clause in their contract that they must have it done in time so as not to delay the track layers, with a heavy penalty in case they were caught. They had some bad luck, and before they could finish their work they were caught, and it nearly broke them.

About ten days before this I had been sent with eight or ten scraper teams to grade a fill on the roadbed, in a little valley under some very high rock bluffs. It was about four miles from the main camp. I got started late, and it was long after dark when we reached the work. Next day the Indians made a rush on a lot of graders all along the line, stampeded a lot of mules attached to scrapers, and shot several teamsters. Fortunately my brother had all the rest of his teams at work in the deep cut, and they were not strung out along the work. The men saw the Indians in time to defend themselves, and drove them off after killing several. None of my brother's men were hurt. Our being late in reaching the spot where we made our camp under the high rock bluffs no doubt saved us from attack, and as we were at work under the bluff out of sight they did not find us. Every teamster on the work had a rifle hung on his near mule's harness hames, and each one carried a belt full of cartridges.

After we had completed the work we were on, we moved the teams back to Denver, and I got a job in an engineer corps as an axeman on the Denver and Rio Grande Railroad that was just starting the survey from Denver south. This was in the spring of 1870. We made our camp at Palmer Lake close to the summit between the Platte and Arkansas Rivers, about fifty miles from Denver, and worked both ways from there. Mr. Holbrook was chief engineer, McMurtry was assistant, and DeReimer was transitman.[6] As soon as we made camp at Palmer Lake I was sent up into the pine timber, about a mile from camp, to make stakes for lining out the road. I had an axe, hatchet, and crosscut saw, but, as I knew

[6]Here and later Breakenridge has slightly garbled the names and jobs of James A. McMurtrie and James R. DeRemer. It was McMurtrie who was later made chief engineer of the railroad with DeRemer as his assistant while H. R. Holbrook was once employed, also, as an engineer for the Denver and Rio Grande. Robert G. Athearn, *Rebel of the Rockies: A History of the Denver and Rio Grande Western Railroad* (New Haven, 1962), pp. 53–57, and O. Meredith Wilson, *The Denver and Rio Grande Project, 1870–1901* . . . (Salt Lake City, 1982), p. 33.

nothing about handling an axe or saw, I was afraid I should not make much of a showing. Taking a lunch with me I started early and returned late, and soon found I could do the work all right. After about a week or ten days Holbrook told a teamster to take our light wagon and bring down the stakes I was supposed to have ready. He sarcastically remarked, 'I don't think there are enough of them to break your wagon down.' The teamster returned with all he could pile on the wagon, and when Holbrook asked him if he got them all, he replied there were two more four-horse loads of them. As there were enough to last some time I was taken out on the line to drive stakes.

One afternoon in a slight rainstorm we were running a long three-degree curve, and Holbrook wanted to complete it before we returned to camp. The head chainman got flustered, could not get in line with the curve, and took some time in getting his rod in the proper place. The transitman was scolding because he was so slow, and the chainman asked me to take the head-end of the chain and let him use the axe, saying his fingers were cold. I changed with him, and having good eyesight, by lining up with the stakes already set, I had good luck and could place the rod exactly right, or nearly right, the first time; and we soon finished the curve with everybody on the run. Holbrook said it was the first good work he had seen us do.

The next morning I was told to take the head-end

of the chain. It was customary for everybody to sit down and rest after putting in a point, and wait until the transitman came up and had his instrument set up for work again, but I liked to try to set up the transit over the point while DeReimer was writing his notes. He and I were good friends, and when he saw that I was taking an interest in the work, he took pains to explain the work of the transit to me, and often, when we were on a long tangent, he would take the head-end of the chain and let me line him with the instrument. In a short time I mastered the work and could run curves. DeReimer taught me all he could. Soon he was promoted to Division Engineer, and McMurtry let me handle the transit until he could get another man. As I was clever with figures I got along well and kept the job.

One day General Palmer, the president of the company, came into camp with a very sick horse, and, as I looked after the welfare of our camp stock, they sent out on the line for me to come in.[7] The General was worried, as the horse was a favorite of his, and was sick with colic. I got there in time and soon had him on his feet, for I had what I thought

[7]Originally from Delaware, William Jackson Palmer (1836–1909) learned railroading on the Pennsylvania, 1858–1861, came out of the Civil War a battle-scarred brigadier general, and served as treasurer of the Kansas Pacific Railroad, before settling down in 1870 to lead the Denver and Rio Grande Railway. Athearn, *Rebel of the Rockies*; Wilson, *Denver and Rio Grande*; and John S. Fisher, *A Builder of the West: The Life of General William Jackson Palmer* (Caldwell, Idaho, 1939).

was a sure cure for colic. The rapid recovery of his horse pleased the General and he soon afterward asked me to take charge of the company corrals and stables at Colorado Springs.

He had sent a contractor, James Carlisle, back to Kansas City to buy a lot of mules and horses, and the company intended to haul their ties and bridge timbers and have the bridges in ahead of the track layers, all the way to Pueblo. General Palmer told me how many head of stock there would be, and told me to make the plans for the stables. He had them set up at once; the bridges were built and the ties distributed long before the rails were laid.

As the road was being built with English and German capital, and there were a great many of the stockholders in Colorado Springs sightseeing, I was often called upon to show them around the country with the company's transportation.

General Palmer married a Miss Mellon. He had a large tract of land in the foothills at the mountains, about five miles from Colorado Springs, where he built a beautiful home which he called Glen Aerie.[8] It was a fine drive through his estate by way of Monument Park and through the Garden of the Gods, and all the sight-seeing parties wanted to take this trip. The end of the railroad for some time was at Palmer Lake, and I frequently drove the General

[8]Palmer married Mary Lincoln (Queen) Mellen of Flushing, Long Island, New York, on November 7, 1870, and built the Glen Eyrie mansion in the early 1870s.

and his wife to the end of the track where they could take the train for Denver.

After the railroad was completed to Pueblo, General Palmer had me fit out an engineering party for a reconnoitering trip below Trinidad, to look for a pass to the Rio Grande through the mountains at the head of the Vermajo River. I was in charge of the teams and saddle horses, and could run levels and take elevations in case it was necessary. Before we left Colorado Springs I sold the rest of the company mules to some contractors, and received more than their first cost.

After I got back from the Vermajo expedition, which was uneventful enough, I bought two fine horses and took a contract to deliver the lumber for a hotel they were building at Manitou. I could make two trips a day between Colorado Springs and Manitou and soon filled the contract.

There was a temporary inn at Manitou while the new hotel was being built, and many tourists came there. There was no trail to the top of Pike's Peak, but there was one to the timber line, and then there was a climb of about half a mile over a very steep grade, over huge sandstone rocks, to the top of the mountain. I got six or eight ponies to take tourist parties to the timber line and then guide them to the top of the Peak.

At one time two young women, who were reporters for Chicago papers, and three gentlemen had me take them to the Peak. They wanted to take their

General William J. Palmer, president
of the Denver and Rio Grande Railroad
and his mountain home, Glen Eyrie.

time on the trip, so we took a camp outfit with us. We started on horseback with two pack horses, and when we got to timber line we camped until morning. Shortly after we had cooked our supper a drizzling rain began. I cut down some small pines, and soon had a comfortable tepee covered with blankets which kept off the fine rain and wind, and placing a lot of pine boughs on the floor for a bed turned the tepee over to the ladies. There was plenty of bedding and it was not raining very hard, so I cut the men a lot of pine boughs and they got along very well. It did not rain very long that night, and after breakfast next morning we started up the mountain. I helped the ladies as much as I could, and they both got to the top. The men did not do so well; two of them reached the summit, but the third one gave out and returned to camp. We stayed at the top for a long time, and the return trip was not quite so hard. When we got back to our camp, the ladies decided to stay there until morning. They were enjoying the trip hugely. As they had plenty of time the men decided to go on to the halfway house, and they drew out and left us.

Next morning after breakfasting and packing up, we started down the trail for Manitou. When we came to where the trail led into the halfway house, the ladies wanted to go in and see if the gentlemen had left there yet. I could see by their horse tracks that they had not stopped, but had kept right on toward Manitou, and I told the ladies so. On our way up, as it happened, I had noticed three horses picketed in front of the halfway house, and as we came to where the trail came out from there I saw that the horses were gone and their tracks were fresh in the trail on the way down to Manitou. I happened to know the horses and their color.

I remarked that three horsemen had gone down that morning, but that they were not of our party. The ladies insisted that I must be mistaken. I described the color of the horses, and when asked how I knew, jokingly replied, I could tell by the tracks. When we reached the hotel we found our party sitting on the porch. Before dismounting, the ladies made inquiries and learned that what I had told them was correct—that three men had passed down just ahead of us riding the horses I had described.

The young women soon left for Chicago, and shortly afterward sent me copies of the papers they were writing for, containing full accounts of their trip, and of the marvelous young guide who told them the color of the horses by looking at their tracks. The boys had a good laugh at my expense.

Nearly all the time I was at Manitou I kept a driving horse and buggy. One day I stopped at the Colorado Springs depot just as the train came in. A very sick young man got off the train and asked for a conveyance to take him to Manitou. I told him I was on my way there and would take him with me. The traveler thanked me and told me that the at-tendant who had come with him from Kentucky had been taken sick in Denver, leaving him to come on alone. We got very well acquainted and I used to take him for a short drive whenever he felt able to go. One day I drove around as usual to take him out, but he said he did not feel strong enough to go out. A good-looking young stranger said he would like to take a ride if I did not object, and I told him to get in. Soon my passenger began to tell me what a wonderful man his father was, how many railroads he owned, what fine horses he had. 'By the way,' I said, 'who is your father?' He spoke up with a good deal of emphasis, 'Cornelius Vanderbilt.' I told him I had never heard of him, and the more the young fellow tried to tell me who he was the denser I got, till at last he realized that I was 'kidding' him.[9]

The temporary inn at Manitou was in charge of an old gentleman named Nye. And one day young Vanderbilt and Mr. Nye climbed up a steep mountain that was just opposite the inn. It was a hard climb, as the sides of the mountain were loose shale and very difficult to get good footing on. Vanderbilt beat the old gentleman and boasted a lot about the fast time he made up and down. When I came in that evening he told me about it and asked if I did not think he had done remarkably well. I told him

[9]Breakenridge's rich young friend was probably Frederick William Vanderbilt (born 1856), an 1876 graduate of Yale who was the grandson (not the son) of Commodore Cornelius Vanderbilt, the developer of the New York Central Railroad. Edwin P. Hoyt, *The Vanderbilts and Their Fortunes* (New York, 1962), pp. 276, 389–91.

he had done well for a tenderfoot, and he wanted to know if I could go up quicker than he had. I forget just how long it took him to make the trip, but I'm sure it was several hours. I told him I could go up in about one third the time it took him to make it, and he immediately offered to bet me a good dinner for the crowd that I could not do it. I took the bet and named the following morning at about sunup as the time when I would attempt it.

Right opposite the inn and across the creek was a long low point of a hill that ended just below the inn, and covered the steep mountain so that you could not see the foot of it from the inn. The trail to Pike's Peak was around the point of this hill, and there was a wood road that went up and around the mountain close to the top. It was about two miles long, but it could not be seen from the inn. I had the man that took care of my saddle ponies take them out before daylight and station them about a quarter of a mile apart on this road.

Next morning everyone was up to see me make the climb. After getting a cup of coffee, I came out ready to go. Young Vanderbilt asked me if I was ready. I told him yes, and he started his stop watch. I stopped to light a cigar, and he told me to hurry, as the time had begun. I strolled across the creek and around the point of the hill until I got out of sight. Then mounting the first pony I ran him to the next, and changed to a fresh one and so on, all the way to the top. And the first they saw of me was when I showed up on top of the mountain and holloed and waved my hands. It was no trouble to come down, as the loose shale would let you slide from ten to twelve feet every stride, and I was soon back on the porch of the inn from where I started, well within the allotted time. They all wanted to know how I had done it, as they had not seen me until I reached the top. After a time I told them and Vanderbilt, who was a good sport, paid the bet, but said it was a regular Yankee trick.

I took him and his companion on several trips, and just before they were ready to start back home, I took them in a democrat wagon with a good team through the south and middle park, and wound up at Idaho Springs, where they bade me goodbye. Young Vanderbilt invited me to return to New York with him as his guest, and told me that if I would go with him he would show me more of New York in two weeks than I could find by myself in two years, but I thought I could not afford it. He said he wanted to show me that I was as big a tenderfoot in New York as he was in Colorado. I have always regretted that I did not go with him.

Soon afterward I sold my horses and returned to the engineer corps, on the survey and construction of the line from Pueblo to Trinidad, and was field engineer while the contractors Orman and Company were grading the roadbed. At the same time, we were running a line down the Arkansas River to Las Animas at the mouth of the Purgatory River.

At a point on this line where a high bluff came to the river there was only room for one right-of-way for a railroad without an enormous expense in cutting the high bluff. The Atchison, Topeka and Santa Fe had also run a line from Las Animas to Pueblo and wanted this right-of-way. Orman's camp was about five miles above this point. One Saturday evening, when I was coming back from Las Animas, I saw some half-dozen teams with plows and scrapers going into camp there prepared to begin grading in the morning, so as to have possession of this point.

Hurrying on to our camp, I had them turn out a dozen teams equipped for road building, and I went back with them that night. Before daylight the next morning, I had the teams strung out all along the right-of-way. When the other camp began to stir, they were startled to find us already on the ground. They at once hitched up their teams and started to grade also. I stopped the first team as it came on the right-of-way and told them they could come no farther. It looked serious for a short time, but their men said they came there to work and not to fight. I advised them to report to their company first and get instructions what to do. There was no one in our camp who had authority to carry on this work. Orman, the contractor, was in Pueblo over Sunday, but I took the authority in my own hands and sent word to General Palmer and Mr. Orman, telling them what I had done. Monday, a lot of officials came down and the ground was staked, a permanent camp

*Grading the right of way
for the Denver and Rio Grande Railroad.*

Courtesy Colorado Historical Society

was set up, and the work of grading this point was completed. General Palmer gave his approval for what I had done.

After the road was graded to Trinidad, Orman turned his mules out to graze and left herders with them and moved to Pueblo. He had with the stock a bell mare that had been captured while running with wild horses some eighty miles east of there. This mare took a notion to return to her former pasture and about eighty mules followed her. It was a week before Orman was notified. He fitted up an outfit to follow them, and, knowing that I was familiar with that part of the country, he asked me to join him. There were four of us with a mount of four horses each, and we had the best saddle horses in the country, besides a teamster with our camp outfit and a cook.

The trail was easy to follow, and we soon got to the range, where we found that the wild stallions had cut the mules up into small herds, with a leader to each bunch of six or eight mules. These mules had become as wild as the horses they were running with. The only way to recover them was to run them down, and keep them moving without letting them stop for feed or water, and if possible get close enough to shoot the stallions.

Wild horses always run in a circle, sometimes sixty or more miles in circumference, and eventually return to their starting point. We made camp near water, and after our mounted men had stationed our remounts so that we should not have to go very far after them, we took our positions several miles apart, so as to take up the chase when the wild herd came near. A band of this stock would start on a run as soon as one of us came in sight. So following up one band, and paying no attention to the others, we would keep the horses in motion. After they had run a few miles, another horseman on a fresh horse would continue the chase. After several hours, we would either get near enough to cut out the mules or shoot the stallions, and the mules soon became quite gentle again. We were able to shoot most of the stallions, but it took about two weeks to recover all the stock.

It was astonishing how wild the mules became in such a short time, and how fast they could run, but as they were work stock they quickly became tired when kept on the move constantly. We saw bands of wild cattle unbranded, but very few antelope. The buffalo had disappeared.

Through some trade between the railroad companies, the Atchison, Topeka and Santa Fe Railroad obtained possession of the line from Las Animas to Pueblo in the winter of 1875, and built into Pueblo from Kansas. Our engineers were idle for some time and I worked as a timekeeper for the contractors laying track on the Atchison, Topeka and Santa Fe. The following spring I returned to La Junta, waiting for the engineers to be called to work.

VI

On to Arizona

A MAN named Cousins from Boston had been to
Arizona. On his return he wrote a book called
'The Marvelous Country,' and gave lectures about
it.[1] In one of his lectures he was quoted as saying that
Arizona was one of the finest lands in the world, and
all they lacked there was plenty of water and good
society. Someone in his audience replied, 'That's all
they lack in Hell.'

The following verse regarding Arizona is reported to have been written some fifty-odd years ago by
Charley Brown, the proprietor of the Congress Hall
gambling saloon at Tucson, Arizona:[2]

[1]Breakenridge is referring to Samuel Woodworth Cozzens,
*The Marvellous Country, or, Three Years in Arizona and New
Mexico* . . . (Boston, 1873), a work that was reprinted at
least two more times.

[2]Born in New York, Charles O. Brown went into the
Southwest as a bounty hunter of Indian scalps then settled
down by 1861 to be Tucson's leading saloon keeper. He
built the Congress Hall in 1867–68. It was the finest building in southern Arizona, and the place where the first territorial legislature met. Brown composed his poem, "Arizona
(or The History of Arizona): How It Was Made and Who
Made It," in the mid-1870s. The version included by Breakenridge varies slightly from that published earlier by Thomas Edwin Farish. Farish, *History of Arizona* (8 vols.; Phoenix,
1915–1918), II, pp. 60, 118–19, 185–88.

ARIZONA

How It was Made and Who Made It

The Devil was given permission one day
To select him a land for his own special sway;
So he hunted around for a month or more,
And fussed and fumed and terribly swore,
But at last was delighted a country to view
Where the prickly pear and the mesquite grew.
With a survey brief, without further excuse,
He stood on the bank of the Santa Cruz.
He saw there were some improvements to make,
For he felt his own reputation at stake.
An idea struck him, and he swore by his horns
To make a complete vegetation of thorns.
He studded the land with the prickly pear,
And scattered the cactus everywhere;
The Spanish dagger, sharp-pointed and tall,
And at last the chollas to outstick them all.
He imported the Apaches direct from Hell,
With a legion of skunks, with a loud, loud smell
To perfume the country he loved so well.
And then for his life he couldn't see why
The river need any more water supply,
And he swore if he gave it another drop
You might have his head and horns for a mop.
He filled the river with sand till 'twas almost dry,
And poisoned the land with alkali;
And promised himself on its slimy brink
To control all who from it should drink.
He saw there was one improvement to make,
So he imported the scorpion, tarantula, and snake,
That all that might come to this country to dwell
Would be sure to think it was almost Hell.
He fixed the heat at a hundred and 'leven
And banished forever the moisture from Heaven;

And remarked as he heard his furnaces roar,
That the heat might reach five hundred more:
And after he fixed things so thorny and well
He said: 'I'll be d——d if this don't beat Hell.'
Then he flapped his wings and away he flew
And vanished from earth in a blaze of blue.

Cousins worked up considerable enthusiasm and raised two crowds of about fifty men each to go out there and colonize on the Little Colorado River. He charged them three hundred dollars each, payable in advance, and was to furnish them transportation for themselves and three hundred pounds of baggage from Boston to Arizona. He got about fifteen thousand dollars out of each crowd he sent out, and it did not cost him over five thousand for each party for transportation, and he still owned the teams he furnished them at La Junta.

One morning there arrived in La Junta a crowd of men with a carload of mules and wagons and a lot of supplies, headed out for Arizona. Mr. Brown, of Chick, Brown and Company, forwarding and outfitting merchants, sent for me and asked me to unload the stock, match it up into teams, and put it into shape for the road. It was one of the Cousins' outfits, and the young men who were in the colony were clerks, mechanics, and school teachers. None of them knew anything about handling stock. A man named Sam Hunt, a school teacher, was secretary of the company, and he was sent out in charge of the party. He hired me to get the outfit together. Hunt had been a teacher of elocution and had tuberculosis.

He came out for his health, and, as the weather was fine, he improved rapidly.

The party had twelve mules, two horses, and four wagons. As soon as I got the stock out of the car, I matched them up into two six-mule teams, with two wagons to each team. The wagons were small, and intended for four-horse and two-horse wagons. The stock was good, and taking a four-horse wagon for a lead wagon and a two-horse wagon for a trailer and coupling them together, we were soon ready to load. Within a few days, and with the help of a teamster I picked up, I had the stock broke to drive with a jerk line. This is a line fastened to the near leader, and running back to the near wheeler, which the driver rides. The leader is taught to come to the left when pulled by the line, and to turn to the right when the line is jerked. The party had about ten thousand pounds of supplies and baggage, as very few had the allotted three hundred pounds.

After the teams were ready to take the road, Hunt asked me to take charge of them and act as guide to their destination. He offered me three hundred dollars a month and expenses until I got back to La Junta and was to send me back on the mail stage. I wrote to Colorado Springs and got a ninety days' leave of absence. Then I hired two teamsters and a night herder, and after putting about five thousand pounds on each team we started. There were forty-five men in the party. Besides two months' provisions some of them had tool chests, shotguns, and rifles; there were a few hoes and garden rakes, and one eight-inch plough, to colonize a country with. I told them before we started that they did not have enough teams to haul them and their baggage, but they said that was all that had been furnished them.

The first two days we had good roads, the mules were fresh, and we made good time, but I made only short drives until the mules had got used to the road and hardened up. The company had furnished Hunt but little money, saying that money to pay the expenses would be in the bank at Prescott when we arrived there. At Trinidad I had to have the mules shod and had to buy grain for them, and paid for it all. From here there was much bad road, and the men had to walk, as the teams were overloaded. They were a fine lot of men to get along with, although they soon learned that the colonization project had been misrepresented to them. By showing them all that they could not possibly get through unless they helped themselves, and by letting some of them ride when they got tired, we got along quite well. We arrived in Albuquerque in good shape, but from there on we had to depend on grass alone for the stock, as there was no grain and we could not haul any.

While in Albuquerque we were told that horse thieves were very busy stealing stock in the country through which we were about to journey, and we would be lucky if we came through without losing some or all of our stock. The men organized and elected a captain, and he appointed a guard each night to guard our wagons. When we came to the dangerous country, as the grass was plentiful, we herded the mules close to camp whenever we could, and a guard of several men would help the night herder hold the stock.

After leaving Albuquerque we traveled along a high plateau and passed near several Pueblo Indian villages. The Indians were mostly shepherds, and their flocks fed on the rich grass that covered the tableland. They built their towns on high mounds or hills, away from the waterways, and had to carry their water up the hill. Their villages were built this way for protection from other tribes, especially the Apaches. The Pueblo Indians and all other tribes, such as the Navajos, Hopis, and Moquis, were at war with the Apaches and were afraid of them. There was no water near the road in many places, and I hired a Pueblo Indian to guide us to water until we reached the next village, where he would quit and I would have to hire another one. It was the same through the Navajo and Hopi country. One man would go only so far and then he would return to his village and another one would take up the job. Sometimes we had to make a dry camp and then drive the stock as far as four or five miles off the road for water. The night herder would then let them graze back toward camp. I always went with him and stayed until the mules were taken care of and were feeding, and would take all the canteens in camp and fill them. We carried a water barrel fastened to the outside of the lead wagon which we kept filled for cooking purposes. We passed through Cubero, Fort Wingate, and Fort Defiance, and at last reached the Little Colorado River, where the party was expected to establish its colony.

Here we found a group of Mormons had already settled and were getting out ditches, building houses, and ploughing the land. This place at that time was called Sunset Crossing, and was near the mouth of Canyon Diablo. It is now known as Saint Joseph.

If there had been no Mormons there, our party could not have located, as they were not prepared, and had provision enough to last them through to Prescott.

After leaving the settlement I had my first trouble or dispute with the men in our party. A troublemaker who had come out in the first party from Boston met us at Sunset Crossing. He told the men how badly they had been deceived by Cousins, and advised them to take possession of the teams and turn them to their own use. We crossed the river at the Mormon village and kept down it until we made camp for noon. The mules were thirsty, and as soon as they were turned loose they made for the river and nearly all of them got mired in the quicksand. We all jumped in and with ropes dragged the stock out, but it was hard work.

One in the party had bought himself a saddle horse in Albuquerque, and as soon as the mules mired he was one of the first to jump in and place ropes around them to draw them out. After all the mules were rescued, it was discovered that his horse had strayed away, and I took its trail afoot and followed it back to the Mormon settlement. A wagon was going down the river and I led the horse behind and rode to where our camp was supposed to be, but when I got there I found the men had hitched up the teams and moved on and left me behind.

I overtook them in camp that evening and told them my opinion of them for playing such a dirty trick. The troublemaker announced that they had seized the outfit and were going to run it themselves from there on. I saw that he had talked a number of the men over on his idea. So that night I went out as usual with the night herder to place the mules on good feed, and, as soon as we got out of sight of the camp, we drove the mules back up the river about ten miles, into the foothills close to where a Mormon family was building a home, and where the night herder could get something to eat. I left him with instructions to keep the mules there until I came after them, and in case he saw any of the men coming after them to drive them farther away. I got back to camp that morning about two o'clock and went to bed, and the next morning there were no mules in camp at daylight, as there usually were, and I was not hurrying the men to break camp.

They came to me and wanted to know why the mules were not in camp. I told them that, as they had decided to take the outfit away from me, I had decided to seize the mules and they could keep the wagons; that the mules were on the way to Prescott, where I intended to attach them for what was due me, and they could get away from there the best way they could. The troublemaker started to run it over me, but I told him I would give him three minutes to get out of camp or we would shoot it out at once. I was mad, and he believed I meant it, and he started back to the Mormon settlement.

After he left, the men took counsel together and came to me and admitted they were wrong, and said that if I would get them out of there and into Prescott they would never interfere again. I could hardly blame them, for they had been deceived; the troublemaker was a good talker, and they were in a humor to be easily persuaded. So I told them that I would have the mules back in camp the next day sometime, and saddled up and went after them, but I took my time, as the animals were run down and needed rest.

We were in this camp three days, and then moved from here to Larue Spring, about eight miles south of the San Francisco Mountain, and the same distance from where Flagstaff now stands. There was no Flagstaff then, and both Sunset Crossing and Larue Spring have been omitted from the late maps. I am told that Flagstaff gets some of its water from this spring. After leaving Albuquerque we followed the Atchison, Topeka and Santa Fe Railroad which had been surveyed for most of the way. At Larue Spring we lay over ten days to allow our stock to rest, and I got through to Prescott without losing a man or a mule.[3]

At that time Larue Spring was a hunter's paradise. There were deer, bear, antelope, and wild turkeys in abundance. The men in the party were not very good shots, and, although they got several deer and turkeys, they soon had the game scared away from that vicinity. Then I took a pack mule and a man with me, and after getting some distance from camp remained overnight and generally returned the next day with a load of meat. I got a brown bear on one trip, and several turkeys, and could always get a deer or two.

One day several of the men left our camp and tramped up to the summit of the San Francisco Peak. They camped overnight on the mountain and we could see their campfire very plainly.

Our mules recovered very quickly and we started for Prescott. We had not seen a human since we left

[3]In 1876, a party of settlers from the Arizona Colonization Company of Boston, lured west—as Breakenridge relates—by Samuel Woodworth Cozzens' overly enthusiastic promotion, had expected to settle on the Little Colorado. Finding that the Mormons had preceded them, they moved on to Flagstaff (named for a towering stripped pine from which the American flag was flown on the July 4th centennial) where they were among the first settlers of the town. Writers' Program of the Work Projects Administration, *Arizona: A Guide to the State* (New York, 1940), p. 189. Platt Cline, *They Came to the Mountain* (Flagstaff, 1976).

the Mormons at the Little Colorado River; nor did we see anyone until we reached the Verde River.

At Hell's Canyon the crossing was so steep we had to lock the hind wheels of the wagons and have the men hold them back with ropes, and after getting down it took all the men and mules to haul them up the other side, one at a time.

There was no water in the creek at this crossing, but a short distance down the creek there was a spring and running water. Here on the side of the rock bluffs were the remains of huge cliff dwellings in a good state of preservation. The approach to them was very steep, and when you got to the floor of the buildings, you needed a ladder to get inside them. They were well protected, and we did not have time to explore them. This place is now called 'Oak Creek.'

On our arrival in Prescott the men scattered.[4] A few remained in Arizona, but most of them went on to California. There was no money in the bank at Prescott to pay my salary and the money I had advanced. I started to attach the outfit when Hunt showed me a bill of sale to him of all the outfit, and

[4]Prescott (named after the great Massachusetts historian of the Spanish conquest of Mexico and Peru, William Hickling Prescott) was settled in the early 1860s. It served as the first territorial capital (1864–67 and also 1877–1889), and, by the 1870s, when Breakenridge was in and out of it, Prescott had become a bustling Arizona mining and commercial center. Writers' Program, *Arizona*, pp. 235–37. See also, Melissa Ruffner Weiner, *Prescott: A Pictorial History* (Virginia Beach, 1981).

proposed that we go into partnership and lease a ranch in the Salt River Valley where he would farm and I go freighting with the teams.

We moved to Phoenix and soon leased a ranch at the southwest corner of town. We got a plough and I ploughed our ranch and then went to freighting, leaving Hunt two teams for ranch use. His idea was that by freighting we could pay the expense of the ranch and have our crop clear in the fall.

After several trips hauling wheat from the Indian Reservation on the Gila River to Hayden's Mill at Tempe, I took a load of flour to Prescott, and from there went to Ehrenburg on the Colorado River, for a load of merchandise. Boats brought the freight up the river from San Francisco.

While I was at Ehrenburg two stage robbers held up the stage near Wickenburg and took all the mail and express. It was soon learned who they were, and Deputy United States Marshal Joe Evans came to Ehrenburg. Soon after he arrived, the robbers came into town. Evans with a posse went to arrest them. They resisted, and one of them was killed and the other one wounded in the street fight. None of the posse were injured.[5]

[5] After the stagecoach robbery near Wickenburg on April 19, 1878, Deputy United States Marshal Joseph W. Evans arrested Andrew Kirby and the popular pioneer, John W. Swilling (1831–1878) who, although believed by many to be innocent, died in the Yuma jail. Larry D. Ball, *The United States Marshals of New Mexico and Arizona Territories, 1846–1912* (Albuquerque, 1978), pp. 110–12, 115, 128.

Gurley Street, Prescott, Arizona Territory, in 1883.

Courtesy Arizona Historical Society Library

On my return to Prescott, I was asked to go to the end of the Southern Pacific Railroad, which was then on the California Desert at a station called Dos Palmos, after a load of freight. The roads were very heavy, mostly deep sand, and water was scarce. I had traded my light wagons for two heavy ones, and carried a large water barrel on each side of each wagon, which we filled at every opportunity; but still our stock suffered for water.

After I had crossed the Colorado River with my team on a ferryboat, and was about forty miles from Prescott, I had to drop my trail wagon on a steep hill and haul up one at a time. While coupling the wagons together again, I caught my fingers in a chain and tore the nails off two fingers and stripped the flesh off the ends of them to the bone. I put the nails and flesh back as well as I could and wrapped my hand up in a clean towel, and as it was very hot weather I got on my horse and started for Prescott just at dusk to have it attended to.

My horse was a sure-footed animal, and the first and only time he ever stumbled with me was that night. I had my hand in a sling and was moving along in an easy trot when he stumbled and threw me over his head. I landed hard on my breast with my hand between me and the ground, and almost instantly the towel was soaked in blood. I had a canteen full of water and kept the wrapping soaked with water and reached Prescott about sunup. After my hand was attended to by a doctor, I sent a man back to the team to help my man bring it into Prescott.

Soon after the team got in, I received a message that my partner Hunt had died that day. I had the team start for Phoenix and at daylight, after breakfast, I mounted my saddle horse and started for that town. I had a noble horse. Going by the Black Canyon route, I reached Phoenix about noon on the following day, but I had to ride nearly all night to make it.

Then my troubles began. After paying all bills I had always sent Hunt the surplus of our earnings with the team. I found that he had raised a good crop of wheat and sold it, and it had been hauled off the place, together with almost everything else. He had borrowed a thousand dollars at the bank and sent it to his father in Boston, who had staked him to make the trip West, and as we had only an oral agreement he had represented the property as belonging to him. I had witnesses to our agreement and he had admitted that we were partners.

After struggling along for some time trying to get out of debt, I made my last trip to Yuma for freight, as the railroad had just reached there. This was in the summer of 1878. Upon my return to Phoenix I sold the outfit to pay our debts, and went to work surveying. As settlers were coming into the valley looking for farms, there was plenty of work to do in my line.

When I first arrived in Phoenix, it was a small village with only a few houses west of where the courthouse now stands, or east of the city hall.[6] On Sunday afternoons it was customary to have horse races and chicken pulling on Washington Street, in the business part of the town. This street at that time had running water on each side of the street, and beautiful large shade trees all along the edge of the sidewalks.

Chicken pulling is a Mexican game. A rooster is buried in the ground, with his head well soaped or greased, sticking up. The game was to put your horse into a run and, stooping from the saddle, try to grasp the fowl by the neck and pull it from the ground. The men were excellent riders and it was an interesting and exciting sport. They would also place bandana handkerchiefs about fifty feet apart on the ground, and with their horses in a run stoop from the saddle and pick them up.

One Sunday while a small crowd was watching the sport, a Mexican on horseback and armed with a saber, ran amuck, and slashed right and left as he charged throughout the crowd. He injured several,

[6]Named after the mythical bird by an English remittance man, Lord Darrell Duppa, Phoenix was an outgrowth of an 1867–68 Salt River irrigation promotion by the Wickenburg prospector, John W. (Jack) Swilling. By the 1870s, Phoenix was flourishing as the seat of Maricopa County. It became the capital of Arizona in 1889, but not before passing through a turbulent early period exemplified by the vigilante episode discussed by Breakenridge. Western States Historical Publishers Inc., *Arizona, the Grand Canyon State: A History of Arizona* (2 vols.; Westminster, Colo., 1975), I, pp. 83–84. On Swilling, see note 5 this chapter.

including the sheriff, who was in the crowd, but fortunately no one was killed, and he kept on and fled into Old Mexico.

Henry Garfias, a brave and fearless officer, was town marshal. He took up the trail, overtaking the Mexican at the customhouse on the San Pedro River just across the line. He brought him back across the line, and after several days' travel delivered him to the sheriff at Phoenix. The Mexican was placed in a cell that was raised about a foot above the ground. The floor of the cell was made out of two-by-six scantling, and one piece about four feet long was left loose so that it could be raised and the dirt swept through it onto the ground. One day before his trial a lawyer wanted to speak to him, and Garfias, with Hi McDonald the constable, went with him to the cell. The Mexican stood with the piece of the floor in his hands behind him, and as they opened the door he raised the scantling and struck at them and would no doubt have killed some one of them except that the scantling struck the top of the door in the cell. Before the Mexican could recover to strike another blow, McDonald shot him twice and he fell dead.

There were a lot of saloons and gambling houses in the village and it was lively. A rancher named Broadway was elected sheriff, and he appointed me a deputy. Crime was rampant, and there were two murders in one week. A rancher named Monahan was shot from ambush while returning home from

town. The murderer was soon tracked down and
placed in jail. Then a day or two later, at a saloon
owned by John LaBar, some men came in for a
drink late one night. They called up everyone in
the house to have a drink with them. While LaBar
was serving them, a bum, who was hanging around,
tried to ring in on them for a drink, but LaBar
ordered him out of the house and refused to let him
have a drink. The fellow went out and as LaBar was
closing up his place soon afterward, he was stabbed
by this man and died within a short time. I arrested
the murderer and locked him up in our jail which
was pretty full.

The following Sunday morning the sheriff told
me to take a prisoner, an old man in for some minor
offense, back out to where he had been working on a
ranch, so that he could get some clothing he had
left there.

While we were out of town, a number of citizens
met at the mill and formed a Vigilance Committee.
At about ten o'clock that morning the Committee
went to the jail and took the two murderers out and
hanged them to the cottonwood trees in front of the
town hall. They took two lumber wagons, placed a
board across the wagon box at the rear end, and had
the murderers stand on the board with the nooses
around their necks and the other end of the rope
fastened to the limb of a cottonwood tree. The first
man to be hanged either fainted or the noose was
too tight. He sank down on the rope, and, as there

was very little slack, his neck was not broken; he just strangled.

The other man, just as the team started to drive from under him, jumped as high as he could and his neck was broken. Everything was very quiet when someone in the crowd spoke up, 'Why, the son of a gun must have been hanged before. He knows just how to do it.'

Phoenix was quiet and peaceful for a long time after this, and the bad element got out of town. An inquest was held on the dead men, but no witnesses could be found who recognized any of the Committee, although none of them were masked. It was all over when I returned with the old man to the jail. I am satisfied that the sheriff knew what the Committee intended to do, and sent me off with the old man to get him out of the way.[7]

[7]The vigilantes were led by Marion Slankard. As Breakenridge notes, they hanged two men: one Keller, the slayer of Luke Monahan (or Monihan), and one McCloskey, the killer of LaBar (or LeBarr). Frank C. Lockwood, *Pioneer Days in Arizona: From the Spanish Occupation to Statehood* (New York, 1932), pp. 273-75.

VII

Prospecting Around Tombstone

DURING September, 1879, the Southern Pacific
Railroad was completed into Old Maricopa.
This was opposite the Maricopa Wells stage station,
and about five miles west of the present station of
Maricopa. The railroad company laid out a townsite here, and ran an excursion from Los Angeles to
this place and sold town lots. At that time it was
expected that all freight shipments and passengers
going to points north of the railroad would depart
from this point. Quite a number of lots were sold,
but there was very little building done. There was
a daily stage running to Prescott, by way of Phoenix,
and another one running to Tucson and the East
from here. Large sixteen-mule teams were hauling
mining machinery and supplies to the points north
and east.

There was much talk about the mines in Tombstone that had been discovered by Ed Schieffelin,
and a rush of miners and prospectors went down
there. I resigned as deputy sheriff, and with Frank
Cox, an attorney, and George Marlow, a ranchman,
started just after Christmas, 1879, for a trip to the
new mines. We had a span of horses and a light
wagon and reached Tucson in two days. We passed

a number of large mule teams loaded with mining machinery for the mines in Tombstone and Bisbee. The railroad graders were strung out for more than thirty miles and had about reached the old overland stage station at Picacho, where we stopped the first night out.

On reaching Tombstone I decided to stay awhile and go prospecting. A pocket of rich ore had been found in a mine called the Mary A in the middle pass of the Dragoon Mountains. There was a good-sized camp in this pass, and I went there prospecting that winter. This was directly under Cochise's stronghold, but as it was winter the Apaches were not troublesome.[1] I found a large cave under a dry creek bank, closed up the front with poles and bear grass, and made it a very comfortable room.

I prospected all winter with little success, as the snow was deep and I knew nothing about the game. But I worked hard.

[1]Cochise (born 1824?) led the Chiricahua Apaches in war (that grew out of a tragic misunderstanding) against Arizona whites and overland travelers from 1861 until in 1872 General O. O. Howard and Cochise made peace. By the time Cochise died two years later even Arizona whites had come to admire the integrity and courage of Cochise, one of whose close friends was the revered pioneer, Tom Jeffords. Cochise's Stronghold is a canyon deep in the Dragoon Mountains about fifteen miles northeast of Tombstone. It is now the Cochise memorial recreational area. Howard R. Lamar., ed., *The Reader's Encyclopedia of the American West* (New York, 1977), pp. 229–30. Writers' Program of the Work Projects Administration, *Arizona: A State Guide* (New York, 1940), p. 440.

In the spring I went to Sycamore Springs, about halfway between the Dragoon Pass and Tombstone, where they were building a reservoir which would supply Tombstone with water, and I worked there a month. Then I returned to Tombstone and worked in that vicinity until the fall of 1880, when I took charge of some teams hauling lumber from the Hauchuca Mountains to Bisbee and Tombstone. I hauled lumber into Bisbee for the first waterjacket smelter.

Tombstone Camp was first started at Waterville, about a mile from where the town now stands. This camp was made because there was running water there at that time. Afterward a townsite was laid out close to the mines and named Tombstone. The first house was built there in April, 1879.[2]

There are several stories as to how the town came to be named Tombstone. But the discoverer of the mines, Edward Schieffelin, prepared a history of his discovery of the mines for the Arizona Pioneers Society, a part of which, with the permission of the Society, is presented on the following pages that comprise this chapter:

[2]Tombstone will figure largely in this and the next eight chapters of *Helldorado*. Laid out and flourishing in 1879, Tombstone was in the midst of a spectacular boom in 1880 and was incorporated and made the seat of Cochise County (named after the heroic Apache chief) in early 1881. The standard general work on the history of the town is Odie B. Faulk, *Tombstone: Myth and Reality* (New York, 1972), a work complemented by John Myers Myers, *The Last Chance: Tombstone's Early Years* (New York, 1950).

HISTORY OF THE DISCOVERY OF
TOMBSTONE, ARIZONA

As told by Edward Schieffelin[3]

In January, 1877, I outfitted in San Bernardino, with two mules and all the necessary apparatus for prospecting, and left there after outfitting, with twenty-five or thirty dollars in money, going to what is called the Hualapai country, on the borders of the Grand Canyon, not far from Hackberry. While I was there prospecting, a company of Hualapai scouts enlisted to go into the southern part of the Territory scouting for Apaches. I had been there about two months and had not found anything, and thinking that would be a good opportunity to prospect, to follow the scouting party about through the country and thus be protected from the Indians, I went down with them, and arrived at Camp Huachuca about the first of April. There the scouts remained for about a month, making preparations for scouting, recruiting, etc. During that time I got acquainted with several of the soldiers and other men of the party, and I took short trips through the

[3]Edward L. (Ed) Schieffelin was born in Pennsylvania in 1847. He made his first prospecting efforts in Jackson County, Oregon, before roaming around the West and, finally, on September 3, 1877, recording his first Tombstone silver discovery. On March 14, 1880, Ed Schieffelin and his brother, Albert (1849–1887), were made wealthy by the $600,000 sale of their Tombstone properties to a Philadelphia syndicate headed by Hamilton Disston. Despite his riches, Al Schieffelin could never overcome the lure of the outdoors, and he died in 1897 while prospecting near Canyonville, Oregon. Lonnie E. Underhill, ed., "The Tombstone Discovery: The Recollections of Ed Schieffelin and Richard Gird," *Arizona and the West*, XX (Spring 1979), pp. 44–67, and *The Silver Tombstone of Edward Schieffelin* (Tucson, 1979).

Ed Schieffelin, who discovered silver near
the town he founded and named Tombstone.

Courtesy Arizona Historical Society Library

country alone, coming back to the camp, until they finally got ready and started out, when I went with them, following them around through the country. But after traveling a short time with them, I found that I could do no prospecting by following the soldiers, so I struck out alone, making Camp Huachuca my base of supplies. . . .

Whenever I went into Camp Huachuca for supplies on one of my trips, some of the soldiers would frequently ask me if I had found anything. The answer was always the same, that I had not found anything yet, but that I would strike it one of these days in that country. The Indians at that time were very troublesome, and many settlers were killed previous to and during the year. Several times in reply to my remark that I would eventually find something in that country, the soldiers said, 'Yes, you'll find your tombstone;' and repeated that several times. The word lingered in my mind, and when I got into the country where Tombstone is now located, I gave the name to the first location that I made. On the organization of the district it was called Tombstone from that location.

I had left the scouts on the San Pedro River, about twenty or twenty-five miles from Camp Huachuca;[4] they went on down the river a few days and then back to the post. I stopped with a man named George Woolfolk, who had come there a few days before to take up a ranch, and I had been there a couple of days when two men came in from Tucson one night (they traveled during the night on

[4]Located about twenty miles southwest of Tombstone across the Huachuca Mountains, Camp Huachuca was established on February 12, 1877, as a United States Army outpost against the Apaches. It became Fort Huachuca in 1882 and is now a strategic communications base. Robert W. Frazer, *Forts of the West: Military Forts and Presidios and Posts Commonly Called Forts West of the Mississippi River to 1898* (Norman, 1965), pp. 9-10.

account of the Indians) who had taken the contract to do the assessment work on the old Broncho Mine, about eight or nine miles from where Tombstone now stands.[5] The next morning they saw me and saw I had a good outfit, a good rifle and plenty of ammunition, and wanted me to stand guard for them while they were at work. I agreed to this, and the next day we went down to the mine. While standing guard I could see the Tombstone hills very plainly with my field glasses and I took a fancy to them, noticing that there was quite a number of ledges in the neighborhood of the Broncho Mine, all running in the same direction, about northwest and southeast. When the two men finished their assessment work on the Broncho Mine, they started back to some ranches that they had located on the river as they were coming down, and I went on a trip through the hills. On the first trip I found some float, and liked the appearance of the country; it was a promising country for mineral. That night I came into the camp of the two men, who were going into Tucson next day to get their pay for their work, and one of them, William Griffith by name, who was the owner of their team, proposed to me to furnish me with provisions

[5]Southeast of Tombstone and about two miles east of the San Pedro River, the Brunchow Mine (often called the Broncho or Bronco Mine) was opened in 1859 by Frederick Brunchow, a well-educated German mining engineer who came to the United States in 1850 as a refugee from the German Revolution of 1848. Brunchow was murdered in an 1860 uprising of Mexican employees. The mine was worked off and on until Schieffelin's strike of 1877 diverted activity to Tombstone. Ownership of the mine was something of a jinx, for in addition to Brunchow two other owners died violent deaths: the prominent pioneer, M. B. Duffield, in 1874 and N. M. Rodgers in 1876. Faulk, *Tombstone*, pp. 10–21. Underhill, ed., "Tombstone Discovery," p. 46, n. 21.

and to have such assays made as were necessary, to pay for
recording, etc., if I would locate a claim for him at the
same time I located one for myself; that is, to make a joint
location and to make the monument or dividing line at
the point of discovery. To this I agreed and told him that
one of us should build the monument and the other have
the choice of claims; that I would not have any partners,
as he knew, from what I had told him before, several
times while they were at work. This was agreed upon,
and the two men went the next day into Tucson.

When they came back, Griffith had changed his mind
regarding the claim; he had met in Tucson a man named
Lee, who had some means; was the owner of a flouring
mill, etc., and who told Griffith if he found a good piece
of land on the river of six hundred acres to take it up
under the Desert Act,[6] which was at that time in force,
and that he would help Griffith to reclaim it; would furnish him money to dig a ditch, etc., and so Griffith said he
would rather do this than go in with me. I said, 'All right,
use your own judgment.' In the meantime, however, while
they were at Tucson, I had found this Tombstone claim
and another one called afterwards the Graveyard, and
had located the two veins, making a location for myself
and one for him.

I took Griffith up and showed him where these claims
were, and he was very grateful to me, but still could not
give up the idea of taking up a desert claim; he wanted

[6]The Homestead Act of 1862 provided for a free grant of
160 acres of federal public domain land, an amount that
proved to be too small for profitable farming in the arid and
semiarid Far West. To remedy this defect the Desert Land
Act was passed in 1877; it allowed a settler to acquire a
640-acre plot for a small fee and the introduction of irrigation water on the land to increase its productivity. Lamar,
ed., *Reader's Encyclopedia*, p. 639.

that, and said he could not keep both. The two men started off and went down the river to within four miles of where Benson is now located and took up a desert claim. I continued prospecting, and sometime afterwards other parties came in there and took up stock ranches, and we all camped together for protection, about thirty miles from where Tombstone is now on the San Pedro River, while this party remained there, about three or four weeks. Of this party, George Woolfolk, Albert Smith, and two brothers named Bullard were members; several others came there and remained a short time, then went on. Also at about that time a party called the Chicago Colony came in from somewhere in the East to a place below Tres Alamos; some of them stopping a few days; others went on without stopping, and they all finally went off. The Indians at that time were infesting all that country. There were also two other men, named Landers and Sampson, on the river below where Fairbanks now stands; they took up a ranch about the latter part of April, at the mouth of the Barbacombe Creek, where it empties into the San Pedro River.

While the above-mentioned party were all camped together on the river, I made trips into the Tombstone country and back to the camp, leaving camp early in the morning of one day, remaining at Tombstone the rest of the day and night, and returning the next day to camp. I made several trips in that way, and thus spent considerable time, but did not go there and make a camp or stay there any longer than one night at a time.

The ledges in Tombstone were pretty hard to find; they did not crop boldly out of the ground, and it was pretty slow work prospecting until you once learned the country; then it went fast enough. All that summer I did not find anything of great importance. I found some good ores and good float, and found several croppings at Tombstone, but did not find any of the principal mines until the following spring. I found enough, however, to satisfy myself that there ought to be good ores there. I was well satisfied of this, but could not go there and stay long enough to do anything, on account of the roving bands of Indians.

Cochise was living at that time,[7] and in his stronghold, within nine miles of Tombstone, across the valley; on a clear day any single house can be discerned from this place in Tombstone now. The place was rather dangerous on this account.

About August, I think it was, Griffith sent up word to me, by a man that was going up the river, to come down and bring some of the ores from those locations we had made, and to bring copies of the notice, and we would go into Tucson and have the claims recorded. I did so, taking some of the ores and copying the notices of these claims, and went into Tucson, I think about the 25th or 26th of August; at all events, there was a feast going on; I think it was the feast of San Juan.

Griffith was somewhat acquainted in Tucson; I was not. He had several pieces of float, some rich ore, which he took around and showed to several parties; there being no assayer in Tucson, we could not get an assay. The rich ore came from one of the ledges I had found, called the Graveyard, which was a small ledge, and afterwards did not amount to much. There was very little interest manifested by the few people that looked at the ore; most of them pronounced it very low-grade; and many would not look at it at all. Griffith became discouraged and did not want to have any of the claims recorded, but I persuaded him that we ought to have at least one of them recorded, and he recorded the Tombstone, and his ledge of which I do not remember the name. The other ores did not look

[7]In 1877 Schieffelin may not have been aware that Cochise had died in 1874.

so well, though they afterwards proved the richest, and those claims were not recorded. . . .

Our experience that day was to say the least disheartening, and toward night Griffith asked me what I thought about the matter, what I should do. I replied, 'I am going back; it does not matter to me what those fellows say; I believe the rock is good, and that one of these days there will be something of importance found there, whether we find it or not. I have seen enough to show me that there are mines there, and I am going back; you may do as you please.' Griffith answered that he did not want any more of the mines, and would stick to his ranch, and go back there in a few days. Said I, 'Well, I am going back to-night;' and I went to another store and obtained such supplies as I needed, a little bacon and a sack of Mexican flour, which was cheaper than American, and having just enough money left to get my mule shod when I passed the military post (where they would do the work for about one-half what civilian blacksmiths would charge). So I left Griffith in Tucson, and started off to the San Pedro River; about where Fairbanks is now. . . .

I was now reduced to the last extremity; without provisions, almost without clothing, and with but thirty cents in money. There was plenty of game at hand, and I subsisted on the deer I killed. After a few days, I thought my best plan was to hunt up my brother Albert, whom I had last heard of as working in the Silver King Mine, and to get him to come to Tombstone with me. He had some money, and we could have assays made, and could obtain supplies. . . .

About that time the company sent a man named Richard Gird to the Signal Mine, to assay for them, and he erected a little office and started his furnace. My brother Al was acquainted with Gird, but I had never seen or heard of him before, as far as I know. One day Al took some of the ore to Gird, and told him to assay it and that he would pay him. After looking at the ore, Gird asked where it had come from. Al replied that he did not know, that I had brought it there from the southern part of the Territory. 'Well,' said Gird, 'the best thing you can do is to find out where that ore came from, and take me with you and start for the place.'[8] Al told him to assay it, anyhow, and he would pay for it. He brought Gird three pieces, and the next day Gird made two assays of the ore. My brother was working on the afternoon shift, and went to work at three o'clock; I came off at seven o'clock in the morning, and as he came into our cabin to change his clothes that day I was asleep. Al had with him the returns for the two assays, and said he, 'That ore of yours—one piece goes six hundred dollars to the ton, and the other only forty dollars.' The latter piece was from the Tombstone, which Griffith had recorded. The other ore assayed very well; in fact a great deal better than any in that part of the country. Gird had said that he would make an assay of the third piece the next day, and the next day I went to his office, and he was just engaged in cupelling the ore down. He asked me what I thought the ore ought to assay and I said I thought about a thousand dollars, to which he agreed. The assay yielded two thousand dollars to the ton; the piece of ore was from the Graveyard claim, which

[8]Richard (Dick) Gird (1836–1910) grew up in New York state and went to California in 1852 where he remained, except for two years in Chile, until 1861. In the latter year he brought to Arizona the talents of a miner, civil engineer, and assayer honed during his California-Chile period. His venture with the Schieffelins lifted Gird into the status of a truly wealthy man, an affluence which he used to accumulate an even greater fortune through activities in land development, beet-sugar production, and cattle ranching during the 1880s and 1890s in the vicinity of Chino, California, and in northern Mexico. Faulk, *Tombstone*, pp. 36–46, 164–65, 188–89, and *passim*.

afterwards did not prove very valuable, although some of the ore was very valuable. . . .

We left Signal City[9] on the 14th of February, just as the noon whistle was blowing. Gird and my brother wanted to get dinner, but I said, 'No, I have been waiting long enough, and we will go at once.' My brother mounted his saddle horse, and Gird and I got upon the wagon, and away we went. We hastened through the country, three hundred or four hundred miles, until we reached our destination. As we passed different stations on the way, we heard of a party that had started out ahead of us. People about Signal could not understand why Gird was going. He had been offered the general superintendency of the company, yet he would not accept it. My brother was known to all the miners, though they did not know me, and they could not understand why the two should leave, especially Gird. They were asked often where they were going, but I had not told them definitely, and they really did not know. . . .

In the afternoon I found where the ore had come from, and was building a monument when my brother returned, having killed a deer. I called to him to come and see what I had found, if he did not think there was rich ore in that country. I had printed the head of my pick down into the rock, and he said, 'Yes, that is rich ore.' It was the claim we called the Lucky Cuss, and the croppings were six or seven inches wide, and probably forty or fifty feet long; it cropped boldly out of the ground, and in many places you could print a half-dollar into it.

From appearances we thought the ore would run twenty thousand to twenty-five thousand dollars to the ton,

[9]The ghost town of Signal (or Signal City), site of the Signal Mine, is in an isolated section of west-central Arizona about forty miles east of present Lake Havasu City on the Arizona side of the Colorado River.

because it was nearly all metal; it assayed fifteen thousand dollars to the ton. Some of it ran twelve hundred to fifteen hundred dollars in gold and fifteen thousand dollars to the ton in silver. I was considerably excited, and there was a change over all from that moment. My brother and I brought some of the ore to the cabin, and I said to Gird, 'I've got some rich ore this time.' Said he, 'I got a rich piece in some of that you brought the other day.' He had assayed a piece of ore that went six thousand or seven thousand dollars to the ton. We had some great large pieces and showed them to him, and he said, 'Yes, that is good ore.'

The next morning we went up and made the locations, and traced it up, staking it out and putting up the monuments. At a point where there was a large cropping Gird took a sample of the ore, from one side of the croppings to the other, which measured thirty feet. That sample yielded two hundred and ten dollars. Gird took the sample that day and assayed it the next, and he said that was the best sample he had ever taken in his life, covering the whole width of the ledge. We were now all perfectly satisfied that we had found all we wanted. . . .

A few weeks passed and we ran out of provisions, about a week after the discovery of the Lucky Cuss. One day I started out, taking the course of the Lucky Cuss ledge, running northwest, to trace it up, and I traced it about a mile and a half down into a gulch, where I found some float and, following this up another gulch, I found the Tough Nut Mine.

That day we were short of provisions, and the next morning my brother and Gird started into Tucson for some. At this time Hank Williams (who had joined the party) had got discouraged; he had not found anything very good; the best assay he got up to this time was seventy dollars. He could not get rid of the idea that the black iron croppings ought to carry the mineral, and since then it has proved that a great deal of it was rich in mineral below the surface. He would not give up this idea, and got discouraged, but Gird showed him some of the ore, and talked him out of leaving, saying, where would he find better ore than that? They did not know then that the Tough Nut was found, that discovery being made the same afternoon.

I brought some of the ore in that evening; it was very rich horn silver ore, and looked even richer than it actually was. It ran twenty-two hundred dollars to the ton. Gird and Al went into Tucson for provisions, and the next morning I overtook Williams going up into the mountains and showed him the ore. I kept prospecting around this Tough Nut, and could not satisfy myself which way the ledge ran. When my brother and Gird came back, about a week after, I had about given up, and made up my mind I would not spend any more time on it. They brought with them a Mexican boy to haul water, and they built a little cabin at the Lucky Cuss Mine, and moved our camp over there. I stopped prospecting in order to help them move over, which occupied two or three days. If I had not done so I should have found the Grand Central, which was discovered by Hank Williams only about a mile from the Tough Nut, and this was the best prospect yet found in the district and it afterward turned out the best. Williams had taken up the location, and taken it all in, without making provision for us, as he should have done according to the agreement with Gird. I spoke to Gird about the matter, and he went up there towards evening, and Hank Williams and Gird contended about the agreement. Gird said, 'Haven't I kept my part of the agreement, and made your assays, etc., and here you have made your location and without saying a word?' Williams acknowledged this, and said he was going to keep it, but finally agreed to cut off fifty or one hundred feet from the end of the claim, which we accepted, and called it the

Contention Mine, because of the dispute over the agreement. This discovery of the best prospect by an outsider rather discouraged me, as regarded prospecting further. The Grand Central and the Contention and the Tough Nut were the best mines in the district, and remain so to the present time. The Lucky Cuss has not proved as good as was reported. . . .

We had begun work in August, 1878, and this was in the early part of 1879. We then incorporated the Tough Nut series into the Tombstone Mill and Mining Company, and Governor Safford[10] and my brother went East to sell the stock. The incorporation was, I think, in February, and they immediately went to Philadelphia and other Eastern points, and during the following summer sold a small part of the stock, but not much. In the meantime Gird was running the mill and I the mine, when I was not engaged in taking bullion to Tucson, until we made the agreement with the stage company to haul the bullion.

About that time my brother returned from the East, and as I was somewhat dissatisfied with the result of our labor, and did not think we had accomplished much, I immediately on his return packed up and went off prospecting, leaving Gird and my brother to run the mine. I was gone about three or four months, and one day, having broken the needle of my gun, I had to come into Tombstone. This was in February, 1880, and I found that letters and telegrams had been sent after me to all parts of

[10]Serving from 1869 to 1877, Vermonter Anson P. K. Safford was one of Arizona's best territorial governors. His investments in Tombstone mining provided Safford with a $150,000 fortune which enabled him to be the founder and main developer of Tarpon Springs, Florida, before his death in 1891. Frank C. Lockwood, *Pioneer Portraits: Selected Vignettes*, introduction by John Bret Harte (Tucson, 1968), pp. 109–27.

the country. A party was on the way from Philadelphia to buy our property; they were Messrs. Disston, Corbin, Ashbury, Hart, and Sheriff Wright, who had chartered a special car and come down to the mines. They made Mr. Disston the spokesman of the party, and he came to me and asked what we would take for our interest in Tombstone, in the two companies, the Tough Nut Mill and Mining Company, and the Corbin Mill and Mining Company. We answered six hundred thousand dollars for our remaining interest in the two companies; our proposition was reported to the other parties and they accepted it. This was in March, 1880, and thus disposed of my own and my brother's interest in the mines, leaving Gird still interested. The first payment, which was about April 1st, was, I think, fifty thousand dollars, and the remainder to be paid in monthly installments. My brother went East, and held the stock in his possession until the money was paid. That closed my own and my brother's connection with Tombstone, excepting one or two small prospects which we sold afterward. The Graveyard we did some work on, but it did not amount to much. The Tombstone claim was sold for a few hundred dollars, and it has never turned out much of importance. Another mine close to it, called the Ground Hog, and another, the Contact, we sold, one for six thousand dollars and the other for fifteen thousand dollars, I think. I have been told that nearly fifty million dollars' worth of mineral has been taken out of the Tombstone district.[11]

[11]According to Underhill, *Silver Tombstone*, p. 53, the Tombstone mining district had, through 1970, produced 1,500,000 tons of silver-bearing ore worth $38,000,000. Much more than half of this yield occurred during the initial and most lucrative phase of Tombstone's mining history down to 1886.

VIII

Appointed Deputy Sheriff

THE interesting period in Tombstone was during the fall of 1879, and the early eighties. In those few years Tombstone was born a mining town, lived a mining town, and died a mining town. Like all mining towns in their beginning, when money came easy and went easy, many kinds of men and women flocked there, and it was soon a lively camp.

The Contention Mill and Mining Company built a quartz mill on the San Pedro River about eight miles from Tombstone, and a town sprang up there called Contention. Then a millsite was selected and a quartz mill built by the Tough Nut Mining Company on the river opposite Charleston, about nine miles from Tombstone, and two miles from the Bronchow Mine. Soon afterward the Grand Central built a mill between Charleston and Contention, at Fairbank. Fairbank is the only town left.[1]

The mines at that time were in Pima County, and

[1]Because of the need for water in the ore reduction mills, the San Pedro river provided the location for these three mill towns. The rather tame Contention and the tough, boisterous Charleston both faded into the status of ghost towns while Fairbank has barely survived. James E. and Barbara H. Sherman, *Ghost Towns of Arizona* (Norman, 1969), pp. 26-27, 40-41, 53-55.

Tucson was the county seat. Charles Shibell was sheriff, and he appointed John H. Behan as his deputy,[2] with headquarters in Tombstone. Behan held this position until 1881 when he was appointed to be sheriff of Cochise County.

In December, 1879, Wyatt Earp came to Tombstone, from Prescott, carrying an appointment as a deputy United States Marshal. His brothers James, Virgil, Morgan, and Warren soon followed him.[3] Doc Holliday, a two-gun man, and noted as a killer, came about the same time.[4]

It is claimed by many that Alfred Henry Lewis, who was in Tombstone in later days getting material for his story of 'Wolfville,' placed Wolfville at Tombstone, and Red Dog at Charleston.[5]

[2]Information about John H. Behan may be found in the Special Biographical Notes at the end of this chapter.

[3]The Earps did come to Tombstone in December, 1879, but it was Virgil rather than Wyatt who held the office of deputy United States marshal. Further information about the Earp brothers may be found in the Special Biographical Notes at the end of this chapter.

[4]Information about Doc Holliday may be found in the Special Biographical Notes at the end of this chapter.

[5]Alfred Henry Lewis (1855-1914) was one of the most successful national political reporters and fiction writers for William Randolph Hearst's publications. Although born and raised in Ohio, Lewis roamed through the Southwest in the 1880s, probably visiting Tombstone in 1883 and 1885 or in 1889. Flournoy D. Manzo, "Alfred Henry Lewis: Western Storyteller," *Arizona and the West*, X (Spring 1968), pp. 5-24. C. L. Sonnichsen, *From Hopalong to Hud: Thoughts on Western Fiction* (College Station, 1978), pp. 41-43.

Wyatt

Virgil

Morgan

James

The Earps, who arrived in Tombstone during 1879 and 1880.
(No picture of a fifth brother, Warren, could be located).
Courtesy Arizona Historical Society Library

Fred White was elected town marshal of Tombstone, January 6, 1880. On November 6, 1880, while a lot of cowboys, with Curly Bill—whose true name was William Brocius—among them, were having what they considered a good time in Tombstone, they began shooting their pistols off into the air. They fired quite a volley, and then started to run with the police after them. They scattered, and Curly Bill ran into an alley, where he was caught by Marshal White and Virgil Earp, whom the marshal had summoned to assist him in making the arrest. The marshal placed him under arrest and told him to give up his pistol. As Brocius was in the act of handing it to him, Virgil Earp grasped Curly from behind around his arms, and, as White took hold of the gun, it went off and White was killed. Curly claimed that White jerked it out of his hand, and, as it was very light on the trigger, it went off accidentally. He gave himself up to Virgil Earp and was taken to Tucson, the county seat, for trial.

He was held in jail there for a month. At his trial Virgil Earp testified that, when White told Curly to give up his gun, he (Earp) grasped Curly Bill from behind around the waist, that White jerked the gun out of Curly's hand, and that it was an accidental shot. He said he examined the gun at the time and there were still five loads left in it, showing that Curly had not been a party to shooting up the town and disturbing the peace. Curly was acquitted. From that time he very seldom came to Tombstone, but made his headquarters at Galeyville. This is the only time I ever heard of Curly shooting anybody, except it was said that he and others had killed some smugglers in Skeleton Canyon. While he was a notorious leader of the rustlers and cattle thieves, none of the stockmen ever swore out a warrant for him, and he was never indicted for any crime.[6]

At this time the Earp party and the cowboys and rustlers were friendly, and Virgil Earp was appointed as town marshal to fill the unexpired term for which Fred White had been elected.

In the fall of 1880 the population of Tombstone had grown to about sixty-five hundred people, and the surrounding country was settling up rapidly. The mining and business men wanted a new county set off from the southeast corner of Pima County. In order for the new county to get as much taxable property as possible, they drew the boundary of the new county so as to take in the railroad about where the station of Pantano is situated, and from there ran the north line of the proposed county due east, and north of the railroad to the line of New Mexico. This made the county eighty-three by eighty-four miles.

The camp was strongly Republican, and most of the taxpayers were Republicans. The mines and the merchants were paying most of the taxes, and they wanted a two-gun man for sheriff of the new county.

[6]Information about Curly Bill Brocius may be found in the Special Biographical Notes at the end of this chapter.

Looking North

Looking South

Tombstone, Arizona Territory, in 1881
Courtesy Arizona Historical Society Library

They asked the Governor, who was a Republican, to appoint Wyatt Earp, who was also a Republican, as sheriff, and Earp had every reason to believe that he would be appointed.

The Territorial Legislature met in Prescott in January, 1881, and formed Cochise County along the lines requested by the people of Tombstone. John H. Behan, a Democrat, was also an aspirant for the office of sheriff, and had a strong backing for the position throughout the Territory. Governor Frémont evidently thought that Behan was the man for the office, and appointed him to hold office for two years. This is what caused the enmity of the Earp party toward the sheriff.[7] The office was worth forty thousand dollars a year, as the sheriff was also assessor and tax collector, and the board of supervisors allowed him ten per cent for collections. The Republicans wanted this plum for themselves. John Dunbar was appointed county treasurer, and Al Jones, recorder. Both were Republicans. Behan then

[7] It was unusual for the Republican Governor John C. Frémont to appoint a Democrat, John H. Behan, to the politically important and lucrative post of Cochise County sheriff, but Behan had a very influential connection in the Republican Party through his Tombstone associates and friends, Thomas and John Dunbar. The Dunbar brothers were from Bangor, Maine, and "were close family friends" of the powerful United States senator, James G. Blaine, also of Bangor, Maine. In addition to his senatorial service, Blaine was the Republican presidential nominee in 1884 and was secretary of state in 1889–92. John Dunbar was Behan's partner in a Tombstone livery stable.

appointed Harry Woods under-sheriff and gave me an appointment of deputy sheriff.[8]

The rich Tombstone mines brought many bad men from all parts of the West into the valleys of the San Simon, Sulphur Spring, and San Pedro Rivers, where stage robbers, outlaws, and cattle rustlers found refuge. But for all that, Tombstone was an orderly, law-abiding town. What little killing was done there was done among the lawless element themselves. This element was very much in the minority, and during the five years I lived there I never heard of a house being robbed, or anyone being held up in the city, and it was perfectly safe for any lady or gentleman to pass along the streets, day or night, without being molested.

Most of the gamblers and card dealers were good citizens, and gambling was as legitimate as dealing in merchandise or any other business. The gamblers had to pay a license the same as the merchants, and they were taxed. The proceeds of the gambling licenses all went to the support of the schools. Several of the gamblers who owned their own games had their families with them, and when they were not on duty at the saloon, would generally be found at their own homes. They were taxed pretty heavily, and when any of the churches wanted a donation,

[8] As a Democrat, Breakenridge was politically acceptable to Behan. In addition, the sheriff had need of Breakenridge's skills as a plainsman in Apache-infested Cochise County with Breakenridge often being required to travel through dangerous country to the east-end town of Galeyville.

John H. Behan
Sheriff of Cochise County, 1881

William M. Breakenridge
Deputy Sheriff

they always called on the gambling fraternity first for a contribution.

Of course there was the usual array of short-card operators and tin-horn sports who hung around the games looking for a chance to pick up a sucker, but they were soon spotted and they did not last long. There were several of the two-gun type of gamblers, but these men never made any gun-play while at their games.

The Clantons—Finn, Ike, Billy, and the old man—had a ranch a few miles above Charleston on the San Pedro River.[9] Tom and Frank McLaury had a ranch in the Sulphur Spring Valley, about twenty-five miles east of Tombstone, and four miles south of Soldier Holes.[10] Galeyville, on the east slope of the Chiricahua Mountains, on the rim of the San Simon Valley, was a refuge for all outlaws. And a number of times they could be seen hanging around Soldier Holes.

Galeyville was a small mining town with a smelter, and employed some thirty or forty men in the mine and smelter. It was here where some sixty or more rustlers, who were engaged in stealing cattle in Mexico, and bringing them across the line into New Mexico and Arizona in large herds, made their headquarters; they knew no law but their own.

[9]Information about the Clanton family may be found in the Special Biographical Notes at the end of this chapter.

[10]Information about Tom and Frank McLaury may be found in the Special Biographical Notes at the end of this chapter.

This town was started when the Texas Mine near there was opened up. Mr. Galey was president of the mining company, and Mr. Wessels built a small smelter and worked the ore from the Texas Mine, and also from a mine managed by a young lawyer named Elliott in Granite Gap, New Mexico, about twenty miles east of Galeyville and just across the line of Arizona.[11]

There was no port of entry between El Paso and Nogales, and the only Mexican custom house, outside of these places, was on the San Pedro River where it flows from Mexico into the United States. Cattle were plentiful and cheap in Mexico, there were few line riders, and it was very easy for smugglers to get across the line from both directions. The Mexicans smuggled Mexican silver into the United States to buy goods, and then smuggled the goods into Mexico, as the duty on merchandise was very high and so was the export duty on silver.

There were but very few cattle ranches in those

---

[11] Among Galeyville's top population of about 400 were many hard-working, honest people who clustered around the smelter of the former Pennsylvania oil man, John H. Galey (1840–1918), but, as Breakenridge declares, the town was dominated by its eleven tough saloons and the outlaw element headed by Curly Bill Brocius. When John H. Galey's Texas Mine closed in the early 1880s, the decline of the turbulent town was swift with the inhabitants rapidly departing, the smelter being moved to Bisbee, and the flimsy wooden buildings being torn down for lumber for the neighboring town of Paradise. Sherman and Sherman, *Ghost Towns*, pp. 58–59.

Loading ore from the mines around Tombstone, early 1880's.

Courtesy Arizona Historical Society Library

valleys at this time. What few there were had not many cattle, and most were willing to buy Mexican cattle whenever they could, and ask no questions.

The outlaws that made Galeyville their head-quarters were most of them cattle rustlers. A party of them would make a raid into Old Mexico where cattle were plentiful, run off a large herd, bring them up through Guadaloupe and Skeleton Canyons, and through the San Simon Valley to near Galeyville. They had squatted on every gulch and canyon near there where there was water, and had built a corral on each of their claims. Here they would divide up the stolen stock, and, placing their brands on them, have them ready for market.

The men were nearly all Texas cowboys whose feeling toward the Mexicans was so bitter that they had no compunction about stealing from them or shooting and robbing them whenever they got an opportunity. One of their men did a thriving commission business acting as the banker and disposing of the stolen stock. Then, while another bunch of rustlers were off making a raid, those left behind would turn themselves loose in Galeyville, having a good time drinking and gambling until they went broke. After the Mexicans found out what they had been doing, there were many of them killed. There was no killing except among themselves while they were drinking, and they confined their crimes to stealing stock and robbing Mexican smugglers who were bringing Mexican silver across the boundary line to buy goods. Most of the time they killed the smugglers. The leaders of the rustlers and outlaws were John Ringo[12] and William Brocius, better known as Curly Bill.

The Clanton family looked after the rustlers' interests along the San Pedro because much stolen stock was brought in from Mexico and moved down the river, and there was nobody patrolling the border for smugglers. The McLaurys looked after all the stock brought up from Mexico through Agua Prieta, where Douglass now stands, into the Sulphur Spring Valley.

The stage robbers, hold-up men, and the other outlaws that made these places a refuge, included Frank Stillwell, Pete Spencer, Zwing Hunt, Billy Grounds, Jim Crane, Harry Head, Billy Leonard, and their followers whose names I have forgotten. At this time the outlaws, rustlers, stage robbers, and certain of the gamblers were good friends.

A good many noted people were living in Tombstone at this time. Tom Fitch, the silver-tongued orator of Nevada;[13] Mark Smith, of Kentucky, who was Congressman from Arizona for many years, and our first Senator to Washington after we became a State;[14] Ben and Briggs Goodrich, of Texas, Colonel Herring, of New York, and many others whose

[12]On John Ringo, see note 7 in chapter X.

[13]One of the West's ablest lawyers was Tom Fitch who later, in November, 1881, was defense attorney for Wyatt Earp in the trial treated by Breakenridge in chapter XI.

[14]On Marcus Aurelius (Mark) Smith, see note 5, chapter X.

names I have forgotten, were practicing law there. Dr. Goodfellow was one of the best surgeons in the West in his day.[15] Mining engineers from all over the world came there.[16]

Among the conspicuous gamblers and fighting men could be found Lou Rickabough and Ed Clark from Colorado; Bat Masterson, Doc Holliday, Wyatt, Virgil, Morgan, and Warren Earp from Kansas and Oklahoma; Luke Short and Charley Storms from Texas; and a number of lesser lights who followed gambling for a living. The principal gambling houses were the Crystal Palace and the Oriental.[17] All kinds of games were played in these saloons, and there was plenty of music. The owners engaged the best talent that could be found, mostly women, to sing in their halls. It was in front of the Oriental Saloon that Luke Short and Charley Storms

[15]On Dr. George Goodfellow, see note 3 in chapter XIV.

[16]Among the top mining engineers in Tombstone was John Hays Hammond. As a recent Yale graduate, Hammond visited Tombstone in 1879. John Hays Hammond, *The Autobiography of John Hays Hammond* (2 vols.; New York, 1935), I, pp. 78–79.

[17]The rival Crystal Palace (founded originally as the Golden Eagle Brewery) and Oriental Saloons were located kitty-corner to each other at Tombstone's busy intersection, 5th and Allen. Lou Rickabaugh, the Oriental's gambling master, hired Wyatt Earp to keep order and Wyatt, along with Morgan Earp, Luke Short, and Buckskin Frank Leslie were among those who dealt faro in the gaudy establishment. Faulk, *Tombstone*, pp. 92–122, 143. Writers' Program of the Work Projects Administration, *Arizona: A State Guide* (New York, 1940), p. 247.

fought a duel with pistols and Storms was killed.[18]

Charleston had very little law and order, and was well-known as a wild and wicked town during 1879 and '80, with a killing there frequently. Jim Burnett was justice of the peace, and a saloonkeeper named Jerry Barton was constable. Barton was a powerful man, and it was reported that he had killed several men with his fist; he was known as a man-killer, with many notches on his pistol handles. He stuttered badly, and at one time, when he was asked why he killed so many men, replied:

'Why, m-my tri-tri-trigger fi-finger stut-stutters.'

[18]In the gambling dispute between Storms and Short, the former was the aggressor as well as the one who paid with his life on February 25, 1881, in the "case of kill or be killed" cited by Breakenridge. Charley Storms had been a professional gambler in Kansas, Colorado, and the Black Hills of Dakota. The dapper dressing Luke Short had a card-playing career frequently punctuated with gun play. Short left Tombstone after killing Storms and returned to Dodge City, Kansas, where, enveloped in controversy in 1883 with reform elements over the management of his Long Branch Saloon, he soon enjoyed the support of his old friends Wyatt Earp and Doc Holliday. Short triumphed over the reformers, but Dodge City was becoming too tame so he left for Fort Worth, Texas, where, in 1887, he killed Jim Courtright, a shakedown artist and professional gunman, before dying quietly himself in Kansas in 1893. George Whitwell Parsons, *The Private Journal of George Whitwell Parsons* (Phoenix, 1939), p. 209. John Myers Myers, *The Last Chance: Tombstone's Early Years* (New York, 1950), pp. 94–95. Ed Bartholomew, *Wyatt Earp, 1879 to 1882* (Toyahvale, Texas, 1964), p. 119. Lamar, ed., *Encyclopedia*, pp. 1106–7. William R. Cox, *Luke Short and His Era* (Garden City, 1961).

John H. "Doc" Holliday

Bat Masterson

Two of the well-known characters
that frequented Tombstone during the 1880's.

At another time, when he was asked how many men he had killed, he deliberated a moment then asked, 'Do you co-co-count M-M-Mexicans?'

After Cochise County was formed, and there was a change in the administration, Barton continued to run his saloon. One day he had a row with a Mexican and shot him, and left at once for Tucson. Sheriff Behan sent Deputy Sheriff Dave Nagle[19] after him and he was arrested and brought back, but the Mexican was not badly hurt, and as soon as he recovered he left for Mexico; so Jerry was not brought to trial.

Earlier he had a fight with a drunken cowboy and had broken his neck with his fist. After the Mexican that he had wounded ran from the country, Jerry's bondsmen surrendered him to the sheriff. He was tried and convicted for killing the cowboy and sent to the penitentiary at Yuma for several years. If he had not seen fit to boast about how easily he could kill a man with his fist, he would not have been convicted, as he could have claimed that it was an accidental blow.[20]

[19]On David Neagle, see note 6 in chapter IX.

[20]The brutish Jerry Barton typified "wild and wicked" Charleston. In 1881, he had wounded the Mexican, Jesus Gamboa, and killed his saloon partner, one Merrill. After shifting his saloon to Fairbank, he used his fists to kill sixty-year-old E. J. Swift on March 16, 1887, was convicted and served time. Barton also killed a Phoenix man with his fists. The Breakenridge reference here to Barton being held for trial evidently refers to 1881 and the shooting of either Gamboa or Merrill. Neither crime, however, resulted in a prison term. Martin, *Tombstone's Epitaph*, pp. 61–64.

While he was in our county jail awaiting trial, the grand jury indicted Milt and Will Hicks for stealing cattle, and a grand larceny warrant was issued for them. I had been told that they were getting ready to leave the country, but that they would be in Tombstone within a few days. I was well acquainted with Milt Hicks, and meeting him soon after on the street, we shook hands and he said he was in town waiting for his father and Will to meet him there. Knowing if I arrested him then, I should not get Will, I decided to wait until I could get them both. In the meantime someone told Milt that I had a warrant for them and he left town at once.

Several days later Sheriff Behan told me that Virgil Earp reported that I told Hicks to get out, as I had a warrant for him. Behan learned that Milt had a sweetheart in town, had come in to see her, and was leaving the next morning. Behan told me to get him before he got away. I knew that he always held out at the Grand Hotel and, going there early in the morning, I saw his horse back of the hotel. As I entered the hotel I met John Ringo, who wanted to talk to me, but I told him I would see him later, and started for the dining room. As I opened the door I met Hicks coming out. Holding out my right hand I said, 'Good morning, Milt,' and shook hands with him. At the same time I grabbed his pistol with my left hand and told him he was under arrest. I then took him to jail. This was on October 22, 1881.

During the evening of October 23rd, at about

five o'clock, three prisoners, Milt Hicks, Charles Thompson, alias Yank, and one named Sharp who was in for murder, made a sensational escape. The jailer, William Soule, left the jail and went uptown leaving the jail keeper, Charles Mason, on watch. Shortly after his departure, the 'trusty' who cleaned up the jail desired to go in where the prisoners were for the purpose of removing some slops. As Mason opened the door and let him in, Sharp caught Mason, and while they were struggling Hicks and Yank ran outside. By this time Sharp managed to break away from Mason, who was inside, and in an instant he, too, was outside, and with Yank was trying to pull the door shut; but they were for a moment prevented by Mason's getting his arm between the door and the jamb. Jerry Barton came to the keeper's help and with his wonderful strength prevented Mason's arm from being broken in the door. Finding that he and Barton could not keep the escaping men from closing the door, Mason threw the lock at Sharp, striking him on the cheek and inflicting a deep cut. Yank and Sharp then locked the door and followed Hicks who had already started down Tough Nut Street.

The keeper yelled for a time before anyone came; finally a Chinaman who lived nearby heard his cries, went to the jail, and was then sent uptown to inform Jailer Soule, who returned and liberated Mason and informed Sheriff Behan of the jail break. In a short time, Behan, City Marshal Virgil Earp, Morgan and

Wyatt Earp, Frank Leslie and myself, were in pursuit, but as darkness came on we were unable to follow the trail any great distance. It led toward Waterville. Next morning, a posse, of Sheriff Behan, Marshal Earp, Dave Nagle, and me, started out to visit the neighboring ranches, as Hicks and Sharp would probably call on some of them for horses, arms, and food. But we could learn nothing of them.

Behan then sent me out in the afternoon of October 24th with a posse consisting of Dave Nagle, Lance Perkins, Charley McLellon, Jack Young, and Si Bryant. We went to Galeyville the night of the 25th, and down to San Simon Cienaga the following day, but could get no trail of the men. While at the Cienaga we arrested a man named Stark who was wanted for grand larceny, but his partner escaped. We took Stark to the railroad station, and Dave Nagle took him on the train to Tombstone, while the rest of us returned to the Cienaga. The hunted men evidently left the country at once, as none of them were ever heard of in Arizona again.

While in San Simon Valley we found two stolen horses, branded with the Chiricahua Cattle Company's brand. Going to Joe Hill's ranch[21] I met Curly

[21] Joe Hill was a close associate of the Clanton-McLaury faction. Later Hill "sought an amnesty" with Wyatt Earp, but before this could be arranged he was killed when thrown from his horse. After Hill's passing, his ranch became the nucleus of the much bigger San Simon Ranch. Myers, *Last Chance*, pp. 150–51, 216. Bartholomew, *Earp, 1879 to 1882*, pp. 137, 145.

Corner, Fifth and Allen Streets,
the center of Tombstone's business section in 1881.

Bill, and told him I found the horses and that they had evidently strayed in there. He helped us round them up and said, 'I wonder who could have stolen them.' But I was pretty sure he was the guilty party.

We led the horses over the mountain to the Chiricahua Ranch, and returned them to the foreman.

Nagle arrived in Tombstone with Stark, who at once gave a bond, and within a few days George came in with a lawyer named Elliott from Granite Gap and surrendered to the sheriff. Both were then brought to trial, but there was no evidence to convict them and they were exonerated of the charge. I never believed them guilty, but they were unfortunate in having their ranch in San Simon Valley, since it was the hangout for all kinds of rustlers and outlaws.

During all this time most of the ranchers were afraid to furnish any information in regard to the outlaws and cattle thieves, and it was impossible to get any help from them. If the outlaws came to a ranch, the ranchmen furnished them such assistance as they asked for, and allowed them to go their way without any interference, thinking they themselves would be immune from rustling. But the outlaws soon found it was easier to steal cattle from the ranchmen and sell them to the butchers and Government beef contractors than to make the hard trip into Mexico after them, especially as the Mexicans were on the alert, ready to shoot on sight, and had killed several of them. The ranchers then found that the rustlers had no respect for anyone's stock, so they began to assist the officers, and the outlaws were soon chased out of the country, and Cochise County was free from them for a long time.

A short time before this, Old Man Clanton, Dick Gray, Billy Land, and several others, were waylaid in Skeleton Canyon as they were returning from Mexico with a herd of cattle they had bought there, and every one of them was killed by Mexicans.[22]

There were many killings in Charleston during

[22]These events came to a head in August, 1881. According to one widely accepted version, Old Man Clanton and Curly Bill Brocius led their outlaw confederates in an ambush of Mexican smugglers headed by Miguel Garcia in Skeleton Canyon that took up to nine Mexican lives and yielded a rich booty of $4,000 in silver, mescal, horses, and cattle. In reprisal on August 13, 1881, Mexican troops from Fronteras, Sonora, attacked a cattle drive being led through nearby Guadalupe Canyon by Old Man Clanton and others. Old Man Clanton was killed in the battle. Skeleton Canyon was a key corridor for rustlers and smugglers operating from both sides of the border. It was also the locale of one of the memorable events in Southwestern history: the final surrender of Geronimo and Nachez to General Nelson A. Miles in September, 1886. Henry P. Walker, "Retire Peaceably to Your Homes: Arizona Faces Martial Law, 1882," *Journal of Arizona History*, X (Spring 1969), pp. 7–9. Writers' Program, *Arizona*, p. 376. Dan L. Thrapp, *The Conquest of Apacheria* (Norman, 1967), pp. 362–63. The folklore of Skeleton Canyon with its baleful history of ambush and sudden death is captured in Walter Noble Burns, *Tombstone: An Iliad of the Southwest* (Garden City, 1927), chapters 6, 8. A dissent has been registered by Ed Bartholomew who in *Wyatt Earp, 1879 to 1882*, pp. 183–85, denounces the "Skeleton Canyon massacre" as a "fiction" fabricated at the time to discredit Old Man Clanton and his supporters.

1880, but I cannot recall the names of those killed. A tin-horn gambler, known as 'Johnny-behind-the-Deuce,' killed Henry Schneider, the chief engineer at the smelter, in Quinn's saloon.[23] A large mob of the smelter men gathered to lynch him, but the constable got him into a buckboard behind a span of mules, and started with him for Tombstone as fast as he could go before the mob could organize. The smelter men, to the number of twenty-five or thirty, followed and were overhauling him when he met a man exercising a race mare, and got him to take the prisoner on behind him and make a run for Tombstone, as the mules had given out. Here the prisoner was turned over to Wyatt Earp, who was a deputy United States Marshal. When the mob, increased by about an equal number of miners from the Hill, came up to take 'Johnny-behind-the-Deuce' away to hang him, Earp stood them off with a shotgun, and dared them to come and get him. It didn't look good to the mob, and Earp took him to Tucson, which at that time was the county seat. 'Johnny' was

[23]Henry (or W. P.) Schneider, chief engineer of the Tombstone Mining and Milling Company, was fatally shot on January 14, 1881, by the very touchy gambler, John O'Rourke (known as Johnny-behind-the-Deuce), in revenge for a fancied insult by the aloof engineer. O'Rourke's nickname stemmed from his habit of bluffing with the deuce in faro. Outrage over this senseless murder caused the highly respectable Tombstone diarist George W. Parsons to write of O'Rourke, "I believe in killing such men as one would a wild animal." Martin, *Tombstone's Epitaph*, pp. 57–58. Parsons, *Private Journal*, p. 199.

bound to the grand jury, but before he was indicted he escaped, on May 17, 1881, after lying in jail nearly a year. The evidence was very clear that it was a cold-blooded murder.[24]

Charleston was a hangout for the riff-raff from Fort Huachuca, Bisbee, Tombstone, and other places where there were officers to see that they behaved themselves. In Charleston they were not molested. The only officers there were Jim Burnett, the justice of the peace, and Jerry Barton, the constable, and they paid little attention to keeping law and order.

[24] According to the *Tombstone Epitaph*, January 17, 1881, it was Virgil Earp, along with Tombstone Marshal Ben Sippy and Sheriff Behan, who prevented the lynching of Johnny-behind-the-Deuce and got him safely to a jail in Tucson from which he escaped in April, 1882. Martin, *Tombstone's Epitaph*, pp. 58–60.

SPECIAL BIOGRAPHICAL NOTES

In order to properly provide background information on the main characters in *Helldorado* but without lengthy footnotes appearing in the text, the following is provided:

JOHN HARRIS BEHAN. Born in Westport, Missouri, in 1845 of Irish parents, Behan came to Arizona in 1863 as a civilian employee of the "California Column" of federal soldiers operating in the Southwest. With a flair for politics and personal relations, Behan held one public office after another (including sheriff of Yavapai and Cochise Counties, territorial legislator, prison superintendent, and customs inspector) and closed his career as a key employee in the commissary department of the Southern Pacific Railroad in Arizona, California, and northern Mexico. He died in Tucson in 1912. In his Tombstone days (1879–1883) he was known as something of a dandy who had a way with women. The latter led to enmity between Behan and Wyatt Earp in their rivalry for the affections of the beautiful young San Francisco actress, Josephine Sarah Marcus, who in 1881 switched from being the mistress of Behan to that of Earp. Moreover, Earp was put out by Behan's reneging on a promise to name Earp as a deputy once Behan became sheriff of Cochise County. John Harris Behan biographical file, Arizona Historical Society, Tucson. Glenn G. Boyer, ed., *I Married Wyatt Earp: The Recollections of Josephine Sarah Marcus Earp* (Tucson, 1976), chapters 1–6.

CURLY BILL BROCIUS (WILLIAM GRAHAM). With "dark, kinky hair" under "a wide-brimmed sombrero" the "tall, rugged" Texas cowhand, William Graham, who sported twin forty-fours on criss-crossed gun belts, was known as Curly Bill Brocius after coming to Arizona in 1878 with a trail herd for the San Carlos Apache Indian Reservation. Moving to the Tombstone area soon after, Curly Bill fell in with the outlaw faction led by Newman H. (Old Man) Clanton. Sherman and Sherman, *Ghost Towns*, p. 58. Howard R. Lamar, ed., *The Reader's Encyclopedia of the American West* (New York, 1977), p. 127.

THE CLANTON FAMILY. Originally from Tennessee, the Clantons came to Arizona in 1873 by way of Missouri and Texas. In the course of their movement through Arizona before settling on their ranch southwest of Charleston in 1878, one of the sons (Peter) was killed in a clash with vigilantes from St. John. The *Arizona Daily Star* (Tucson) of March 26, 1882, described the Clantons as being "fine specimens of the frontier cattle man" who, although quite well off, "lived on horse-back, and led a life of hardship." In individual terms, the family patriarch, Newman H. (Old Man) Clanton, had the look of a hard-bitten bearded pioneer, young William H. (Billy) Clanton was a strapping six-footer, and Phineas F. (called Finn by Breakenridge) and Joseph Isaac (Ike) Clanton were "wiry, determined-looking men." Farewell to the Clantons—file in Arizona Historical Society, Tucson. Manuscript U.S. Census Returns, Charleston, Pima County, 1880, p. 190. *Arizona Daily Star* (Tucson), March 26, 1882, p. 1, c. 3-5.

THE EARP FAMILY. Nicholas Porter Earp (1813-1907) went overland to California from Iowa in 1864 with his wife, Virginia Ann Cooksey (1823-1893), whom he had married in 1840 and who became the mother of five sons, James, Virgil, Wyatt, Morgan, and Warren, and three daughters, Martha, Virginia Ann, and Adelia. There was also a half brother, Newton Jasper Earp, who was the son of Nicholas P. Earp and his first wife, Abigail Storm.

Newton, James, and Virgil Earp served in the Union Army during the Civil War. Thereafter, the clannish Earp brothers roved through such tough western towns as Lamar, Missouri, Wichita and Dodge City, Kansas, and Las Vegas, New Mexico, during the 1860s and 1870s. The Earps came to Tombstone in December, 1879, with Virgil carrying an appointment as deputy United States marshal. Later, Virgil held two concurrent appointments as town marshal of Tombstone (in which he was sometimes referred to as chief of police). Wyatt was first employed as a Wells, Fargo stagecoach guard and soon became active, also, as a gambler and saloonkeeper and, with Virgil and the other Earps, as a prolific investor in mine and town-lot properties. Wyatt also served for a time as a deputy sheriff of Pima County before Cochise County (including Tombstone) was sliced off from parent Pima County in early 1881. Contrary to repeated statements by Breakenridge (and other writers), Wyatt Earp, as Larry D. Ball shows, was never a deputy United States marshal in Arizona until his last few months in Tombstone. Wyatt and Virgil, had checkered careers which produced contradictory views on their characters. Thus, their backgrounds as officers of the law in the Kansas boom towns put them on the side of order and cast them in a favorable light to many respectable, propertied citizens. On the other hand, their often high-handed, gun-slinging behavior as law officers and their active involvement in gambling, saloon life, and prostitution (through some of the Earp women in Kansas) planted a deep distrust and dislike of the Earps in the hearts of many honest citizens. Wyatt's past was the shadiest of all with an arrest for horse theft, a name for bunco-artistry, and a persistent pattern of womanizing in his pre-Tombstone background. Wyatt may have tried to turn over a new leaf in Tombstone, for he stood in well there with such pillars of local society as diarist George W. Parsons, mining executive E. B. Gage, Mayor John P.

Clum, and the Reverend Endicott Peabody. The following apt characterizations of the five Earp brothers (in order of age) during their Tombstone period were published by the Tucson *Arizona Daily Star*, March 26, 1882 (years of birth and death are inserted): *James C. Earp* (1841–1926), saloonkeeper by profession, was the most agreeable of the five brothers [who, although in Tombstone with the others, took no part in the troubles there]. *Virgil W. Earp* (1843–1906) was a "raw-boned six-footer" of "bold, daring" appearance and "sinister expression" who was "not to be trifled with." *Wyatt Berry Stapp Earp* (1848–1929) was "cold and calculating" and the "brains" of the brothers as well as having a "more refined appearance" than the others. *Morgan Earp* (1851–1882) was both the most handsome and the most reckless of the five [and also the favorite of his older brother, Wyatt]. *Warren B. Earp* (1855–1900) was the youngest and the only brother who was dark complected. With all the other brothers being blue-eyed and "decided blondes" (who were generally clean shaven except for long sandy mustaches) and of about the same six-foot build, it was often difficult for outsiders to tell them apart.

JOHN HENRY (DOC) HOLLIDAY was a cynical, quarrelsome, hard drinking gambler-dentist who, knowing his tubercular condition doomed him to an early death, took wry satisfaction in his famed career as a deadly gunfighter. Holliday's one redeeming quality was loyalty to his friends, which he more than demonstrated to Wyatt Earp and his brothers in Tombstone. Born in Georgia in 1851, Holliday left there with a dental degree and went on to gain a top reputation as a gambler and gunfighter (with his dental practice a sideline) in such Great Plains cowtowns as Dodge City before accompanying the Earps to Tombstone. In 1887, Holliday died of tuberculosis in Glenwood Springs, Colorado, at the age of thirty-six. He was survived by his alcohol-prone companion and wife, the former prostitute, Kate Elder (1850–1940), who had been born Mary Katherine Horony, with whom he had a long, stormy relationship. Kate's autobiographical declaration about Doc that "if he was crowded, he knew how to take care of himself" was an understatement. Pat Jahns, *The Frontier World of Doc Holliday* (New York, 1957). A. W. Burk and Glenn G. Boyer, eds., "The O.K. Corral Fight at Tombstone: A Footnote by Kate Elder," *Arizona and the West*, XIX (Spring 1977), pp. 65–84.

FRANK AND TOM McLAURY. Robert Franklin (Frank) and Thomas (Tom) McLaury (often given as McLowry in the 1880s) were sons of a Tama County, Iowa, farmer and lawyer, Robert Houston McLaury. Tom and Frank left Iowa to join their brother William (Will) McLaury, a lawyer, in Ft. Worth, Texas, with whom they intended to study the law. Instead, they came to Arizona and established themselves on the ranch mentioned by Breakenridge. Josephine Sarah Marcus (who later married Wyatt Earp) described Frank McLaury as a self-regarded "lady-killer" and "a little strutter" who was "a troublemaker" while Tom was "quiet and pleasant" and reputed to be "the hard worker in the family." *Des Moines Sunday Register*, November 1, 1981. Boyer, ed., *I Married Wyatt Earp*, p. 68.

IX

Vignettes of Life in the '80's

IN THE spring of 1881, a bunch of rustlers brought out a large herd of cattle from Mexico through Skeleton Canyon. After holding them in San Simon Valley, where the feed was good, until they had recovered from their trip and were in good order, they sold them at San Carlos to the contractor who had a contract with the United States Government to supply beef to the Apache Indians at that post and to the troops stationed there.

Among the cowboys that delivered the cattle at San Carlos were John Ringo, Curly Bill, Old Man Hughes, his son, Jim Hughes, Joe Hill, who changed his name when he left Texas, Tom Norris, and several others whose names I have forgotten.

After receiving their money for the cattle and dividing it among themselves, they returned to Fort Thomas on the Gila River[1] and at once entered

---

[1]Named after Brigadier General Lorenzo Thomas (d. 1875) and located on the Gila River about seventy-five miles northeast of Tucson, Fort Thomas (1876–1891) was maintained as a United States Army strong point against the Apaches on the nearby San Carlos Indian Reservation. Robert W. Frazer, *Forts of the West: Military Forts and Presidios and Posts Commonly Called Forts West of the Mississippi River to 1898* (Norman, 1965), p. 12.

into a poker game in Jack O'Neil's saloon. Ringo
and Joe Hill were expert poker players, and it was
only a matter of a short time until they would have
all the money and the balance of the rustlers would
have to start out on another raid into Mexico for
more cattle. The game was running for several days
and nights, and whenever anyone dropped out for a
few hours' rest, there was always someone to sit in
and fill his place.

Dick Lloyd, a Texas cowboy who worked for J. B.
Collins at the Bear Spring Ranch, was in the habit
of coming to Fort Thomas every few months and
getting on a rip-roaring drunk. After a few drinks
he would get on his horse and with a Texas cowboy's 'Whoop-ee!' dash through the streets on a run
firing his pistol into the air. He was considered
quarrelsome when he was drinking.

On the second day of the poker game, he came
into the fort and at once started drinking. The gang
of rustlers that were playing cards did not like him,
and I guess he soon found out that they did not
want him around, for he left O'Neil's saloon and
went to one kept by Ed Mann. Mann and he got
very drunk. They soon got into a quarrel, and staggered out of the saloon onto the street. Mann gave
Lloyd a push and he nearly fell down, and Dick
cautioned him not to do it again. Mann gave him
another shove, and this time he did fall, but it was
on account of his drunken condition. Lloyd drew
his pistol and took a shot at Mann, but Mann

dodged and the bullet caught him just across the back of the neck. He fell as if he were dead, but the shot just creased him and knocked him out.

Lloyd got on his feet and, after looking at Mann, whom he thought he had killed, started to run for his horse which was tied to a tree close by. He was so drunk that he fell down several times before he reached it. Placing his six-shooter back in the scabbard, he drew his rifle from the saddle and with another loud 'Whoop-ee' yelled:

'Here is where Dick Lloyd is away for Texas!'

He then rode his horse into a store next to the saloon and fired a few shots into a lot of tinware hanging on the wall, while the proprietor dropped down flat on the floor behind the counter. Dick rode in at one door and out of another and started toward O'Neil's saloon, but, when meeting a man he knew, threw down on him and ordered him to go to the store and get him some cartridges and to be quick about it.

Then the idea struck him that he had better get himself a better horse than the one he had, so, riding into the corral back of O'Neil's saloon, he dismounted and, pointing his gun at Johnny Boyle who was in charge of the corral, he ordered him to take the saddle off his horse and place it on a fine horse standing there belonging to Joe Hill. He then mounted the Hill horse, and rode into O'Neil's saloon. As he entered the door it was supposed that everyone at the poker table took a shot at him.

He fell from the horse riddled with bullets, one of which went through the horn of the saddle. The horse, badly scared, ran off into the brush, with Joe Hill after it, but it soon returned to the corral, and Hill returned to the poker party.

Lloyd was lying dead on the floor all crumpled up and they left him there until the coroner took charge of the body. The poker game continued, and the players started a 'kitty' from their jackpots to buy a suit of good clothes for Lloyd to be buried in and to pay for the funeral expenses. They also hired a couple of Mexicans to dig a grave up on a little hill near by. Next morning the poker game stopped just long enough for the funeral. The cowboys, all mounted, rode behind the corpse, which, wrapped in a blanket, they lowered into the grave with their lariats. After placing about a dozen empty bottles at the head of the grave, they fired a salute over it, and returned to the poker game!

Frank Leslie, known as 'Buckskin Frank,' was a noted figure in Tombstone. He was a bartender for Colonel Hafford, claimed to have been a scout, and was a good shot and rider. When in the saddle, he used to wear a buckskin suit. He was considered a very treacherous man when drinking, and made few friends. On June 2, 1880, he attended a dance at the opera house, and walked home with Mrs. Killeen, the Commercial Hotel housekeeper, who had separated from her husband. While they were sitting on the front porch of the hotel above the street,

"Buckskin Frank" Leslie,
one of the fighting men of Tombstone.
Courtesy Arizona Historical Society Library

her husband, Mike Killeen, also a bartender, came out on the porch, and after a few words Leslie shot and killed him. He afterward married the widow.[2]

During the winter of 1881, Leslie went to work for Milt Joice, proprietor of the Oriental Gambling Saloon, tending bar. One day he was serving two men over the bar, when a cowboy named William Claybourn, known as the Kid, came in drunk and started to argue with the two men. Frank ordered him out of the house. Claybourn left and went to the corral and got his rifle, saying he was going to kill Leslie. He stepped behind a fruit stand on the sidewalk near the door of the saloon. Someone went into the saloon and told Leslie that the Kid was out there with a rifle and meant to kill him when he came out. Leslie, taking his pistol in his hand, came out of a side door behind the Kid and spoke to him, and as the Kid turned Leslie shot and killed him.

[2]Franklin (Buckskin Frank) Leslie told conflicting stories about his origins, but it is probable that he grew up in Texas and had some training as a pharmacist. Be that as it may, he turned up in 1877 at the San Carlos Indian Reservation in Arizona as an army scout after having perhaps served the military from Texas to the Dakotas in the 1870s. In civilian life he settled down to bartending and an 1880 partnership in owning the Cosmopolitan Hotel on Allen Street. Leslie's nickname came from his customary garb of a fringed buckskin jacket. Leslie was an interesting, well-informed conversationalist, but there were two sides to him: "sober, he was courteous as a preacher, but drunk, he was like primed lightning." Colin Rickards, *"Buckskin Frank" Leslie: Gunman of Tombstone* (El Paso, 1964), pp. 4–12. Douglas D. Martin, *Tombstone's Epitaph* (Albuquerque, 1951), pp. 79–87.

He stood there with his pistol in his hand until the city marshal came and arrested him. As the marshal reached for the pistol, Leslie cautioned him to be very careful, as it was very light on the trigger. After carefully letting the hammer down, he handed it to the officer. Leslie was tried and acquitted, as it was claimed he acted in self-defense.

Claybourn, a short time before this in Quinn's saloon in Charleston, had killed James Hickey, another bad man. Hickey was drunk and abusing everybody that came into the saloon. The Kid came in and when asked to fight drew his gun and went to work. He killed Hickey and was acquitted.[3]

In the summer of 1883, Joice bought a ranch in the Horseshoe Pass in the Swisshelm Mountains, and put Leslie in charge of it. He had his home in Tombstone, but was at the ranch a great deal of time, and kept a woman there, and a young man by

[3]Born in Mississippi in 1860, William F. (Billy or The Kid) Claiborne drifted into Arizona as a teenage cowboy with a chip-on-his-shoulder. By 1881, Claiborne had become a member of the Clanton-McLaury outlaw faction. Buckskin Frank Leslie, John Ringo, and Claiborne had been drinking companions, but Claiborne apparently blamed Leslie, unjustly it seems, for the death of Ringo in July, 1882, (see note 6 in chapter XIV.) When he returned to Tombstone from work in a Globe, Arizona, smelter, Claiborne went gunning for Leslie at breakfast time on November 14, 1882, but, as Breakenridge declares, Claiborne's first shot missed while Leslie's found its mark. Bill O'Neall, *Encyclopedia of Western Gunfighters* (Norman, 1979), pp. 60–61. Martin, *Tombstone's Epitaph*, pp. 88–93. Rickards, "*Buckskin Frank*", pp. 15–23.

the name of O'Neil, hired to look after the stock. One day he returned to the ranch from Tombstone drunk, quarreled with the woman, and shot her to death. He then shot at the boy and wounded him, but he got into the brush and escaped, and Leslie could not find him. Thinking he had killed them both, he rode back to town and reported that the boy had killed the woman in a quarrel, and that he had shot the boy in self-defense. The young man got to a neighbor's ranch, was brought to town, and Leslie was arrested for murder. He was tried, convicted, and sentenced to the penitentiary for ten years—which sentence he served.[4]

Mrs. Leslie got a divorce from him,[5] and while he was serving his sentence he got in correspondence with a woman living in San Francisco. Shortly after he was released from prison, she met him in Yuma

[4]Buckskin Frank's paramour was former prostitute and Bird Cage Theater entertainer Molly Williams (or Bradshaw) whom he killed in a drunken quarrel on July 10, 1889, at the Magnolia Ranch. It was James Neal upon whom Leslie tried to pin the crime. Rickards, *"Buckskin Frank,"* pp. 25-32. Martin, *Tombstone's Epitaph*, pp. 93-95.

[5]According to Tombstone old-timers, Buckskin Frank was wont to stand his wife, May, up against their house to improve his marksmanship by shooting her profile with bullets. Known in Tombstone, therefore, as "the silhouette girl," May understandably lived in fear of her husband and was granted an uncontested divorce from Leslie on the grounds of adultery, battering, and his failure to provide for her. Rickards, *"Buckskin Frank,"* pp. 23-24, 26. C. L. Sonnichsen, *Billy King's Tombstone: The Private Life of an Arizona Boom Town* (Caldwell, Idaho, 1942), pp. 34-35.

and married him. As soon as he got out of prison, I got him a position with Professor Dumbell, who was the geologist for the Southern Pacific Company. He was looking for coal in Mexico, and wanted a man to attend to getting his supplies in to him. The Indians were rather bad in that vicinity, and I recommended Frank for the job. He was down there about three months and then came back to Yuma, was married, and went to San Francisco to live, but it was not long before his wife got a divorce.

In 1925, thirty-five years later, I was at Bartlett Spring, California, and met a man from Oakland. He told me that he ran a poolroom in Oakland, and that Leslie came to him down and out. He gave him a bed in his rooms, and a light job looking out for the poolrooms. Leslie remained there about six months, and one night when this man went home he found that Leslie had skipped out and stolen a six-shooter from him. He learned that Leslie went north, but did not try to follow him up. I was up there in October, 1926, but could get no trace of him.

While there, I learned that Dave Nagle[6] died at his home in Oakland in the spring of 1926. Nagle was much in evidence in Tombstone in the early eighties, and was elected city marshal in January,

[6]Well respected by all in strongly factionalized Tombstone, David Neagle (1847?–1926) was an efficient lawman and gun handler and sometime miner, saloonkeeper, and politico who spent most of his career in California to which he returned from Cochise County in 1882. His principal residence was San Francisco.

1882. Before that he was a deputy under Sheriff Behan. He was a fearless officer and a good one.

The few law-abiding citizens in Charleston had a small adobe building which they used for a church. One Sunday evening when they were gathered there for their evening service, Curly Bill and a bunch of cowboys came to town, and some of them suggested that they attend church. They agreed, and, armed as usual, all trooped into the church. The good people, fearing trouble, began to leave, and soon the place was empty except for the gang. The preacher started to leave also, but he was told that they came to hear him preach and intended no harm. So he remained, and preached them a sermon, hitting them as hard as possible. They asked him to line out a hymn, and they all sang. Then they asked him to pass the hat and take up a collection, and they filled his hat with Mexican dollars; it was the largest contribution ever taken up in that church!

Next morning as Curly was dozing in front of a saloon, Justice Burnett[7] came around the corner of the building with a shotgun in his hands and arrested Curly. He tried him right there on the spot, and fined him twenty-five dollars for disturbing the

[7]Famed, as Breakenridge notes, for his arbitrary justice levied, often, at the barrel of a shotgun, Jim Burnett was born in New York state about 1832. According to C. L. Sonnichsen, Burnett "had hair to his shoulders, a beard right out of the old testament, and an eye as hard as a ball bearing." Sonnichsen, *Colonel Greene and the Copper Sky-rocket* (Tucson, 1974), pp. 28–30.

peace the night before at the church. Curly paid, but said no more church for him, it was too expensive.

After Burnett had been justice of the peace for a couple of years, the board of supervisors of Pima County called on him for a settlement. He told them he kept no books, that he did a cash business in assessing fines, and that the county did not owe him anything, as his office was self-sustaining! This was the condition of things up to the time Cochise County was created.

The board of supervisors from Cochise County cleaned house and appointed all new officers in Charleston. Sheriff Behan appointed William Bell as deputy sheriff there. Bell made a good officer, but it was almost impossible to get a conviction. If a man was arrested for murder, there were always witnesses to swear it was in self-defense, and if it were cattle-stealing, he could always prove an alibi.

Shortly after Cochise County was formed, Jim Burnett moved onto a ranch he had taken up on the San Pedro River above Charleston. W. C. Greene, a cattleman, had a ranch a short way above him. Along in the nineties they had a dispute about water rights, and Greene placed a dam in the river to impound the water. One day it was stated that Burnett blew up the dam with giant powder. Greene's little daughter was down playing in the sand in the river bottom at the time, and was caught in the flood of water and drowned. Greene and Burnett were bitter enemies after that and each threatened

William C. Greene and his daughter, Eva.
Courtesy Arizona Historical Society Library

the other. One day they met on the street in Tombstone. Both went for their guns, but Greene was too quick for Burnett and shot him dead in his tracks before he could get his gun into play. Greene was acquitted. He soon after got possession of the copper mines in Cananea, Mexico, and made an immense fortune, and everyone who had stood by him during his trouble was handsomely rewarded by him.

He was a great lover of fine horses, and always took pride in having the best. One day while he was driving a span of half-broken colts, they ran away. He was thrown from the buggy and killed.

The Tombstone city officers elected January 5, 1881, were John P. Clum, mayor,[8] and Ben Sippy,

[8]John P. Clum (1851–1932) was a key figure in Tombstone in the early 1880s as both mayor (1881–1882) and the editor of Tombstone's famed newspaper, the *Epitaph*. Clum was a strong friend of the Earps and a vigorous opponent of the Clanton-McLaury "cowboy" faction of outlaws and of Sheriff Behan whom Clum accused of aiding and abetting the outlaws. Born in New York state, Clum attended Rutgers College and then went west to New Mexico in the Army Signal Corps, and in 1874–1877 made a name for himself as organizer of the first Apache reservation, the San Carlos, in Arizona. Clum left Tombstone in 1882, spent time in Alaska, and eventually went into retirement in Los Angeles. A strong Republican like his life-long friend, Wyatt Earp, Clum revisited Tombstone during the first annual Helldorado Days in 1929 and left his own incisive pro-Earp memoir of Tombstone's turbulent days, "It All Happened in Tombstone," *Arizona Historical Quarterly*, II (October 1929), pp. 46–72. John P. Clum manuscripts, Special Collections, University of Arizona Library, Tucson. Woodworth Clum, *Apache Agent: The Story of John P. Clum* (Boston, 1938).

city marshal. Sippy defeated Virgil Earp by forty votes. Some four or five months later Sippy resigned the office, and Virgil Earp was appointed by the city council to fill his place. He at once had his brother Wyatt appointed as a deputy city marshal, another brother, Morgan, appointed as a city policeman, and Doc Holliday as a special officer, thus making them all peace officers sworn to obey the laws and to enforce them.[9]

Sheriff Behan's office was for a short time in a corral on Fifth Street. He had in a back room a prisoner whom he had arrested for stage robbing. The man was to be taken to Tucson within a few days, as the crime was committed in Pima County. I was seated at the desk in the office, and Behan was in a chair close to me leaning back against the wall, when a shot was fired so close to me that a grain of powder struck my temple and set the blood running freely. The bullet passed me and entered a bunch of papers in a pigeonhole in the desk.

I thought the shot had come from outdoors, and had been fired in an effort to rescue the prisoner. I jumped to the door with a loaded shotgun that was standing next to the desk, but could see no one. I then saw what had happened. Behan's pistol had dropped from his belt and fallen on the floor and accidentally discharged. When the excitement was

[9]Not until shortly before the shootout with the Clantons and McLaurys on October 26, 1881, did Virgil Earp deputize his brothers, Wyatt and Morgan, and Doc Holliday.

Mr. and Mrs. John P. Clum.
He was elected mayor of Tombstone in January 1881.
Courtesy Arizona Historical Society Library

over, I took a cartridge from my pistol and placed the hammer on an empty chamber, and never carried but five shots in it from that time. I was always careful to see that the hammer was on an empty chamber whenever I put the gun on.

On March 15, 1881, the Sandy Bob stage plying between Benson and Tombstone was fired upon by stage robbers near Drew's station on the road to Benson, and Bud Philpot, the driver, was killed along with a passenger who was riding in a seat on top of the stage. Bob Paul who was the Wells, Fargo shotgun messenger and Philpot the stage driver, for some reason unknown, had changed places. The team ran away, but kept to the road, and in a short time were under control, and the murderers got nothing.[10]

Jim Crane, Harry Head, and Billy Leonard were accused of the crime, and were searched for diligently, but their trail was lost. A short time afterward it was reported that they were at Cloverdale in

[10]The attempted robbery of the stagecoach resulting in the deaths of driver Eli (Bud) Philpot and passenger Peter Roerig was not only a local *cause célèbre* but led to a bitter rupture between the Earp-Holliday and the Clanton-McLaury factions with Wyatt Earp and Ike Clanton each agreeing, after the October 26, 1881, shootout, that the ill will on each side went back to the attempted stagecoach robbery. Tombstone public opinion tended to reflect these animosities with Earp partisans thinking the Clantons and McLaurys were behind the stagecoach holdup while the Clanton-McLaury partisans saw the evil genius of Wyatt Earp and Doc Holliday behind the event. On Bob Paul, see note 4 in Chapter XI.

New Mexico, near the Mexican line. This was a cattle ranch and an outlaw rendezvous. Sheriff Behan started with Frank Leslie and myself to hunt them. Wyatt Earp, as deputy United States marshal, sent his brothers, Virgil and Morgan, and another man whose name I have forgotten, as a posse to hunt for the stage robbers.[11] After leaving Galeyville, we rode to the San Simon Cienaga, and stopped all night at Joe Hill's ranch.

As none of us had ever been in that part of the country before, we had to inquire the way to Cloverdale, and were directed wrongly as we ought to have expected. Next morning, taking a lunch with us, we started on the trail we were directed to take, and that night reached a deserted ranch house called the double 'dobe. This was forty miles from the Cienaga. The following day we started out early and, on passing through a gap in a mountain, found ourselves on a wide open plain with neither trees nor water in sight. We made a dry camp that night and next morning found the stakes of the Atchison, Topeka and Santa Fe Railroad line that was being surveyed toward Benson. We followed them and then about noon came in sight of the double 'dobe, where we had stayed the first night out.

We had seen no one since we left Joe Hill's; we

[11]Wyatt Earp did not become a deputy United States marshal until early 1882. At this time, March, 1881, it was Wyatt and Morgan who joined their brother, Virgil Earp, in the posse in the latter's capacity as deputy United States marshal.

had run out of provisions, having eaten the last of our lunch the night before, so we let our horses graze and rest until evening. Although both posses camped together at night, we did not travel together, as our party was better mounted and we were more inclined to the saddle. We reached the water some time before the others. Our horses were tired and we did not know the way, or where there was a ranch at which we could get aid, and after a consultation I decided that my horse was as able to carry me back to the San Simon Cienaga that night as he would be in the morning. Behan and Leslie thought the same, but the marshal's posse decided to wait until morning. We saddled up and struck out after dark, and reached Joe Hill's ranch about daylight. We got Hill's people up and hired a man to take some provisions back to the marshal's party. We lay at Hill's one day, then returned to Tombstone.

The stage hold-ups, Crane, Head, and Leonard, were in-hiding in New Mexico, and that summer they were all three killed at Hachita, New Mexico, by some cowboys who were after the reward.[12]

It got to be a common rumor that Doc Holliday,

[12]Head and Leonard were killed in Hachita (formerly Eureka), New Mexico, on June 22, 1881, while attempting to rob the Haslett Brothers' Store. It was claimed that Curly Bill Brocius and John Ringo later retaliated by slaying the Hasletts. Myers, *Last Chance*, p. 151. Not all authorities agree with Breakenridge that Crane was killed at Hachita with Head and Leonard. Some feel that Crane died in the ambush at Guadalupe Canyon (see note 22 in chapter VIII).

the gambler, was with these men when they tried to rob the stage; that it was he who fired the shots that killed Bud Philpot, the stage driver, and the passenger who was riding on top of the stage; that he was drunk at the time and the others could not restrain him, and that he returned to Tombstone, while the others fled south to the San Jose Mountains near where Naco now stands.

The Tucson, Arizona, *Weekly Star*, of March 24, 1881, copies from the Tombstone *Nugget* of March 19, 1881, as follows:

Luther King, the man arrested at Redfield's ranch charged with being implicated in the Bud Philpot murder, escaped from the sheriff's office by quietly stepping out the back door while Harry Jones, Esq., was drawing up a bill of sale for a horse the prisoner was disposing of to John Dunbar. Under-Sheriff Harry Woods and Dunbar were present. He had been absent but a few seconds before he was missed. A confederate on the outside had a horse in readiness for him. It was a well planned job by outsiders to get him away. He was an important witness against Holliday. He gave the names of the three that were being followed at the time he was arrested. Their names were Bill Leonard, Jim Crane, and Harry Head.

The Star later said:

It is believed the three robbers are making for Sonora, via some point near Tucson. The fourth is at Tombstone and is well known and has been shadowed ever since his return. [This is Doc Holliday.] This party is suspected for the reasons that on the afternoon of the day of the attack, he engaged a horse at a Tombstone livery stable, at about four o'clock, stating he might be gone seven or eight days, and he might return that night, and he picked the best animal in the stable. He left about four o'clock armed with a Henry rifle and a six-shooter. He started toward Charleston, and about a mile away from Tombstone cut across to Contention, and when next seen it was between ten and eleven o'clock riding into the livery stable at Tombstone, his horse fagged out. He at once called for another horse, which he hitched in the streets, for some hours, but did not leave town. Statements attributed to him if true, look very bad, indeed, and if proven are most conclusive as to his guilt, either as a principal actor, or an accessory before the fact.

On July 6, 1881, Sheriff Behan arrested Doc Holliday on a warrant sworn out by Kate Elder, who was Holliday's mistress, for killing Bud Philpot. He was released on a bail bond for five thousand dollars given by Wyatt Earp and two other men. The next day Virgil Earp arrested Kate on a charge of being drunk, and she was fined $12.50–her punishment for having Holliday arrested. At his hearing before the justice of the peace, Holliday was discharged on account of insufficient evidence.[13]

[13]Whether Doc Holliday participated in the attempted stagecoach holdup is one of Tombstone's enduring controversies. The 1881 legal finding of insufficient evidence against Holliday has far from settled the matter. Kate Elder withdrew her charge against Holliday who stated that if he had been involved he would not have bungled the job. Wyatt Earp's widow later held that the accusation against Holliday had been fabricated by supporters of Sheriff Behan in order to embarrass the Earp-Holliday clique. Glenn G. Boyer, "Postscripts to Historical Fiction about Wyatt Earp in Tombstone," *Arizona and the West*, XVIII (Autumn 1976), 225-33.

X

Endicott Peabody Builds a Church

URING the summer of 1881, there came into
Tombstone one day on the stage, a young
Episcopal minister right from Boston, Massachusetts. He had just been ordained, and was what one
would call 'a live wire.' His name was Endicott Peabody.[1] He was about twenty-four years of age, and
full of vim and energy. He immediately got busy
building up a membership for his congregation and
getting funds together to build a church. He was a
good mixer and soon got acquainted not only with
the very best element of society in Tombstone—
and there were some educated people there—but he
undertook to get acquainted with everybody; with
the mining magnates and managers, the federal,

[1] Not yet ordained and still a student in the Episcopal
Theological Seminary in Cambridge, Massachusetts, Peabody was in Tombstone from January 29 to July 7, 1882, at
the behest of a Tombstone mine superintendent who knew
Peabody's brother, Francis, and felt that Endicott's robust
Christianity would go over well in tough Tombstone, a con-
jecture that proved valid. Born into a wealthy old aristocratic family of Massachusetts, Endicott Peabody was educated
at Cambridge University in England and then, back in
America, abandoned the family banking business to study
for the Episcopalian ministry. Henry P. Walker, "Preacher
in Helldorado," *Journal of Arizona History*, XV (Autumn
1974), pp. 223-48.

county, and city officials, the professional and business managers, the miners and muckers, the ore
haulers or teamsters, and the saloonkeepers and
gamblers. He soon had a large congregation and had
the money donated to build his church. When it
was completed, he had the money to pay for it, and
the church has never been in debt since.

Peabody was a fine athlete, and was soon named
the official referee in all baseball games and other
outdoor sports that were carried on by the young
men of Tombstone. His decisions were never ques-
tioned, as he was known as being absolutely square
and he had no favorites. He loved a good horse race,
and frequently attended the gymnasium, where he
kept himself in fine physical condition by exercise;
he never refused an invitation to put on the gloves
with anyone, and never was bested.

W. K. Meade, a mining man, who in 1885 was
appointed United States marshal of Arizona Territory,[2] told the story that at one time, shortly after
Peabody arrived, he was with E. B. Gage, the general manager of the Grand Central and Contention
Mines,[3] Charley Leach, a mining superintendent,

[2]On Marshal Meade, see note 12 in chapter XV.
[3]E. B. Gage was one of the few leading men of Tombstone
in the boom of the 1880s who was still active there after the
turn of the century. In 1902, Gage collaborated in the re-
opening of the flooded mines with a new and better pumping
system. As the Tombstone Consolidated Mines Company,
this venture had, however, failed by 1909. Odie B. Faulk,
Tombstone: Myth and Reality (New York, 1972), pp. 180-85.

The Reverend Endicott Peabody.
Courtesy Groton School Archives

St. Paul's Episcopal Church, Tombstone,
built through the efforts of its first minister,
the Reverend Endicott Peabody.
Courtesy Buehman Photo Collection, Arizona Historical Society Library

Mr. Durkee, who had the contract for hauling the ore, Ham Light, and several other mining promoters, playing poker one afternoon in the back room at the hotel. There were two tables, and it was a pretty stiff game. Frequently there would be a thousand dollars or more in the pot.

Gage was an Episcopalian. Mr. Peabody came back where they were playing, and introduced himself and asked them for a donation to help build a church. He explained that it was something needed badly, and the only way it could be built was to get everybody he possibly could to subscribe toward building it. Gage counted out about a hundred and fifty dollars from his pile in front of him, and everyone else in the room followed his example. Peabody was dumbfounded for an instant, and then told them that it was a much larger contribution than he had expected, but it was for a good cause and he knew they would never regret it.

There was a musical society in Tombstone, and a lot of good talent in it. Some of the members had sung in opera. They conceived the idea of putting on the comic opera 'Pinafore,' although the expense of staging it was very high, as they had to send to San Francisco for their costumes. Yet with all the expense they cleared about two hundred and fifty dollars, which they turned over to Mr. Peabody for the church building fund.

Mr. Vaughan once said that when he was teaching school in Charleston during the summer of 1881, the Reverend Mr. Peabody was invited to deliver a sermon. His subject was the evil of the drinking and carousing cowboys and the cattle-stealing rustlers. Billy Claybourn, the would-be bad man who had killed one or two in saloon fights in Charleston, and who was afterwards shot down by Frank Leslie in Tombstone, heard of the sermon and sent word to Mr. Peabody that if he ever came to Charleston again and preached such a sermon he, Claybourn, would come to the church and make him dance. Peabody told the man who delivered the message that he expected to return to Charleston in about two weeks, and would preach a sermon that he thought appropriate, and if Mr. Claybourn would come to the church and listen, and then thought he could make him dance, to try it.

George Parsons, now living in Los Angeles,[4] told me he heard that Mark Smith, a young attorney in Tombstone,[5] and a Mr. Stebbins, who represented the New York stockholders in the very rich mines,

[4]The prolific Tombstone diarist George W. Parsons was a good friend of Endicott Peabody. Both were strong admirers of Wyatt Earp.

[5]Marcus Aurelius (Mark) Smith was a rising lawyer and Democratic politician in Tombstone from 1880 to 1886. In the latter year, he was elected Arizona territorial delegate to Congress, a post to which he was often re-elected. As Arizona's leading Democrat he was a champion of statehood, and when statehood finally came his career was crowned with election to the United States Senate. Steven A. Fazio, "Marcus Aurelius Smith: Arizona Delegate and Senator," *Arizona and the West*, XII (Spring 1970), pp. 23–62.

were one Saturday afternoon playing a game of 'seven up.' Mark won twenty dollars.

The next morning they went to church and Stebbins passed the contribution plate. When he came to Mark, he stood there shaking the plate until he attracted the attention of the whole house, and would not leave until Smith contributed the twenty dollars he had won from Stebbins the night before. That was the kind of people living in Tombstone.

Peabody was known to go into the saloons and gambling houses and go up to the gambling tables when they were in operation, with a crowd around them, and say, 'Gentlemen, I am going to preach a sermon on the evil of gambling Sunday night, and I would like to have you all come to the church and listen to it.' All who could get away went to hear him. He had large audiences always.

One day that summer I had to go to Bisbee to serve some papers for the sheriff. It was in July, I think, and a very hot day. I engaged an outside seat on the stage, and when it drove up to the express office I saw that the Reverend Mr. Peabody was on it. He had an outside seat also and was going to Bisbee. When the stage stopped, he got down and went into Bob Hatch's saloon and came out with two bottles of beer wrapped up in paper to keep them cool, and he and I drank them on the way there. They were very refreshing. He was not one to go behind the door to cover up his acts, but was open and aboveboard at all times.

My business called me into the saloon and gambling houses frequently, and I never heard Peabody spoken of except in the highest terms of respect. He was well liked, and everyone regretted when he was called away at the end of six months. He returned about five years ago, and preached a sermon in his old church. Members of his flock, who were scattered all over the State, came to listen.[6]

Tombstone has a reputation as a wild and wicked city, with a man for breakfast every morning. This is all a mistake. Tombstone was an orderly town, with very little crime. The large majority of the inhabitants were law-abiding. Yes, there were a few tough outlaws there, but they mostly confined their quarreling and shootings to themselves. Even though there were a few killings, as happened in all frontier towns, practically none of the law-abiding citizens were ever injured.

[6] Endicott Peabody followed his successful stint in Tombstone by concluding his seminary studies, gaining ordination, and going on to found in 1884 and head for fifty-six years, the exclusive Massachusetts preparatory school for boys, Groton. Although a Republican himself, Peabody was extremely proud of Groton's most illustrious graduate, Franklin D. Roosevelt, who invited his schooldays mentor, Peabody, to conduct services at St. John's Church, Washington, D. C., on the days of his first and second inaugurations as President in 1933 and 1937. Peabody was never forgotten in Tombstone, and he never forgot Tombstone to which he returned in February, 1941, to celebrate the fifty-ninth anniversary of his arrival in Tombstone. Frank D. Ashburn, *Peabody of Groton: A Portrait* (New York, 1944). Walker, "Preacher in Helldorado."

*Memorial Day observance in Tombstone
during the 1880's.*

Courtesy Arizona Historical Society Library

About the first work I did after I was appointed deputy sheriff was to assess property in and around Tombstone, because the sheriff was also assessor and tax collector.

Soon after I got through assessing the property in Tombstone, in the spring of 1881, I was sent to San Simon, a station on the Southern Pacific Railroad, to serve a summons on a merchant there. I went by train, and while waiting for a return train, I went into a saloon kept by a man they called 'Shorty.' There was a gang of cowboys and rustlers in there playing cards, and Curly Bill was lying on a card table. I had never seen him before. He was fully six feet tall, with black curly hair, freckled face, and well built. Shorty brought in a bucket of water and filling a tin cup said, 'Here's how, boys,' and lifted the cup to drink from it.

Curly, who had raised up on his elbow, shot the cup out of his hand, saying, 'Don't drink that, Shorty, it's pison.' The bullet went through the wall of the board house and killed Curly's horse.

Soon after this trip I was sent out to assess and collect taxes on the personal property in the valleys and mountains east of Tombstone. There had never been any taxes collected in this part of the county, even when it was Pima County, and nearly all the property was personal. There were but few ranches that had any title. There were a great many teams hauling lumber from the Chiricahua sawmills to Bisbee and Tombstone mines, and for building purposes

in the different town sites. I was told by many that
I would have no success, but I started out to try.

I went alone as usual. The Indians were out in
the mountains and valleys and committing all kinds
of depredations, and it kept me rather busy looking
out for them, but I got along finely, and collected
quite a sum of money in taxes. Where the teamster
did not have the money to pay, he gave me an order
on the mining company or party he was hauling for.
After assessing through the Sulphur Spring Valley
as far as Willcox, I returned to Prue's ranch and
remained overnight. Next morning I started over
the trail to Galeyville, where no taxes had ever been
collected, and where the rustlers held full sway.
The merchants and saloonmen had no title to the
land on which their buildings were built. The taxable property was all personal.

I had already made my plans, and as soon as I
reached Galeyville I hunted up a Mr. Turner, the
banker for the rustlers, and asked him to introduce
me to Curly Bill. He took me to Babcock's saloon
and corral where Curly was, then Turner called
him out and introduced me to him. I told him who
I was and what I was, and said I wanted to hire him
to go with me as a deputy assessor and help me
collect the taxes, as I was afraid I might be held up
and my tax money taken from me if I went alone.

The idea of my asking the chief of all the cattle
rustlers in that part of the country to help me collect taxes from them struck him as a good joke. He

thought it over for a few moments and then, laughing, said, 'Yes, and we will make everyone of those blank blank cow thieves pay his taxes.'

Next day we started and he led me into a lot of blind canyons and hiding places where the rustlers had a lot of stolen Mexican cattle, and introduced me something like this:

'Boys, this is the county assessor, and I am his deputy. We are all good, law-abiding citizens and we cannot run the county unless we pay our taxes.'

He knew about how many cattle they each had, and if they demurred, or claimed they had no money, he made them give me an order on their banker Turner. Curly had many a hearty laugh about it. He told them that if any of them should get arrested, it would be a good thing for them to show that they were taxpayers in the county.

I was treated fine by all of them, and I never want to travel with a better companion than Curly was on that trip. He was a remarkable shot with a pistol, and would hit a rabbit every time when it was running thirty or forty yards away. He whirled his pistol on his forefinger, and cocked it as it came up. He told me never to let a man give me his pistol butt end toward me, and showed me why. He handed me his gun that way, and as I reached to take it he whirled it on his finger, and it was cocked, staring me in the face, and ready to shoot. His advice was, that if I disarmed anyone to make him throw his pistol down.

I learned one thing about him, and that was that he would not lie to me. What he told me he believed, and his word to me was better than the oaths of some of whom were known as good citizens.

After assessing the town of Galeyville, I left there with nearly a thousand dollars tax money, with which I arrived safely in Tombstone, and was much relieved when I did so. But I should never have done it if I had tried to assess the rustlers alone.

After that, whenever there was anything to be done in Galeyville or the San Simon Valley, I was sent to do it, and I was kept in the saddle a good portion of the time. I always went alone, as I did not believe in a suddenly picked-up posse. I could depend on myself, but did not always know about the other fellow.

During the summer of 1881, Zackendorf and Company, of Tucson, sent an agent to Tombstone to get out an attachment against an Eastern mining company that had a group of three mines in Bisbee and a smelter at Hereford. The smelter had been shut down for some time and the mines were lying idle. The agent arrived in Tombstone on a Sunday evening, and was in a great hurry to get out the attachment; he got the clerk of the court to sign the papers right after midnight. About one o'clock on Monday morning they were given to me to serve.

I came into Hereford about half after five that morning, and after seeing my horse was well fed and watered, I went to the smelter, which was in the hands of a caretaker, and placed an attachment on the building and contents, with all machinery and tools, and then placed the caretaker in possession as keeper. Then, getting breakfast, I was on my way to Bisbee before seven o'clock. I arrived there about ten thirty, and had my horse taken care of while I ordered a lunch put up at the restaurant so that I could eat it while riding on my return trip. I went to the mines, where I posted the notices of attachment, and returned to the corral where my horse was. I could not find a horse there that I thought would carry me to Tombstone as quickly as my own. So I saddled up and was on my way home before noon, reaching the recorder's office ten minutes before five that evening. The course I rode over was in the shape of a triangle, a distance of eighty miles. Both I and my horse were very tired. The sheriff's office was a fee office, and his fees for this trip amounted to about fifty dollars. Zackendorf's agent paid me well for making the trip. I was in the saddle a little over fourteen hours. The fees at that time were twenty cents a mile both ways, and five dollars for posting each notice of attachment on each piece of property, and one dollar for a copy of each notice, besides other fees for service of papers on the agent of the mining company.

John Ringo and Curly Bill were the big chiefs among the rustlers in and around Galeyville. Ringo was a mysterious man. He had a college education, but was reserved and morose. He drank heavily as if to drown his troubles; he was a perfect gentleman when sober, but inclined to be quarrelsome when drinking. He was a good shot and afraid of nothing, and had great authority with the rustling element. Although he was the leader on their trips to Mexico after cattle and in their raids against the smugglers, he generally kept by himself after they returned to Galeyville. He read a great deal and had a small collection of standard books in his cabin.[7]

One night, while drinking, he got into a poker game with some miners in a Galeyville saloon and lost about a hundred dollars. He asked for an advance of a hundred on his watch and chain, but as he was drinking they were afraid of him, and told him that they were about to close the game as it was late, and to come around the next night and they would give him revenge. After leaving the saloon, he got his horse and came back. On entering the saloon where there were two poker games still going on, with ten or twelve players, he threw down

[7]The mystery and myths surrounding John Ringo's life have largely been dispelled by a recent article by Jack Burrows who shows that Ringo was born in Indiana in 1850, spent most of his teen years in San Jose, California, lacked any college education (contrary to one of the myths about Ringo), went off to Texas in 1869, fell in with a cutthroat gang headed by Scott Cooley, and fled to Arizona in 1879. Although he was a hardened outlaw, Ringo's reputation as a killer has been greatly exaggerated as Burrows shows. Jack Burrows, "John Ringo: The Story of a Western Myth," *Montana: The Magazine of Western History*, XXX (October 1980), pp. 2–15.

on them with his gun and held them up. They were playing with money and no chips.

He remarked, 'You fellows held the top hand all the evening, I hold it now,' and took all the money on both tables, then left and went to Joe Hill's place in the San Simon Cienaga.

By the time he reached there he was sober and told Joe what he had done. He said that if he had not been drunk he would not have done it, as they were all friends of his, and asked Joe to return the money to the saloon. The players got their money back and were satisfied, as they all liked Ringo.

Some dissatisfied person came to Tombstone several months later, and went before the grand jury. As a consequence Ringo was indicted for robbery and a warrant was issued and given to me to serve.

I had met Ringo frequently on my trips to Galeyville and was very well acquainted with him, and we had had many pleasant visits. I was advised to take a posse with me, as they thought he was sure to resist arrest, but I said that if I could not get him alone it would take a troop of soldiers to get him, as he had fifty or sixty followers who would stay with him. Because I was certain that I could arrest him alone, I refused to go if they wanted me to take a posse.

Mounting my saddle horse, I got to Prue's ranch late that night, and the next morning I started over the mountain for Galeyville. I reached there before Ringo was up, and knocked on the door to his room. He came to the door with his six-shooter in his hand. He invited me in, and I told him I had a warrant for him for holding up the poker game.

'What,' he said, 'are you going to arrest me for that? Why, that was all settled.'

He dressed and we went to breakfast together, and he asked me not to say anything about it, as he did not want any of the boys to know he was under arrest. He said that he would have to wait until Turner, their banker, came in that afternoon, to get some money, and if I would head back to Prue's ranch, he would meet me there in the morning. I considered his word as good as a bond, so I went back to the ranch, and next morning Ringo was there for breakfast. He had come in the night and rather than disturb us he had slept in the haystack.

We rode into Tombstone that day, and Ringo told me enough about his family for me to know that they were not aware that he was an outlaw.[8] We were both heavily armed, for the Indians were out and we had to be on the alert all the time. On reaching the town we put up our horses, and as it was about dark we first got supper at a restaurant and then went to the jail. I asked the jailer, who I knew had an extra room, to let Ringo keep his arms and sleep in his house across the street from the jail, and I would be down early next morning and help

[8]Perhaps out of shame, Ringo misled Breakenridge, for Ringo's sisters in San Jose were well aware of Ringo's criminal career and were deeply mortified by it to the extent that they totally rejected Ringo when he paid a visit to San Jose in 1881 or 1882. Burrows, "John Ringo," p. 5.

him get his bond. After Ringo waived examination and his bond was fixed, John Dunbar, county treasurer, Al Jones, county recorder, and one of Ringo's gambler friends were ready to sign it.

There was a law and order committee formed in Tombstone that stood in with the gang that was opposed to the sheriff, and it was reported that some of them had gone toward Charleston to arrest Curly Bill and a lot of cowboys and bring them to Tombstone. Ringo was anxious to get down there and be with his friends. While waiting for Judge Stillwell to approve the bond, Ringo's attorney came to the sheriff's office and said, 'All right, Johnny, the bond is approved,' and Ringo got on his horse, which I had brought to the office for him, and went to Charleston. He got there before the law and order party did; in fact they never got there.

That evening the judge met Sheriff Behan and remarked that he would look into the matter of Ringo's bond in the morning and to have him in court. Behan told him that Ringo's attorney had said that the bond had been approved and that he had turned him loose. The judge replied that he had not approved it and that he held Behan responsible for the prisoner. The judge then issued a warrant for Ringo and gave it to two of the so-called law and order committee to serve.

They proceeded to Charleston that same night to arrest Ringo. On their arrival they were held up at the bridge going into town by a bunch of cowboys who were guarding it, as they were expecting some of the law and order gang and were watching for them. The cowboys disarmed them and took them to a saloon while they awakened Ringo, and told him what was up, and that the men were there with a warrant for him. He told them there were not enough of them to arrest him, that it looked like a put-up job by the sheriff, and to hold them there until he got across the bridge. He rode back to Tombstone and came to my room and told me what they had tried to do. As it was nearly morning I took him to the sheriff's office and made him a bed on the lounge and informed the sheriff.

The law and order posse in the meantime remained in Charleston until the next day and did not return until afternoon. Next morning when court opened, the judge told Sheriff Behan to bring Ringo into court and he would look into the bail matter. He did not know at that time that Ringo was in custody. Behan told me to bring him in, and I called him from the office and, as the bondsmen were perfectly good, the judge had to approve the bond, and Ringo returned to his friends. At this time the Republican officials were making a strong fight against Sheriff Behan. The case of highway robbery against Ringo was dismissed, as they could find no witnesses to appear against him. This was the only warrant that was ever issued against him as far as I could learn.

XI

The Shootout Near the
O. K. Corral

A GREAT deal has been written and said regarding
the feud between the Earps and Doc Holliday
on one side, and the Clantons and McLaurys on the
other. While none of the Earps were ever elected
to office in Cochise County, some were appointed as
peace officers so that they had the law to back them
up. After Holliday was accused of being one of the
stage robbers and shooting Bud Philpot, the Earp
party was very bitter toward the cowboys.

In September, 1881, the stage running between
Tombstone and Bisbee via Hereford was held up by
two masked men. The passengers were robbed and
the mail and express taken. Sheriff Behan sent Dave
Nagle and me to do what we could toward tracking down the highwaymen. We went to the place
where they held up the stage, and we were able to
get a good view of the tracks of both men and horses.
We had no difficulty in following the horse tracks
toward Bisbee until they were obliterated by a drove
of cattle passing over them.

On our arrival in Bisbee, where we would spend
the night, we interviewed several of the passengers.
They told us that the smaller of the two robbers did
most of the talking, and asked each one if he had

any sugar. This was a well known expression of
Frank Stillwell's, who always called money 'sugar.'[1]
We learned also that Stillwell had had his high
heels taken from his boots and low heels put on in
place of them. The shoemaker gave us the ones he
had taken off and they fitted the tracks at the scene
of the hold-up. Pete Spence[2] and Frank Stillwell
had come into Bisbee together and were still there.
After we had gathered what evidence we could, we
were of the opinion that Stillwell and Spence were
the guilty parties.

Wyatt Earp, Morgan Earp, Marshall Williams, a
Wells, Fargo agent at Tombstone, and Fred Dodge,
a gambler,[3] as a United States marshal's posse, left

[1]On Frank C. Stilwell's background and death, see note 4,
chapter XIII.

[2]Pete Spence (or Spencer), whose real name may have
been Lark Ferguson, may have been a friend of the Earps.
He lived in Tombstone with his Mexican wife, Marietta, but
also had a well-known wood-cutting camp in the southern
Dragoon Mountains. In addition, he was Frank Stillwell's
partner in a Bisbee livery stable. Spence survived the Cochise County troubles to serve, it is said, two or three years
in the Yuma prison for an undisclosed conviction. Odie B.
Faulk, *Tombstone: Myth and Reality* (New York, 1972), p.
148. John Myers Myers, *The Last Chance: Tombstone's Early
Years* (New York, 1950), pp. 182, 216. Glenn G. Boyer, ed.,
*I Married Wyatt Earp: The Recollections of Josephine Marcus
Earp* (Tucson, 1976), pp. 20, 26, 59, 76, 85.

[3]Unbeknownst to Breakenridge and others, the occupation of Frederick J. (Fred) Dodge as a faro dealer in Hafford's
saloon was a cover for his status as a secret agent for Wells,
Fargo whose shipments in and out of Tombstone were highly
vulnerable to robbery. Myers, *Last Chance*, pp. 128, 181.
Fred Dodge, *Under Cover for Wells Fargo* (Boston, 1969).

Tombstone some time after we did. They came direct to Bisbee, where we met them and told them what evidence we had, and wanted Williams to swear out a warrant for Spence and Stillwell. He refused at first to do so, and fearing the men might leave town before we arrested them, I went to the corral where they were stopping and put them under arrest while Nagle went before the justice and got a warrant for them.

When the Earp party saw that we had arrested the men, they prevailed upon Williams to swear out a Federal warrant for them for robbing the mail and express, and all of us went to Tombstone together with the prisoners.

Stillwell and Spence were taken before Justice Spicer who set bond at two thousand dollars which they paid. They were then rearrested by Wyatt Earp, as deputy United States marshal, charged with robbing the mail, and were bound to the grand jury in the sum of five thousand dollars which they also secured and were given their liberty.

The feud between the two gangs was growing very bitter. A short time after Nagle and I arrested Spence and Stillwell, Virgil Earp told me that the McLaurys had threatened to kill everyone who had a hand in arresting Stillwell and Spence and advised me to shoot them the first time I met them or they would get me sure. I laughed at him, as I knew about the feud between them.

A few days later I met Tom McLaury in town

and, in conversation with him, told him I was going to start for Galeyville that afternoon. He invited me to ride out with him and spend the night at his ranch. I did so, and in talking about the arrest of the cowboys, he said he was sorry for them, but it was none of his fight and he would have nothing to do with it, as he had troubles enough of his own. As long as I was in the sheriff's office I never knew of any warrant being issued for any of the McLaurys or Clantons. If there had been I would have known, as I served most of the warrants outside of Tombstone.

Pony Deal and Sherman McMasters were accused of holding up a stage near Globe, Arizona. They had separated, and Deal was arrested in Tucson by Bob Paul, the United States marshal.[4]

McMasters came to Tombstone, Virgil Earp recognized him, and wired Paul asking if McMasters

[4]Robert H. (Bob) Paul (*c.* 1830–1901), a native of Massachusetts, made a round-the-world whaling voyage at the age of fourteen but left a second cruise in 1849 to join the California gold rush. He was an effective two-term sheriff of Calaveras County and then in 1872 went to work for Wells, Fargo which sent him to Arizona in 1878. He next served as the highly regarded sheriff of Pima County and then as a detective for the Southern Pacific Railroad (on the latter see chapter XVII). Contrary to Breakenridge's statement, Paul, a Republican, was not appointed United States marshal for Arizona until 1889 when Benjamin Harrison became President. Paul served until the Democrats recaptured the White House in 1893. Robert H. Paul—clipping file, Arizona Historical Society, Tucson, Larry D. Ball, *The United States Marshals of New Mexico and Arizona Territories, 1846–1912* (Albuquerque, 1978), p. 167.

was wanted. But before he got an answer, McMasters left town, and it was reported that it was he who stole a valuable saddle horse from the Contention Mine. The horse belonged to E. B. Gage, general manager of the mine, and he was anxious to get it back. It was rumored that Earp told McMasters to leave, and, as he joined the Earp party later, it looked as if it might be so. The sheriff sent out several parties to search for the horse. I went with one party to San Simon Valley, but could not learn anything about either the horse or McMasters, except that McMasters had stolen the horse and traded it to Milt Hicks.

One afternoon Ike Clanton met me on the street and told me that if I wanted the Contention horse to get to McLaury's ranch before dark and I should find him there. Ike passed on with no further information. I had just come in from a hard trip and my horse was tired, so, going to a livery stable, I hired a pony to make the trip.

I did not arrive at the ranch until after dark, as the pony was very slow and lazy.

As I rode up, I saw that there was a large crowd of cowboys there, and the place in front of the house was covered with water from an irrigating ditch. Not wanting to come on them unawares, I holloed and asked if it was safe to ride through the water. Frank McLaury came to the door. When I told him who I was, he asked me in, and upon entering I found Curly Bill and some ten or twelve rustlers there with him. They were nearly all strangers to me. I went out with Frank to put up my horse in the corral, and told him what I was there for.

I said: 'Frank, I am not the only one who knows that the horse is here. Half of Tombstone knows it. You are posing here as honest ranchmen. It is well known that you are harboring rustlers and outlaws and dealing in stolen cattle, and you dare not let me go back without the horse. You are under suspicion, and if I go back without the horse and tell that you would not give it up, you will have to quit ranching here and join the rest of the rustlers.'

He thought it over and said the horse was not there at that time, but would be there before morning; he would not tell me who stole it. He asked me to remain overnight and we entered the house. It was crowded, and Curly and some of the others divided blankets with me and I slept on the floor with them all night. I was up at daylight and the horse was in the corral. Several parties came in during the night, but I did not know who they were.

As I started for the corral to catch up the horse, Frank said he would catch him for me. On our way to the corral he told me I was all right and safe while I was at the ranch, but the fellow who had the horse was sore about my taking him, and he and his gang intended to hold me up after I left the ranch and take the horse away from me.

After breakfast, I saddled my pony and led the Contention horse. While I was in sight of the ranch

I felt perfectly safe. However, I saw several cowboys leave the ranch and swing through the pass toward Antelope Spring, where I believed they would try to get me, as I had to go through a narrow canyon.

As I reached the road to Tombstone, I saw a lumber wagon just ready to break camp. I rode in behind it out of sight of the horsemen that I supposed were after me, and quickly changed my saddle onto the Contention horse. I asked the driver to lead my pony into town and quickly rode across country for Tombstone.

The cowboys saw me and rode after me for a short distance and fired a few shots in my direction, but I stopped to return a shot or two, which landed close to them. They then gave up the chase, as they knew their horses could not catch the one I was riding, and after a long ride, I reached the Contention Mine without meeting anybody else.

A short time afterward I met Billy Clanton and John Ringo in Sulphur Spring Valley. They knew all about my getting the horse, and laughed and said, 'You had better look out or you will get caught the next time.'[5]

It was on October 25, 1881 that Ike Clanton and

[5]This story of the recovery of the valuable horse belonging to the leading Tombstone mine manager, E. B. Gage, is an illustration of what made Breakenridge such an effective deputy sheriff: his personality and his mastery of outlaw and cowboy psychology which made it possible for him literally to ride into a den of thieves and emerge unscathed with stolen property recovered or taxes collected.

Tom McLaury came into Tombstone in a light wagon from Antelope Springs. They were leading a saddle horse. The following day Billy Clanton and Frank McLaury came riding in from Charleston and met them there.

Late the night that he arrived in town Ike Clanton went into the Eagle Brewery for a lunch. Doc Holliday followed him in and began abusing him. He tried to get Ike to fight, and asked him to draw his gun. Ike told him he had no gun. Holliday called him a blank blank liar, saying he was too big a coward to leave his gun off. Ike claimed he looked around and saw Morgan Earp, a policeman, standing on the other side of the lunch counter. He also abused Ike and dared him to fight.

Clanton went out of the house and saw Virgil Earp, the city marshal, on the sidewalk just outside the door. Morgan Earp and Holliday followed him out and continued to abuse him, although they were both peace officers. They claimed he had been talking about Holliday and the Earp party. Ike first got drunk, then went to the corral where he had left his team and arms, and went to bed.

Next morning, expecting trouble, he got his gun from the corral and said he thought the Earps and Holliday intended to murder him. As he was walking up the street, Virgil and Morgan Earp came up behind him and knocked him down with a blow from a pistol and arrested him for carrying arms. They took him to the justice's office after disarming him, and soon Wyatt Earp and Doc Holliday came there. Although they were sworn peace officers and had taken Clanton's gun away from him, they were said to have called him all the names they could lay tongue to, and dared him to fight, offering him a gun. However, Clanton believed that the moment he reached for it he would be shot down.

Then Wyatt Earp left to go uptown. The story of his first meeting with Tom McLaury is told in the testimony that Bauer, the Tombstone butcher, gave at the trial of Wyatt Earp and Holliday:

'I was with Mr. Hines, a cattleman,' said Bauer, 'when I saw Wyatt Earp and Tom McLaury meet near Judge Wallace's courtroom. They spoke, but I did not hear what they said. Earp raised his left hand and ran it into Tom McLaury's face. Tom had both hands in his pants pockets. Earp said, "Are you heeled or not?" Tom answered, "No, I am not heeled, I want nothing to do with anybody," and took his hands out of his pockets to ward off the blow. Tom backed off the sidewalk toward the middle of the street. Mr. Earp followed him up. Earp then drew his pistol out of his coat pocket with his right hand and hit Tom McLaury on the head with it and Tom fell in the middle of the street. He got up and Earp hit him several times with the pistol, and knocked him down again. I saw no pistol or arms of any kind on McLaury. He was staggering and bleeding and someone led him away toward Everhardy's shop.'

The account of what followed is contained in the evidence given later at the trial of Wyatt Earp and Doc Holliday for the killing of Billy Clanton

and Tom and Frank McLaury, as reported in the
Tombstone *Nugget*:[6]

Sheriff John H. Behan was sworn and testified: 'I was in
the barber shop getting shaved. The barber was talking
about the probability of there being a fight between the
Earps and the cowboys. It was about half past one or two
o'clock. Saw a crowd gathering on the corner of Fourth
and Allen Streets. I asked the barber to hurry up and get
through, as I intended to go out and disarm and arrest the
parties. I got out and crossed over to Hafford's corner.
Saw Marshal Earp standing there and asked him what was
the excitement. He is Virgil Earp. He said there were a

[6]What followed was the Tombstone gunfight of October
26, 1881, in which Virgil, Wyatt, and Morgan Earp along
with Doc Holliday aligned themselves about six feet in front
of Billy Clanton and Frank and Tom McLaury and exchanged shots (Tom McLaury was, however, unarmed) resulting in the deaths of Clanton and the McLaurys, the
wounding of Virgil and Morgan Earp, and the grazing of
Holliday. Perpetuated by the title of a classic (and pro-
Earp) movie, *The Gunfight at the O.K. Corral* (1957), it is
the common, but erroneous, view that the shootout took
place at the O.K. Corral. In fact, it took place between 3rd
and 4th Streets on Fremont Street and on a contiguous va-
cant lot between the lodging house and photography shop of
C. S. Fly and the Harwood dwelling. The O.K. Corral
(where the Clantons and McLaurys stabled their horses) was
a block away on Allen Street between 3rd and 4th Streets,
but a passage ran through the block from Allen to Fremont
so that the O.K. Corral had a rear entrance on Fremont that
was located three lots away from the outbreak of the gunfight. Thus, it is accurate to say that the shooting took place
near but not *at* the O.K. Corral. Alford E. Turner, *The
O.K. Corral Inquest* (College Station, 1981) has meticulously
diagrammed the positions of the participants at the beginning of and during the gunfight.

lot of s—— of —— in town looking for a fight. He did not mention any names. I said to him, "You had better disarm the crowd." He said he would not; he would give them a chance to fight. I said to him, "It is your duty as a peace officer to disarm them rather than encourage the fight." He made no reply, but I said I was going down to disarm the boys; I meant any parties connected with the cowboys who had arms.

'Marshal Earp at this time was standing in Hafford's door. Several people were around him, I don't know who. Morgan Earp and Doc Holliday were then standing out near the middle of the street at Allen and Fourth Streets. I saw none other of the defendants there. Virgil Earp had a shotgun.

'I went down Fourth Street to the corner of Fremont and met Frank McLaury holding a horse. I told McLaury that I would have to disarm him, as there was likely to be trouble in town and I proposed to disarm everybody in town that was carrying arms. He said he would not give up his arms, as he did not intend to have any trouble. I told him he would have to give up his gun all the same. I said, "Frank, come along with me." We went down to where Ike Clanton and Tom McLaury were standing. I told them they must give up their arms. Billy Clanton was there. When I got down to where Ike was, I found Tom McLaury, Billy Clanton, and Will Claybourn. I said to them, "Boys, you have got to give up your arms."

'Frank McLaury demurred; he did not want to give up his arms. Ike told me he did not have any arms. I searched him and found he did not have any arms. Tom McLaury showed me by pulling his coat open that he was not armed. Claybourn said he was not one of the party; he was trying to get them out of town. I said, "Boys, you must go to the sheriff's office and leave your arms, and stay there until I get back." I told them I was going to disarm the other party.

'I saw the Earps and Holliday coming down the sidewalk. They were a little below the post office. Virgil, Morgan, and Wyatt Earp, and Doc Holliday were the ones. I said to the Clantons, "Wait here awhile, I will go up and stop them." I walked up the street twenty-two or three steps and met them at Bauer's butcher shop under the awning in front and told them not to go any farther; that I was down there for the purpose of arresting and disarming the McLaurys and Clantons. They did not heed me. I told them to go back. "I am sheriff and am not going to allow any trouble if I can help it."

'They brushed by me and I turned and went with them, begging them not to make any trouble. When they arrived within a few feet of the cowboys, I heard Wyatt say, "You s—— of ——, you have been looking for a fight and you can have it." Some one of them said, "Throw up your hands," and then the fight commenced. Some twenty-five or thirty shots were fired. Billy Clanton said, "Don't shoot me, I don't want to fight." Tom McLaury threw his coat open and said, "I have got nothing." Billy Clanton and Frank McLaury were the only ones armed, they had their horses ready, leading them, and were leaving town. Their rifles were on their saddles.

'They had their hands up when the Earp crowd fired on them. Doc Holliday shot Tom McLaury with a shotgun and killed him instantly, Morgan Earp shot Billy Clanton while their hands were up.'

W. C. Claybourn was sworn. His evidence corroborated Behan's. He stated that 'Wyatt Earp said, "You —— of ——, you have got to fight." City Marshal Virgil Earp said, "Throw up your hands." All three cowboys done so, and then the shooting commenced. Doc Holliday shot Tom McLaury and Morgan Earp shot Billy Clanton while their hands were up. After Billy Clanton was shot he said, "Don't shoot me, I don't want to fight." I saw him draw his pistol after he was shot down. Tom McLaury

The O.K. Corral, Tombstone.
Near the scene of the gunfight which pitted the Earps
and "Doc" Holliday against the Clantons and McLaurys.

threw open his coat, and stated, "I am not armed." Wyatt Earp shot Frank McLaury in the belly. He staggered into the street trying to pull his pistol. There was about six shots fired by the Earps before this, and Tom McLaury was killed and Frank and Billy were mortally wounded before they fired a shot.'

Ike Clanton swore that 'the Earp party commenced shooting after the cowboys had all of them threw up their hands as ordered to do.'

Mrs. M. J. King testified: 'I was at the meat market and saw the Earps and Holliday passing in front. Holliday had on a long coat. He had a long gun under his coat. One of the Earps said as they passed, "Let them have it," and Holliday said, "All right." I turned to run, but before I got to the center of the room the shooting commenced.'

R. J. Coleman swore: 'Saw Sheriff Behan try and stop the Earp party, but they kept on until they came to the cowboys, and one of them said, "Throw up your hands," or, "Give up your arms," and then the shooting commenced. The Earp party shot first.'

James Kehoe testified: 'Saw the Earp party pass by the sheriff up to the Clanton party, then heard two shots, and saw Frank McLaury run into the street drawing his pistol after the shots were fired. He was staggering.'

Andy Mehan swore: 'Tom McLaury left his pistol with me in my saloon just as soon as he came to town. I still have it.'

B. H. Falleha swore: 'I saw the sheriff and the marshal talking. The marshal said, "These men have made their threats. I will not arrest them, but will kill them on sight." Virgil Earp said this.'

West Fuller swore: 'Heard the Earps say, "Throw up your hands," and at the same time they commenced shooting. Saw Billy Clanton throw up his hands and heard him say, "Don't shoot me, I don't want to fight." There were five or six shots fired by the Earp party before

Billy Clanton or Frank McLaury fired, and they were both mortally wounded before they fired a shot. They were the only ones in the Clanton party that I saw fire a shot.'

Thomas Keefe testified: 'After the fight I heard Billy Clanton say, "They have murdered me," loud enough for everyone present to hear him. I helped carry him in the door. I examined Billy Clanton's body. He was shot through the arm and right wrist. He was shot in the right side of his belly. Also below the right nipple, and the lung was oozing out of the wound. He was shot through the pants, right leg.'

Addie Boland swore: 'I am a dressmaker; live opposite the entrance to Fly's lodging house. I first saw five men opposite my house leaning against the small house west of Fly's. They were cowboys. One man was holding a horse. Four men came down the street toward them, and a man with a long coat on walked up to the man holding the horse and put a pistol to his stomach, then stepped back two or three feet, and then the firing became general. That was all I saw. I don't know which party fired first, did not see any of the cowboys throw up their hands. I watched them until the firing commenced, then I got up and went into the back room. It looked to me as if they were all shooting at the same time. I saw no parties fall.'

J. H. Lucas swore: 'I was in my office on the opposite side of the street, and about two hundred or three hundred feet from the Fly building. I was sitting in my office. I heard a couple of reports of a gun or a pistol. I hesitated a moment and I heard a couple of more reports. I then started to the upper hall door. While going, I heard four or five more reports. When I got to the hall door, I cast my eyes up and down the street and saw a man I suppose to have been Billy Clanton standing in front of the little house just below Fly's building. He had his pistol up and I thought was firing, and for fear of a stray bullet I drew

Tom McLaury

Frank McLaury

Ike Clanton

Participants in the gunfight near the O.K. Corral.
Courtesy New York Historical Society

my head in for an instant. I looked again and still saw him standing there with his pistol and I thought fighting. I drew my head in again. I looked again and still saw him with his pistol. I continued to look at him, then looked about to see if anyone else had weapons. I did not see anyone else that I thought had weapons. I think his pistol was discharged twice from the time I thought he was hit till he was down on the ground. About the same time he got to the ground the firing ceased. I heard some considerable shooting, but could not see any of the parties except Billy Clanton. I am satisfied the shooting came from the other parties besides Billy, though I could not see them.'

Sills, another witness, swore: 'I was across the street about three hundred feet away from there. I could not tell which side fired first; the firing was almost simultaneous.'

The report in the *Nugget* continues with the statement of Wyatt Earp (not sworn to):

'My name is Wyatt S. Earp. Thirty-two years old last March. Resided in Tombstone since December 1st, 1879. Am a saloon keeper. Have been deputy sheriff and detective. The difficulty which resulted in the death of William Clanton and Frank and Tom McLaury originated last spring. [Here prosecution objected to defendant reading a prepared statement. Overruled and excepted to.] A little over a year ago I followed Frank and Tom McLaury and two other parties who had stolen six Government mules from Camp Rucker—myself, Virgil and Morgan Earp, Marshal Williams, Captain Hurst, and four soldiers. We traced these mules to McLaury's ranch. [Here prosecution moved to strike out above as irrelevant. Overruled and excepted to.]

'They had branded the mules DS changing the US to DS. After we arrived at McLaury's ranch, Captain Hurst came to us boys and told us he had made a compromise. By so doing he would get his mules back. We insisted on following them up. Hurst prevailed upon us to go back to Tombstone, so we came back. Hurst told us, two or three weeks afterward, that they would not give up the mules to him after we went, saying that they only wanted to get us away, that they could stand the soldiers off. Captain Hurst cautioned me and my brothers Virgil and Morgan to look out for these men, that they had made some hard threats against our lives.'

Several of the old-timers still living in that part of the country tell the following story regarding these mules: Curly Bill, Zwing Hunt, and Billy Grounds stole the mules and ran them down into the Sulphur Spring Valley near McLaury's ranch. At Soldier Holes they sold the mules to a freighter, who hurried them back into the Chiricahua Mountains, and went to hauling saw logs for Morse's sawmill. He kept them there in the tall pines until their fresh brands healed up and their manes grew out long and then got a Government contract hauling supplies to the different posts and Indian reservations. They told me they had often heard him laugh about it and tell how he got a fat contract to haul Government freight with the stock that was stolen from the Government at Camp Rucker, and that none of the mules were ever recognized by any of the Government officers or employees.

Justice of the Peace Wells Spicer, before whom

they had their hearing, was regarded as a partisan of the Earps, and an enemy of Sheriff Behan.[7] While six witnesses swore that the McLaurys and Clanton held up their hands as directed by the Earps, and three swore that they did not see them throw up their hands, four of the witnesses heard the Earp party say that the cowboys would have to fight, and heard Virgil Earp tell the sheriff he would not arrest them, but would kill them on sight, Justice Spicer rendered his opinion in part as follows:

'Addie Boland, who saw distinctly the approach of the Earps and the beginning of the affray from a point across the street where she could correctly observe all their movements, says she cannot tell which side fired first, that the firing commenced at once from both sides upon the approach of the Earps and that no hands were held up. That she would have seen them if there had been. Judge Lucas states he saw Billy Clanton fire or in the act of firing several times before he was shot, and he thinks two times afterward. Sills asserts that the firing was simultaneous. He cannot tell which side fired first.'

[7]Wells Spicer, born in 1832, apparently in Illinois, began his Western career as a non-Mormon lawyer in Utah where he was as an aggressive but unsuccessful defense attorney for John D. Lee, organizer of the Mountain Meadows massacre of the members of a California-bound wagon train in 1857. In 1878, Spicer's affinity for the mining industry brought him to Tombstone where he was an active Republican and involved in many profit-seeking endeavors that included his legal practice, a United States court commissionership, a partnership with Wyatt Earp in a liquor and tobacco store, and the office of justice of the peace. Gary L. Roberts, "The Wells Spicer Decision: 1881," *Montana: The Magazine of Western History*, XX (January 1970), pp. 64–65.

The Judge then continued as follows:

'I cannot resist the firm conviction that the Earps acted wisely, discreetly, and prudently to secure their own self-preservation; they saw at once the dire necessity of GIVING THE FIRST SHOT to save themselves from certain death. They acted: their shots were effective, and this alone saved the Earp party from being slain.

'I conclude the performance of the duty imposed upon me by saying in the language of the statute; There being no sufficient cause to believe the within named Wyatt Earp and John H. Holliday guilty of the offense mentioned within, I order them released.'

After Judge Wells Spicer had rendered his decision, Wyatt Earp and Doc Holliday were turned loose. The Tombstone *Nugget* came out in an editorial and said, 'The sentiment of the community was that justice had not been done.'

It is my belief that the cowboys were not expecting a fight, as only Billy Clanton and Frank McLaury were armed. They had their pistols on, and their rifles were on their saddles, as they were about to leave town. If they had expected that the Earps were coming to kill them, they could have shot down the whole Earp party with their rifles before they got within pistol-shooting distance.

At the time of the shooting, Sheriff Behan shoved Ike Clanton, who had been disarmed by the Earps, into the open door of Fly's photograph gallery, and he ran through the house and out of the back door. He was unarmed and had to flee for his life.

EDITOR'S SPECIAL NOTE

Breakenridge laconically states his own opinion—one shared by others and that has been, in effect, the classic anti-Earp interpretation of the gunfight ever since it occurred: that the Earps (assisted by Holliday) premeditated the killing of the Clantons and the McLaurys and used their legal authority to catch their opponents off guard and unprepared for effective resistance to their superior fire power. To this indictment is added the charge that the order to the Clantons and McLaurys to put up their hands was followed by a fusillade from the weapons of the Earp party. Breakenridge quotes testimony (mainly from John H. Behan, William Claiborne, R. J. Coleman, West Fuller, and Thomas Keefe) to support his case against the Earps and Holliday. Although the Earps and Holliday denied (during the month-long trial) having fired first on October 26th, Wyatt Earp's widow, writing in the 1930s after Wyatt's death, declared that, in private conversations within the family circle, Wyatt and Virgil admitted that Doc Holliday and Morgan Earp had, indeed, fired first, but this was justified on the grounds that Clanton and the McLaurys had their weapons on display with the clear intention of using them and that, therefore, it was a kill-or-be-killed situation. This, indeed, was the interpretation adopted by Justice of the Peace Wells Spicer whose decision maintained (in the passage quoted by Breakenridge) that even if the Earp group had fired first they were entitled to do so in the interest of "self-preservation." Boyer, ed., *I Married Wyatt Earp*, pp. 88–93. Roberts, ed., "Wells Spicer Decision." Except for one perfunctory, ineffectual effort in early 1882, there was no further attempt at litigation. This is not to say, however, that the Clanton-McLaury faction viewed the matter as settled. Instead, it resorted to a campaign of ambush and murder against the Earps that led to the explosive events of December, 1881–March, 1882, portrayed by Breaken- ridge in the next two chapters.

XII

Aftermath of the Feud

AFTER THE Earps and Holliday were released from custody, they went into the Oriental Saloon, ranged up to the bar, and called for drinks. M. E. Joice, proprietor of the saloon, and a county supervisor, who was unfriendly toward them, made the remark, 'See who's here. I expect there will be another stage robbed before morning.'

One of them slapped him across the face, and they drew their guns. Joice backed toward the door and said to them, 'You won't get to shoot me in the back as you have shot everyone else, and I don't think you have the nerve to shoot me when I am looking at you.' He backed out the door and got away.

The next day he came into the saloon where the Earps were, and, with a six-shooter in each hand, asked them if they wanted to fight as bad as they did the night before. Sheriff Behan followed Joice into the saloon and coming up behind him grasped him around the waist, turned with his back toward the Earps and carried Joice out of doors, and arrested him for carrying weapons. He was fined fifteen dollars for carrying the guns. Up to this time Joice and Behan were close friends, but from this time out Joice was very bitter toward him.

The *Epitaph* had the following notice of the affray: 'It is understood that a little unpleasantness occurred in the Oriental Saloon yesterday, which under any circumstances is regretable. Under the present state of public excitement it should become all good citizens to avoid provocation for a disturbance.' The next day it stated that 'M. E. Joice was arrested for carrying arms, and fined fifteen dollars.'

Soon after this, Doc Holliday, while on a drunken spree, came to Joice's saloon and began shooting. He shot the bartender through the foot and shot Joice through the hand. Joice rushed to Holliday and knocked him down and took his pistol away from him, and was trying to shoot him through the head with the wounded hand when the bystanders separated them and took Holliday away from him.

From the time the McLaurys and Billy Clanton were killed there was continuous war between the two factions. One stormy night along about the first of the year 1882, someone fired a load of slugs from a shotgun across the street at Virgil Earp, and hit him in the arm and body. He was badly injured and was laid up for a long time.[1]

[1] Virgil Earp was shot outside the Oriental Saloon at about 11:30 p.m., December 28, 1881, as he walked from the Oriental to the Cosmopolitan Hotel. Virgil was badly wounded (especially in his left arm) and thereafter was consigned to the sidelines in what Breakenridge accurately calls the "continuous wars between the two factions." Some believed that attorney Will McLaury vengefully master-minded the attack on Virgil Earp and later (see the next chapter) on Morgan Earp.

From this time on, the Earp party consisted of five to eight men, and they were always together heavily armed. Wyatt Earp, as deputy United States marshal, asserted that they were a posse under him, and that they were looking for mail robbers.

I was told to patrol near the Bird Cage Theatre at night, as the sheriff expected trouble to break out there between the two factions at anytime.

The Bird Cage Variety Theatre was opened in Tombstone on December 21, 1881, by William and Lotty Hutchinson. It was the only resort of the kind in town, and was well patronized. The Hutchinsons brought their talent from San Francisco, and the place was filled up every night. The actresses sold drinks between acts, and when the show was over the seats were moved back and there was dancing.[2] It was a great resort for both factions, and the bar did a rushing business. Although no one had been killed there, and Hutchinson ran it in an orderly manner, we looked for trouble between the two factions to come off at anytime.

One dark rainy night I was tired and decided to go home, and before doing so took a walk up the street to the corner opposite the Bird Cage, to see if everything was quiet. At McKnight's store on the

[2] Among troupers playing at the Bird Cage who later became famous was Eddie Foy. Actor James O'Neill, father of playwright Eugene O'Neill, appeared in 1880 and, with other gullible performers, lost money in a bogus property known, derisively, as "The Actors' Mine." Odie B. Faulk, *Tombstone: Myth and Reality* (New York, 1972), pp. 116–20.

corner opposite the theater, as I was hugging close to the building because of the rain, I ran up against a gun-barrel which was placed against my breast. Looking up, I saw it was Frank Stillwell.

I asked him what he was trying to do, and he said that a certain party had boasted that he was going to get him that night, and that he would not do it if he saw him first. I told him that it was much too late for him to kill anyone that night, that he was in enough trouble already, and to go home. He did as I told him, and I turned back wondering who he was after. About the middle of the block I met Doc Holliday, who roomed a short distance up the street, on his way home. It flashed through my mind that I had inadvertently saved Holliday's life that night.

During the fall of 1881, Bat Masterson, who had been dealing faro bank at the Oriental Saloon, left Tombstone. I next heard of him in the early nineties when I was told he had been appointed a United States marshal at Washington, D.C., and that he got the appointment through President Roosevelt.[3]

[3]In 1905, President Theodore Roosevelt appointed William Barclay (Bat) Masterson (1858–1921) to be a deputy United States marshal in New York City. Afterwards, Masterson remained in Gotham where he finished his career as the successful sports editor of the *Morning Telegraph* with a particular expertise on boxing. The Canadian-born Masterson, a good friend of Wyatt Earp and Luke Short on the basis of their Dodge City days, had gained fame as a gambler, policeman, and sheriff in Kansas, Arizona, and Colorado during the 1870s and 1880s. Robert K. DeArment, *Bat Masterson: The Man and the Legend* (New York, 1979).

Crystal Palace Saloon

Remains of the Bird Cage Theatre
A couple of Tombstone's recreation centers.
Courtesy Arizona Historical Society Library

Luke Short, soon after he killed Charley Storms, left Tombstone and went back to Texas. What became of him after this I never learned.[4] The Earp crowd were the only gunmen left in Tombstone.[5] The rustlers and outlaws, who were supposed always to be ready for a gunfight, very seldom came to town.

After the killing of Billy Clanton and the McLaurys, the Earp party made their headquarters at Bob Hatch's saloon on Allen Street,[6] and whenever a bunch of cowboys came to town, their headquarters were at the Grand Hotel about opposite Hatch's saloon. One day John Ringo was standing in front of the hotel alone. Seeing the Earp party coming

[4]On Luke Short's post-Tombstone life, see note 18 in chapter VIII.

[5]The "Earp crowd" was bolstered by new legal authority when Wyatt was appointed to be deputy United States marshal on January 6, 1882. Wyatt used his new appointment to appoint members of the Earp faction to serve as a federal posse on into February and March, 1882: Morgan and Warren Earp, Doc Holliday, Sherman McMasters, "Texas Jack" Vermillion, and "Turkey Creek Jack" Johnson. Charles Smith and Dan Tipton may also have been posse members. McMasters, Vermillion, and Johnson were all members of Tombstone's gambling and gunfighting element. Larry D. Ball, *The United States Marshals of New Mexico and Arizona Territories, 1846-1912* (Albuquerque, 1978), pp. 123, 132. Ed Bartholomew, *Wyatt Earp, 1879 to 1882* (Toyahvale, Texas, 1964), pp. 293-96.

[6]Robert S. (Bob) Hatch, known in Tombstone for his fine singing, was well liked by all and was not a member of the Earp faction. He served as county sheriff later in the 1880s and eventually as assistant superintendent of the Yuma jail.

down the street to their headquarters, he crossed to where they were, and accosting Wyatt Earp, said:

'Wyatt, let's end this row. It has gone on long enough. Let Holliday and me get out here in the middle of the street and shoot it out. If you get me, the cowboys will go on home and consider the feud ended. If I am the winner, you agree to do the same and it will be all over.' And turning on his heel he started for the middle of the street.

This arrangement, however, was not acceptable to the Earps, and they all went into the saloon.

Someone came to the sheriff's office and told him that Ringo was uptown trying to start a fight, and I was told to go and bring him to the office. When I got to Allen Street, the only man in sight was Ringo. He was walking up and down in front of the hotel with his hands in the side pockets of his overcoat. I told him that Behan wanted him, and asked him what he was up to. He said he was trying to end the feud, but that the others were not game to meet him man to man and face to face, that they would rather wait for a chance to shoot him in the back.

When we got to the office, Behan told him he would have to give up his arms, as it was against the law to carry arms in town. Ringo handed him two pistols from his pockets, and Behan put them in a drawer in the desk, and walked out of the office.

'What are you going to do with me?' asked Ringo. 'Am I under arrest?' I told him he could go wherever he pleased.

'But John took my guns, and if I go uptown without them and they [the Earps] find it out, I won't last longer than a snowball in hell. I was about ready to leave town when you came after me.'

I told him I could not help his being disarmed, and, when he was ready to leave, no doubt the sheriff would return his pistols. I walked over to the drawer and pulled it out to see if the guns were still there, and, forgetting to close it, I walked out also. On my return Ringo and his guns were gone, and he left town right away.[7]

During the fall of 1881, I was sent over through the Chiricahua Mountains and into San Simon Valley and Galeyville, to summon witnesses and jurymen for the fall term of court. The Indians had stolen and run off nearly all the horses in that vicinity. It was about sixty miles from Galeyville to Tombstone by the trail, and where the trail passed over the Chiricahua Mountains and through the deep canyons and gulches, it was covered with snow during the winter. Business was dull and money scarce in Galeyville, and the only way for the people living there to get away was by horseback over the trails or by the mail stage to the San Simon railroad station, from there to Benson by the railroad

[7]Ringo departed for Charleston which was visited by two posses (one led by the Earps and Holliday) bent on bringing him back to answer for violation of the Tombstone regulation against carrying guns. Both posses failed, but Ringo came back on his own and paid a $30 fine. Bartholomew, *Wyatt Earp, 1879 to 1882*, pp. 289-91.

and then from Benson to Tombstone by stage. It was a hard trip, and none of them cared to take it at this time of the year.

In going to Galeyville I always made my ride so as to stop at a ranch at the foot of the mountains on the west side, and then to get an early start and get over the mountain and into Galeyville early in the forenoon next day. No doubt they were expecting me, for, as I reached the foot of the hill where the road led to the town on top of the mesa, Joe Hill, a ranchman living at the San Simon Cienaga, was just starting down the hill on his way to his ranch.

As soon as he saw me he turned back and yelled, 'Here comes the sheriff, boys;' and by the time I reached the top of the hill a great many of the inhabitants were running to cover in the gulches and thick brush, hoping to hide from me and thus avoid a summons. However, by remaining there that day I served the papers on all that I was after. As soon as I got a few of them served, they helped me find the rest, and although it was rather hard for some to leave home, they took it good naturedly.

A few who had saddle horses that the Indians had failed to steal returned with me over the trail, and the rest made the trip by way of the railroad. On our arrival in Tombstone some of them told of the chase I made after them, and Frank Ingoldsby, a draftsman, drew a cartoon of the affair showing the men scattered out in every direction trying to hide, while the officer was after them on horseback trying to catch them with a riata. He sent it to the *Police Gazette* in New York, and they published it under the title, 'How the Sheriff Serves Papers on Jurymen and Witnesses in the Mining Camps in Arizona.' There was a big demand in Cochise County for that issue of the *Police Gazette*.

While in the San Simon Valley I saw a fine mare belonging to John Dunbar, the county treasurer, that had been stolen by Zwing Hunt. She was with six other well bred horses that had undoubtedly been stolen. I was alone and under orders to report as soon as possible, but I did rope the mare and brought her to Tombstone. If I had not been in a hurry, I should have brought the whole bunch.

There was a lot of horse stealing going on, and if you had a good horse you had to guard him carefully. One day a cowboy from New Mexico came into Tombstone riding a splendid horse. He put up at the O.K. Corral, said he was broke, and offered to sell the horse for about half what it was worth. He soon found a purchaser, and, after he had received his money, the buyer asked him,

'What about the title?'

The cowboy replied, 'The title is perfectly good as long as you go west with him, but don't take him east; it is not so good in that direction.'

In the latter part of September I was out serving some papers in Willcox and the Sulphur Spring Valley, and, after visiting Willcox and Dos Cabezas, wound up at the home ranch of Persley and Woolf, at the Sulphur Spring, at one time a great resort for the Apaches.

Early the next morning Mr. Woolf and I started for Tombstone, through the middle pass in the Dragoon Mountains. This pass is but a short distance from Cochise's stronghold in the same mountains. In the meantime nearly one hundred Indians belonging to Sanchez's and Geronimo's bands had left the reservation. After attacking Samaniego's wagon train on the morning of October 2, 1881, near Cedar Spring, about fifteen miles northwest of Fort Grant, and killing Samaniego's brother and five teamsters, the Indians separated into several smaller parties and left for the Sierra Madres, in Mexico.[8] On the morning of October 6th, as we entered the pass, we saw fresh tracks where fifteen or twenty Indians had gone in ahead of us that morning, and, as we reached the mouth of the pass on the other side of the mountain, we saw where they had stampeded a team hauling wood.

The wagon was about a hundred feet off the road, broken down; the harness had been stripped from the four animals; the stock had been driven off, and about a hundred yards away we found the body of

[8]The slaying of Bartolo Samaniego and the others was a part of the first of Geronimo's three outbreaks (1881–83, 1885–86, 1886) within a six-year period; the first outbreak is described and analyzed in Dan L. Thrapp, *General Crook and the Sierra Madre Adventure* (Norman, 1972). Breakenridge's participation in the aftermath of Geronimo's final outbreak appears in chapter XVI.

Geronimo (left horseman) and Nachez (right horseman) in 1886.
Geronimo's son is standing by his side.

the teamster, who must have jumped from his wagon and tried to escape by running away. His head was smashed in with rocks.

We learned later that the Indians had been closely pursued by the troops, with whom they had had a skirmish the night before. Part of the Indians kept down the north side of the mountains, while the others went into the pass and waited until morning. The troops followed the Indians that went down the north side. They were headed for Camp Rucker in the Chiricahua Mountains, and those troopers followed them until they reached Soldier Holes Ranch, where they went into camp and waited for their pack mules to come up.

We saw that the Indians had passed ahead of us and were evidently in a hurry to get into Mexico, as they did not deviate from their course to commit depredations, but gathered up all the horses and mules that came in their way, and hurried on. Their tracks were very fresh and seemed headed toward Antelope Springs, about thirteen miles to the east of Tombstone. As it was still early in the forenoon, the murder must have occurred only a short time before we got there. We hastened to Tombstone and reported it, and the authorities sent out and had the body of the murdered man brought into town.

That afternoon a posse of volunteers was formed to go after the Indians, and Sheriff Behan and I went with them. The party was composed of John P. Clum, Charles Reppy, Frank Ingoldsby, Ward

Priest, George Parsons, Marshal Williams, Wyatt and Virgil Earp, Cy Bryant, Sheriff Behan, and myself, with several others whose names I have forgotten. Couriers were also dispatched through the mountains and foothills to warn the isolated ranchers that the Apaches were out on the warpath, and in their vicinity.

It was late in the afternoon when we got started and was nearly dark when we reached Antelope Springs, where we located the trail of the Indians, headed toward the McLaury Ranch in the Sulphur Spring Valley.

It began to rain about the time we struck the trail, and before we reached the Frink Ranch we were thoroughly wet. This was one of the heaviest rains that had come to that part of the country. We reached the ranch about nine o'clock at night, wet, cold, and hungry.

Mr. Frink gave us some hot coffee, and told us the Indians had driven off all his horses, except one saddle horse he had in the corral, late that afternoon, and had gone across the valley. They took twenty-seven head of horses from him and the McLaury boys.[9]

Mr. Frink's cabin was very small, and we had to sit up all night, as there was no room to lie down. It

[9]These events occurred while Frank and Tom McLaury were still alive and about two to three weeks before they were shot to death in Tombstone (see chapter XI) on October 26, 1881. Thrapp, *General Crook*, pp. 53–57.

rained very hard all night. The posse had started out without any supplies, and most of them were not used to the saddle.

In the morning the rain had stopped, but it had washed out all the tracks, and there were two or three inches of water all over the ground. We saddled up at daylight, Mr. Frink going with us, and crossed the valley to the mouth of the Horseshoe Pass in the Swisshelm Mountains, now known as Leslie Canyon.

At the mouth of the pass we held a council of war and decided that Frink and I would reconnoiter up the pass and learn if the Indians were in there, while the rest of the party would wait at the mouth until we returned. We took opposite sides of the pass looking for signs or Indians, and, after going about a mile and a half, Frink found their fresh tracks where they had passed out of the pass over a low divide that morning. They were going south on his side of the canyon. He signaled me to come to him and we crawled up to the summit of the low hill and saw them not more than a mile away. There were fifteen bucks ahead, and a few squaws driving the stolen stock, bringing up the rear.

We at once returned to where we had left the posse, but found they had got tired of waiting, and were several miles from us on their way to McLaury's ranch. I started after them and overtook them at the ranch, where they were cooking beef, bread, and coffee for breakfast. There we learned that the other bunch of Indians had passed on the north side of the mountain going toward Camp Rucker, and on toward Skeleton Canyon, and that Colonel Bernard,[10] with several companies of cavalry, had followed them up as far as Soldier Holes and gone into camp waiting for the ground to dry up so that it would not be so hard on his horses to follow them.

Here the posse separated, some of us going to Tombstone, and Sheriff Behan and the rest going to Soldier Holes to report to Colonel Bernard that the Indians were only a few miles away.

In the meantime Mr. Frink, seeing that we were not returning, again took up the trail, and by a short cut through the hills got to a point between the Indians and the squaws. Then he rushed in and cut off nearly all of the stolen stock and stampeded them back into the valley. The Indians did not even follow him up, but hurried on for Old Mexico.[11]

[10]This was Captain Reuben F. Bernard, commanding officer of Company G, 1st Cavalry Regiment, who was a hard-fighting, grizzled veteran of wars against Cochise's Apaches in Arizona (1869-70), Bannocks and Paiutes in Idaho and Oregon (1878), and Sheepeaters in Idaho (1879). Thrapp, *General Crook*, p. 53. Robert M. Utley, *Frontier Regulars: The United States Army and the Indian, 1866-1891* (New York, 1973), pp. 173-74, 201-2, 324-29, 330-32. Breakenridge's reference to Bernard's colonelcy may have been based on a Civil-War brevet rank of colonel for Bernard.

[11]With Mexican permission, General George Crook pursued the Indians deep into the wild Sierra Madre Mountains of northern Mexico and, making good use of a large force of Apache scouts, eventually obtained Geronimo's surrender in 1883-84. Thrapp, *General Crook*.

XIII

"Curly Bill" is Wounded

IN MAY, 1881, I was sent out with Mark Ezekiels,
traveling salesman for Zackendorf and Company,
to Galeyville, to serve an attachment on a store
owned by Rynerson and Wilkins. After serving the
papers, we started to take an inventory of the goods.
We were in a hurry, because we wanted to return on
the stage that afternoon. It happened that Curly Bill
and quite a number of his followers were in town
that day, and a rustler from Lincoln County, New
Mexico, named Jim Wallace, rode in on a fine sorrel
horse with a wide white stripe in his face.[1] Wallace
joined in with the rest of the crowd, and they were
drinking and playing cards.

A constable named Goodman, who lived there
came past, took note of the fine horse and asked
Wallace where he got it. This was not considered
good form unless you had a reason for asking it, and
the Lincoln County man drew his gun and said, 'If
you want that horse more than I do, take him.' And

[1] Although Jim (or Jake) Wallace, "a horseback drifter,"
had been in Las Vegas, New Mexico, in 1879, he seems,
despite what Breakenridge was later told in Galeyville, not
to have been a participant in the Lincoln County War in
New Mexico. Ed Bartholomew, *Wyatt Earp, 1879 to 1882*
(Toyahvale, Texas, 1964), p. 161.

he fired a shot into the ground close to the officer's heels. Goodman got around the corner of the building as fast as possible, and the gang thought it was great sport.

Soon after this I had to take a trip down to the Shortridge store and had my pistol inside my waistband. As I passed the saloon where the cowboys were, somebody told Wallace that I was a deputy sheriff from Tombstone. As I came back on my way to the Wilkins store, he was on the saloon porch. Evidently expecting to have some fun he called me to the porch and asked me if I was after that horse.

I told him, 'No, I am riding a better horse than that.'

He started to draw his gun, but I was too quick for him and grasped his hand, at the same time, placing my gun against his stomach, I told him to drop his own weapon, which he did. Stepping up on the porch I took his gun, but, knowing that he could get another, I thought it best to run a bluff on him. I handed the gun back to him and told him he was making a fool of himself, and to put it back in his scabbard. Then I turned my back on him and walked into the saloon. I asked the crowd to have a drink and went on to the store where I was taking the inventory.

A lot of the boys saw the occurrence and told Curly about it. Curly, who was about half drunk, took Wallace to task for trying to pick a fuss with the officers, and every time he looked out the door and saw the horse with the white face he threatened to shoot it, but the others talked him out of it.

Later Wallace came to the store where we were at work with the door locked, and rapped. Wilkins went to the door and came back and said there was someone there to see me, and I told him to let the man in. It was Wallace. He told me that Curly was very angry with him, and told him he had to apologize to me. He wanted me to go to the saloon with him so that he could square himself with Curly. I went with him and he apologized, and I thought everything was all right, but Curly, who was still drinking, wanted to have a row with Wallace and still threatened to shoot the horse.

After a time Curly went across the street to Babcock's saloon, where his horse was, and said he was going to camp. Wallace followed him and they had some words. Curly told him to keep away and not bother him anymore or he would shoot him as well as the horse. Wallace left Babcock's saloon, and soon afterward Curly came out and stepped off the porch. Just as he was getting on his horse, Wallace stepped up behind him and shot him. The bullet hit him in the cheek and knocked out a tooth coming out through his neck without cutting an artery.

Someone came up and told me that Curly was shot. I went ahead and met some of the men carrying Curly to the doctor's office. He could talk, and said, 'Billy, someone shot me; who was it?' I told him I would find out, and when I got to Babcock's corral

I saw that the gang was in there. I asked them who did the shooting, and they pointed to Wallace. I told them I wanted him and they said for me to take him. They had already arrested him and taken his pistol and belt.

I took him to the office of the justice of the peace, G. W. Ellenwood, which was down under the hill from the town, and the justice told me not to allow any armed men to come into court. As everyone went armed those days, I went back, after getting the constable to guard the prisoner, and met the boys coming down to the justice's office. I told them what the magistrate had said, and that I had rather they did not go down to the trial unless they were sent for as witnesses. They replied that they did not care to go down, for if Curly died they would hunt Wallace up, and if Curly lived he could hunt him up himself.

The only witness called was Babcock, who told what was said and what happened. The justice, after looking through several law books, said, 'I discharge the prisoner; he did it in self-defense.' Wallace then asked me to get his horse and arms, as he did not want to go back uptown. I got them for him and he left at once.

On account of the delay we got the stage to wait for us and left Galeyville just before sundown. Just outside of town the road crossed Turkey Creek, and then climbed a steep hill, and as we reached the summit I saw the head of the white-faced horse and had my gun ready and covered Wallace as he came into view. He was standing in the road, holding his horse, and said he was waiting to learn how Curly was getting along and if he was expected to die. I had him get in the stage and Ezekiels drove the team, while the stage driver rode the horse to the stage station in the valley where we changed horses and got supper.

Here I left Wallace to go on his way. He told me he was broke, and I paid for his supper and gave him ten dollars. I never did see him again, but he mailed me the money soon after I got to Tombstone. Later I heard that he was killed in a fight near Roswell, New Mexico. Curly was laid up only about two weeks, and was as well as ever.

The cowboys at Galeyville told me that Wallace was one of the outlaws who had been hired as fighting men during the Lincoln County War. This war was a fight between cattlemen who were trying to gain control of the Pecos Valley in Lincoln County. John Chisholm, a Texas stockman, came to New Mexico in 1867 just after the Civil War, with nearly a hundred thousand head of cattle, and made his home ranch on the Pecos River at Bosque Grande. He was able to get fat contracts let by the Government to supply the Indians and troops with beef.

During the Civil War cattle had been running wild in Texas. At the time Chisholm came to New Mexico there were thousands of maverick or unbranded cattle. These cattle belonged to the first

man that got his brand on them. Chisholm's brand
was a 'Long Rail' on one side of the animal, and his
earmark was known as the 'Jingle Bob.' He hired a
lot of cowboys to round up this maverick stock and
drive them to New Mexico. It was claimed by them
that he also had offered them a bonus on all cattle
branded by them. This he denied, and refused to
pay them anything except their wages.[2] This helped
to start the Lincoln County War.[3]

Major L. G. Murphy, who came to New Mexico
with the California troops and had been mustered
out of the service about the time that Chisholm
moved in there, started a store in Lincoln, and
within a short time got to be a powerful politician
and controlled all the offices in that county. He
then began to break in on the business that Chisholm was doing with the Government, and to establish a stock ranch on the range that was covered
with Chisholm's cattle. He hired an army of cowboys as fighting men to rebrand these cattle in his
brand. Because Chisholm had fallen out with the

[2]The best account of the legendary, larger-than-life John
Simpson Chisum (1824–1884) and his ranching empire is
Harwood P. Hinton, Jr., "John Simpson Chisum, 1877–
84," *New Mexico Historical Review*, XXXI (July 1956), pp.
177–205, (October 1956), pp. 310–37, XXXII (January
1957), pp. 53–65.
[3]Two outstanding books on the Lincoln County War are
Maurice G. Fulton, *History of the Lincoln County War*, ed.
Robert N. Mullin (Tucson, 1968) and Frederick W. Nolan,
The Life and Death of John Henry Tunstall (Albuquerque,
1965).

cowboys, Murphy had no trouble to get them to work for him. This was the beginning of the Lincoln County War.

Chisholm sent to Texas and soon enlisted a lot of fighting men, paying them big wages, to protect his cattle from the ravages of the Murphy gang, and at the same time to steal what stock they could from the Murphy herds—and the killing began. Murphy controlled all the peace officers, and had them appointed or elected, and nearly all of them were outlaws. Wallace was hired by one side and Billy the Kid by the other, and this feud was kept going for several years.

After Pat Garrett was elected sheriff, he soon had the war stopped and the principal people connected with it who had not been killed off were indicted. At the time Wallace came to Galeyville he was hiding out from the officers in New Mexico.

The Arizona *Weekly Star* of May 26, 1881, has the following from its correspondent in Galeyville:

CURLY BILL

This Noted Desperado 'Gets It in the Neck' at Galeyville

The notorious Curly Bill, the man who murdered Marshal White at Tombstone last fall, and who has been concerned in several other desperate and lawless affrays in southeastern Arizona, has at last been brought to grief, and there is likely to be a vacancy in the ranks of our border desperadoes. The affair occurred at Galeyville Thursday. A party of eight or nine cowboys, Curly Bill and his partner Jim Wallace among the number, were in town enjoying themselves in their usual manner, when Deputy Sheriff Breakenridge of Tombstone, who was at Galeyville on business, happened along.

Wallace made some insulting remarks to the deputy, at the same time flourishing his revolver in an aggressive manner. Breakenridge did not pay much attention to this 'break' of Wallace, but quietly turned around and left the party. Shortly after this Curly Bill, who it would seem had a friendly feeling for Breakenridge, insisted that Wallace should go and find him and apologize for the insult given.

This Wallace was induced to do, and after finding Breakenridge he made the apology, and the latter accompanied him back to the saloon where the cowboys were drinking. By this time Curly Bill, who had drunk just enough to make him quarrelsome, was in one of his most dangerous moods, and evidently desirous of increasing his record as a man-killer. He commenced to abuse Wallace, who, by the way, has some pretensions himself as a desperate and 'bad' man generally, and Curly Bill finally said, 'You d——d Lincoln County s—— of a b——, I'll kill you anyhow.' Wallace immediately went outside the door of the saloon, Curly Bill following close behind him. Just as the latter stepped outside, Wallace, who had meanwhile drawn his revolver, fired. The ball penetrated the left side of Curly Bill's neck and passing through came out the right cheek, not breaking the jawbone. A scene of the wildest excitement ensued in the town. The other members of the cowboy party quickly surrounded Wallace, and threats of lynching him were repeatedly made by them.

The law-abiding citizens were in doubt what course to pursue. They did not wish any more bloodshed, but were in favor of allowing the lawless element to 'have it out' among themselves.

But Deputy Sheriff Breakenridge decided to arrest

Wallace, which he succeeded in doing without meeting any resistance. The prisoner was taken before Justice Ellenwood and, after examination into the facts of the shooting, he was discharged.

The wounded and apparently dying desperado was taken into an adjoining building, and a doctor summoned to dress his wounds. After examining the course of the bullet, the doctor pronounced the wound dangerous, but not necessarily fatal, the chances for and against recovery being about equal. Wallace and Curly Bill had been partners and fast friends for the past five or six months, and, so far as is known, there was no cause for the quarrel, it being simply a drunken brawl.

A great many people in southeastern Arizona will regret that the termination was not fatal to one or both of the participants.

Although the wound is considered very dangerous, congratulations at being freed from this dangerous character are now rather premature, as men of this class usually have a wonderful tenacity of life.

In March of 1882, some time after the Earps and their followers had been acquitted of gunning down the McLaurys and Billy Clanton, they had been to a concert at the opera house, and, on returning from there, went into Bob Hatch's saloon. Morgan Earp challenged Hatch to play a game of pool, and the rest of the party sat down to see them play. A shot was fired through the back door and Morgan Earp was shot down and killed. He was most foully assassinated. On investigation they found where someone had stood on a box and fired the shot through the upper half of the door, which was of glass.

The Earps suspected Frank Stillwell of committing the crime,[4] with two half-breed Indians that
worked in Pete Spence's wood camp twelve or fifteen miles out of town, and near the South Pass in
the Dragoon Mountains. The next day they started
with the corpse to take it to Colton, California,
where their parents lived. Virgil Earp, whose arm
was slowly recovering from a gunshot wound, was
to take the body to Colton from Tucson, and the
rest of the party went with him as far as Tucson. Ike
Clanton and Frank Stillwell were at the Tucson depot when the Earps came in on the train. Clanton
saw them and warned Stillwell to get away from
there at once; then he himself left for downtown.

As it was reported at the time, Stillwell waited at
the depot, went around the rear of the train, and
walked up toward the front on the opposite side
from the depot. The Earps apparently saw him and
followed. A number of shots were heard and the
next morning Stillwell's body, riddled with bullets,

[4]Frank C. Stilwell (c. 1857–1882), who came out of the
Kansas-Missouri border country, was the younger brother of
a rugged and respected Indian scout and United States marshal in present Oklahoma, "Comanche Jack" Stilwell.
Frank Stilwell drifted through Dodge City when Wyatt
Earp was also there and came to Arizona as a miner and
teamster at Signal before moving on to the Tombstone country. He served in 1881 as an effective deputy sheriff for John
H. Behan in Charleston and Bisbee before being relieved
after his arrest (see chapter XI) for the Bisbee stage robbery
in September, 1881. Bill O'Neal, *Encyclopedia of Western
Gunfighters* (Norman, 1979). Bartholomew, *Wyatt Earp,
1879 to 1882*, pp. 148–49, 210–11.

was found lying alongside of the railroad tracks.

It is seventy-five miles from Tombstone to Tucson. Morgan Earp was killed about eleven o'clock at night, and Stillwell was seen in Tucson the next morning. There was no positive proof that he had done the killing of Morgan Earp—only suspicion. But it was generally believed that he went down along the side of the train so that he might get a shot at some of the Earps as the train passed.

Wyatt Earp and the members of his party sent Virgil on with the body of Morgan, and then took the back track afoot and walked to Esmond, the first station out of Tucson. There they flagged a freight train and rode to Benson, and from there took the stage for Tombstone and arrived there in the afternoon. They had evidently decided to resist arrest and leave the country. They first gathered up their baggage and equipment and placed it in a light wagon, and, with 'Harelip' Smith as the driver of the wagon, started it out toward Sycamore Spring, about eight miles north of Tombstone, and began making preparations to get out themselves. Soon after they arrived, a warrant from Sheriff Bob Paul, of Pima County, where Stillwell was killed, was wired to Sheriff John Behan, of Cochise County, to arrest them for the killing of Stillwell.

A man named Howard, who was telegrapher in the Tombstone office, told me a couple of years ago that the manager of the telegraph office at Tombstone was a friend of the Earps, and he showed them the warrant first. They asked him to hold it up until they could get ready to leave. After they had their horses saddled and brought up in front of the hotel where they were stopping, the manager took the warrant to Behan.

Behan told Deputy Sheriff Dave Nagle and me to get our shotguns and come back as soon as possible, as he had to arrest the Earps again. We had not gone a block on our way after our weapons when they came out of the hotel. Behan met them on the sidewalk as they were getting on their horses and tried to arrest them alone. (This was about eight o'clock at night.) There were six of them: Wyatt Earp, Doc Holliday, Sherman McMasters, Johnson, who was a mysterious man called 'The Unknown,' Tipton, and Texas Jack. Behan was unarmed.

They drew their guns on him, and told him they had seen him once too often and rode out of town as fast as they could go.

The Tombstone *Epitaph*, in the issue of March 22, 1882, had this to say:

Last evening Wyatt Earp, Doc Holliday, Sherman McMasters, Texas Jack and Mysterious Johnson came into town and at once went to the hotel. About eight o'clock they were joined by Charley Smith and Tipton. They at once left the hotel and got on their horses that were tied in front of it. Sheriff Behan stepped up to them and said, 'Wyatt, I want to see you for a moment.' Earp replied, 'I have seen you once too often,' and they rode quickly out of town.

Next morning, soon after sunrise, they came into

Bob Paul, sheriff of Pima County and later U.S. marshal.

Courtesy Arizona Historical Society Library

Pete Spence's wood camp, where they expected to find the two half-breeds whom they accused of being with Stillwell when Morgan was killed. They were told that only one of them was there. Indian Charley was up on the side of the hill chopping wood, and the other one was in town. According to the report of the men at the wood camp, the visitors at once rode up the hill and soon afterward several shots were heard. When the men in camp went to look for Indian Charley, they found him dead with several bullets in his body.[5]

From there the Earp party rode to Mescal Spring in the Mustang Mountains, where they were to meet a man who was to bring them some money from Tombstone. The members of the party claimed that as they rode up to the spring they found Curly Bill with nine or ten other rustlers camped there, and that all but Wyatt rode away. But Wyatt Earp, who was out in front, rode up to within about thirty feet of the outlaws where they were encamped behind an embankment, and getting off of his horse opened fire on them and killed Curly Bill.[6] The outlaws

[5] Florentino Cruz alias Indian Charley was found dead on March 22, 1882. Douglas D. Martin, *Tombstone's Epitaph* (Albuquerque, 1951), p. 214.

[6] According to Wyatt Earp, he engaged in a shotgun duel with Curly Bill at less than ten yards. The supposed shoot-out took place on March 24, 1882, at Iron Springs (later called Mescal Springs) about twenty miles west of Tombstone. On word from Earp's posse the killing was reported in the *Tombstone Epitaph* on March 25, 1882. Stuart N. Lake, *Wyatt Earp: Frontier Marshal* (Boston, 1931), pp. 338–42.

returned his fire and killed Texas Jack's horse and hit the pommel of Earp's saddle, but, although they were only a short distance away and all expert shots and fired twelve or fifteen shots, they did not hit Wyatt, and he got on his horse and rode away.

Just a short time before this a couple of cowboys named Pink Truly and Alex Arnold, whose true name was supposed to be Bill Alexander, were accused of robbing a store in Charleston. They got away, but Pink Truly was soon arrested for the robbery, and at his trial a number of his cowboy friends proved their usual alibi for him. They all swore that he was at their ranch the night of the robbery playing poker with them, that it was an all night game, and that Truly never left the house that night. So he was acquitted, and the matter dropped.

Arnold, however, had gone into hiding at Mescal Spring with two cowboys. As soon as Pink was free, he took some provisions out to the spring where they were hiding, and was there when the Earp party rode up. Both Truly and Arnold told the following story about the fight as soon as they came to Tombstone: They stated that Curly Bill was not there; that he had been in Mexico for the past two months. As the Earp party rode up to the spring the four cowboys took refuge behind an embankment, and all except Wyatt of the Earp party turned and rode away. Wyatt, however, rode up rather close to them and dismounted, and with the bridle rein over his arm stepped in front of his horse, raised his rifle and fired at them. They returned the fire. Alex Arnold reported that Earp was wearing a white shirt which made a splendid target. He was only a short distance away and drew a fine bead on Wyatt and fired. Earp turned partly around and staggered back toward his horse which he mounted and rode away after the others of his party. Both Truly and Arnold claimed that Wyatt Earp had a steel vest on under his shirt which deflected the bullet. They also stated that they shot the horn off Earp's saddle, and killed Texas Jack's horse, and that Jack got on behind one of the other men and rode away.

To corroborate the story as told by Arnold and Truly, a prominent citizen who, at the time, was a deputy sheriff under Sheriff Behan, was at what is now known as the McKittrick Ranch, about twelve miles north of Willcox, when the Earp crowd were seen in the distance coming toward the ranch. The wife of the ranch owner was very sick, and he asked the deputy to go into the granary out of sight until they got away from there, as he was afraid that if they made any row it would endanger his wife's life. The rancher met the Earps as they rode up, explaining his wife's condition, and asked them to move on, as he was afraid that if the sheriff's posse should come while they were there the excitement would kill his wife. They said that they were very hungry, and if he would give them some supper they would move on as soon as they ate.

While the cook was getting them supper, Wyatt

Earp, Doc Holliday, and one other came and stood right at the partially open door of the granary, not three feet away from it. The deputy reported when he returned to Tombstone that he could see plainly that Earp's overcoat had a bullet hole through each side of the front of it, and he heard them say, 'The steel saved you that time.'

As soon as they finished supper, the Earp party pulled out from the ranch a short distance and made camp for the night, and the next day rode to the Bonita Ranch owned by H. C. Hooker.[7] The next morning the deputy sheriff went to Willcox and got Mr. Stewart, of Norton and Stewart, to wire the information to Sheriff Behan in Tombstone.

A reliable merchant and rancher living at Safford told me that about two weeks after the Earp party reported killing Curly Bill, Curly himself came to his home and said he had just got back from Old Mexico; that he was leaving the country and going

[7]The Sierra Bonita ranch house of Henry Clay Hooker (1828–1907), located about sixty miles north of Tombstone, combined a fortification with elegant living quarters in the Spanish-Mexican hacienda style and was a show place of Arizona that was featured in Augustine Thomas' Broadway drama, *Arizona* (1889). Hooker, a New Englander who came to Arizona by way of California, established his ranch in 1872 and during the 1870s and 1880s built it into a fabulous spread of more than 800 square miles with over 10,000 blooded cattle. Howard R. Lamar, ed., *The Reader's Encyclopedia of the American West* (New York, 1977), p. 511. Janet Ann Stewart, "Territorial Ranch Houses of Southern Arizona, 1863–1912." *Journal of Arizona History*, XI (Winter 1970), pp. 240–41.

H. C. Hooker's Sierra Bonita Ranch near Willcox.

Courtesy Arizona Historical Society Library

to Wyoming where he was going to get work and try to lead a decent life, as he was tired of being on the dodge all the time. The merchant gave him a good saddle horse to ride away on. A Mr. Vaughn, now living in Tombstone, told me that ten years later Curly Bill came through Benson on the train bound for Texas, and stopped off long enough to visit the postmaster, whom he had known in his earlier days in Arizona.[8] I never heard of Curly Bill being accused of any crime except cattle-stealing, and I never knew of any warrant being issued for him. I most certainly should have heard of it if there had been any, as all warrants for any of the rustlers were given me to serve.

It took a couple of days for the sheriff to get a posse together to go after the Earp party, as good horses were scarce, and the chase was likely to be a long one. Moreover, the sheriff had to be careful in choosing his posse, as the Earp party had a great many friends and followers. He at first told me to

[8] Another version of the conclusion of Curly Bill's Arizona career is that he went back to his home state of Texas in the summer of 1881 after recovering from the wound inflicted on him by Jim Wallace. Bartholomew, *Wyatt Earp, 1879 to 1882*, pp. 169–70. Whether or not Curly Bill was actually killed by Wyatt Earp in 1882 is another one of the unresolved controversies growing out of the Tombstone troubles of the early eighties. Two recent authorities who accept the Earp claim are John D. Gilchriese and Gary L. Roberts. Lamar, ed., *Reader's Encyclopedia*, p. 127. One important piece of circumstantial evidence bolstering the Earp claim is that no primary-source documentation of Curly Bill's existence after the spring of 1882 has been found.

get ready to go with him, but later he said I had better stay, as I was likely to be needed in the office. He asked me to loan my horse and rifle to Johnny Ringo, who had left his rifle at a ranch close to the town, and who with several others of the cowboys and rustlers made up the posse. He took these men knowing that the Earp party would resist arrest, and, on account of the feud between them, he believed the cowboys would stay and fight.

Just before he was ready to start, Behan told me to get myself an outfit and go with him, and when I asked for my own horse and rifle he told me to get another outfit together. I refused to go unless I could have my own, and they left without me. This was the first and only time I ever had any trouble with Behan. While he was gone on the trail of the outlaws, I went to the Chandler Ranch after Hunt and Grounds.

The posse followed the Earp party to near Fort Grant and the Hooker Ranch. Hooker, who had suffered severely from the rustlers staking his cattle, was friendly with the Earps, and when Behan came with a posse composed mostly of rustlers and cowboys, with John Ringo and Finn and Ike Clanton among them, he would give them no help or information. At the fort, Behan tried to get Indian scouts to follow the trail, but the commanding officer would not let him have them, and he had to return without finding the Earp party. They got out of the country, and so far as I know none of them ever returned. They went on to Colorado, and Bob Paul, the sheriff of Pima County, where the crime was committed, got extradition papers for them and went there after them, but the Governor of Colorado would not honor them.[9]

From this time on Cochise County became peaceful and quiet, and Tombstone settled down to be normal once more. A lot of the rustlers had been killed by the Mexicans in rustling stock, and in quarrels among themselves when they were drinking. The stockmen had organized for self-protection, and the rustlers got out of the country as quickly as possible. With most of the bad men run off there was no more

[9]What happened to the Earps after they fled to Colorado in the spring of 1882? Wyatt Earp roved through boom towns in Colorado and Kansas (including a brief return to Dodge City in 1883). He married Josephine Sarah Marcus (in 1882 or 1883) before his second wife, Mattie (whom he deserted in 1882) died in 1888; lived for a time in San Francisco where he refereed the Sharkey-Fitzsimmons prize fight in December, 1896; went through the gold-mining booms of Nome, Alaska, and Tonopah and Goldfield, Nevada; and in 1906 settled down in Los Angeles where in the 1920s he became a friend of the cowboy movie stars William S. Hart and Tom Mix. He died on January 13, 1929, about a year after the publication of *Helldorado*. Warren Earp returned to Arizona and was slain in a saloon fight in Willcox, Cochise County, in 1900. Until his death in 1905, Virgil Earp lived, among other places, in Cripple Creek, Colorado; Colton, California; Prescott, Arizona; and Goldfield, Nevada. Lamar, ed., *Reader's Encyclopedia*, p. 329. Glenn G. Boyer, ed., *I Married Wyatt Earp: The Recollections of Josephine Sarah Marcus Earp* (Tucson, 1976). Frank Waters, *The Earp Brothers of Tombstone: The Story of Mrs. Virgil Earp* (New York, 1950), pp. 208–13. Lake, *Frontier Marshal*.

trouble, and there was no more cattle rustling than there is today.

Sheriff Behan had more to contend against than any other officer. He was a brave and fearless lawman, who could see something good in even the worst of men. He did not persecute anyone, but he would try to serve any warrant that was given him.

XIV

The Mines Begin to Close Down

ONE OF the worst outlaws was Zwing Hunt. He
came from Kopprel, Texas, and was from a
good family. His father and brother were merchants
there and good citizens. Zwing first worked as a
cowboy for the Chiricahua Cattle Company, and
was so well liked by them that they staked him to a
six-yoke team of oxen, and he went to hauling lumber to the mines in Tombstone. He was making
good money when he decided to quit and go into
rustling.

Hunt joined in with a young man named Billy
Grounds, as reckless as himself.[1] It was claimed not
only that they rustled stock, but they ambushed in

[1]Like Zwing Hunt, William A. (Billy) Grounds (1862–
1882) grew up in a respectable family of central Texas.
Some personal difficulty, apparently, in his home town of
Dripping Springs caused Grounds to become a sixteen-year-
old refugee in New Mexico in 1879 where he made his way
to the wild town of Shakespeare which had attracted such
members of the central-Texas outlaw element as John Ringo
and Joe Hill. Homesick for Texas and his family, Grounds
soon got into a shooting scrape, bought a horse from Ringo,
and briefly ran a saloon before moving on to Tombstone and
Charleston, and membership in the cowboy-outlaw faction
of Cochise County. Janaloo Hill, "Yours Until Death, William Grounds," *True West*, XX (March-April 1973), pp.
14–15, 54–57, 60–61.

Skeleton Canyon a party of Mexicans who were smuggling silver bullion and silver dollars out of Mexico, and killed everyone in the party. It was said they buried their spoils in the canyon, and forty-seven years afterward there are people still looking for the silver.

In the fall of 1881, Persley and Woolf, of Sulphur Spring Ranch, had thirty head of cattle stolen. The tracks of the cattle led toward the San Pedro River. Woolf came to Tombstone and got a John Doe warrant, and I went with him to try to trace the stock. We followed them to Charleston and found them in a corral where they had been sold to a butcher, and one head killed. The thieves had not been gone over an hour. The man who had bought them turned them back over to Woolf and paid him for the one killed. From the description given of the men who sold the stock we were satisfied that they were Hunt and Grounds, and they were indicted for grand larceny, but were never arrested, as they left the country for a time and went to Mexico.

The following spring M. R. Peel was murdered by two masked men in the office of the Tombstone Mining Company at Charleston. Just after darkness two men opened the door of the office with rifles in their hands, and without saying anything one of them fired and shot Peel through the heart. The men ran and disappeared into the dark. Peel was a quiet young man and well liked, and was not known to have any enemies. It was always my belief that the men came there to rob the safe, and that being nervous they fired accidentally. Next day two men came out of the hills to a ranch near Lewis Spring and asked for something to eat. They claimed they had had nothing to eat for the past twenty-four hours. They were fed, and soon a company of soldiers came past looking for Indians. The men were badly scared and did not go out until after the soldiers left. They slept there the rest of the day, and at night went away. Hunt and Grounds were suspected of doing the killing. A few days later word was received at the sheriff's office that they were at the Chandler Ranch, about nine miles out of Tombstone.

Hunt and Grounds went to the Chandler Ranch March 25, 1882.[2] There was no one there but the man in charge. The proprietor was in Tombstone. There were two Mexican families living in a house about a hundred yards from the home ranch house. The outlaws claimed that the owner of the ranch owed them seventy-five dollars and they sent a note to the owner in Tombstone by the man in charge asking him to send them the money by bearer, as they were about to leave the country. Instead of sending them the money, he informed the sheriff's office where they were. In the meantime a man called

[2]Providing milk for Tombstone and owned by J. J. Chandler, this dairy ranch was a leading local landmark located about ten miles east of Tombstone. Ed Bartholomew, *Wyatt Earp, 1879 to 1882* (Toyahvale, Texas, 1964), p. 201.

Bull Lewis, a teamster, came to the ranch, and was the only one in the house with the outlaws at the time we got there. The sheriff was away with the posse chasing the Earp gang, and the warrant for grand larceny was given me to serve. I was told to take a posse with me, and when I demurred, thinking I could get them more easily alone, I was told that if they had shot young Peel they would resist arrest. The office got two miners to go with me, and I got one of the guards at the jail. His name was Allen, and he was a very courageous man. The other two were Jack Young and a Mr. Gillespie.

We reached the ranch just before daylight, and, after tying our horses a distance from the house, crept up. I stationed Young and Gillespie at the back door behind a pile of wood, and told them to lie quiet until daylight. Knowing the habits of the cowboys, I said they would come outside at daylight to look for their horses. If Young and Gillespie would then cover them with their guns, they would surrender. Allen and I were to guard the front door. I took the front of the house, as there were both a door and a window there, and only a door on the rear side. Allen and I started for the front of the house, and just as we got there I heard Gillespie knock on the door. When asked who was there, he answered, 'It is me, the sheriff.' The men inside opened the door and shot him dead and shot Young through the thigh. Neither Young nor Gillespie ever got a chance to fire a shot.

Just then the front door opened and Bull Lewis came running out crying, 'Don't shoot, I am innocent.' A shot came from the front door and creased Allen across the neck. It knocked him senseless. I heard someone step toward the door from the inside, and I grabbed Allen by his collar and dragged him under the bank of the dry creek in front of the house. The bank was about a foot high. I jumped behind a small tree just as someone fired from the front door, the bullet hitting the tree. The person who fired it stepped to the door to fire the second shot, I fired one barrel of my shotgun, loaded with buckshot, into the opening. Just as I fired I remembered an old adage always to aim low in the dark, and I pulled down thinking I would hit him in the stomach. But I hit him in the head and heard him strike the floor. In the meantime Allen had come to, and Hunt came around from the back of the house, calling, 'Billy, Billy.'

Allen and I both fired at him, Allen with a rifle, and I with a pistol, and he disappeared. He was only about fifty yards from us, and we both thought he was shot. It was not daylight yet. Young, who had got about thirty yards from the house, holloed that he was shot, and I ran to him and helped him to another house about a hundred yards from where we were. Allen lay behind the creek bank and he guarded the front door so that no one could come out and take a shot at me. All the shots were fired inside of two minutes.

On my return to Allen after getting Young where he could have attention, I told him I was sure Hunt was wounded, and as I could trail very well I would go up the creek and look for him, and for him to guard the house. It had become daylight by this time and we could see Billy Grounds's feet sticking just out of the door.

I went up the creek some hundred yards or more when I heard the bear grass rustle. Not knowing what caused it, whether a rabbit or a calf, and thinking it might be Hunt, I threw down my gun on it and cried, 'Throw up your hands.'

Up came a pair of hands, and a voice said, 'Don't shoot; you've got me anyway.'

I guess I cried out rather loud, for Allen came running. I ordered Hunt to lie down and place his hands in front of him, all the time covering with my gun. He did as I told him, and I went up and took his guns away from him. I sent Allen back for a milk wagon that was at the other house, and to get the men there to come up and take Hunt to the house. He was shot through the left lung, and every breath he drew whistled out through the wound in his back where the bullet came out. I asked him why he did not shoot when I came onto him. His reply was that he was burning up for a drink of water, and if he shot me he would not get any.

I took off my coat and made a pillow of it for him, and by this time I was getting rather shaky myself. Allen soon came back with the wagon and we carried Hunt to the house, but before he came he sent Bull Lewis with a message into Tombstone, asking for the ambulance and a doctor to be sent out as soon as possible. We found Gillespie dead at the back door. Grounds was still alive, but he never recovered consciousness. We placed both Hunt and Grounds on a mattress, made a fire and put hot water bottles at their feet, and did what we could to make them comfortable.

When the doctor got there a crowd came out also, and a lot of my friends came with them because they got the idea that I had been killed. When we took Hunt through the narrow two-foot door to place him in the ambulance, we squeezed his shoulders together and the blood spurted from his lung. Forcing the blood from his lung probably saved his life. Allen was suffering from the wound in his neck, but he would not give up until the doctor came, and he was taken care of at once.

On our return to Tombstone we had Gillespie dead in one wagon, Hunt and Grounds badly wounded in another, Young and Allen in the ambulance, and myself the only one not injured and able to ride in the saddle.

I learned from Jack Young that Gillespie was an aspirant for the sheriff's office at the next election, and that he thought I was too cautious or afraid, and that he could go in and make the arrest alone and get credit for it. Hunt told me that they thought it was the Earp party after them, and if he had known who it was, he would never have made a fight. Grounds never recovered consciousness and he died that night.

I was with Dr. Goodfellow[3] when the hospital attendant notified him that Grounds was dead, and he asked me to go to the hospital with him, as he wanted to learn how he could have lived so long with the buckshot in his brain. Some of the buckshot lodged in a silk handkerchief he had around his neck and did not go through it.

When we got to the hospital the doctor asked me to hold the light while he dissected the head. About the time he was ready my hand began shaking and I nearly dropped the lamp. Placing it on the table I told him to hold it himself; I was not curious as to where the shots went.

The ranchman where the two men stopped after Peel was killed identified both the men as the two

[3]Dr. George E. Goodfellow (1855–1910), Cochise County Coroner, was one of Tombstone's leading professional men. It was said that he had a larger practice in abdominal bullet wounds than any other civilian doctor in America. He could, however, lighten his baleful duties with such examples of humor as his finding that the bullet-riddled dead body of one McIntyre was "rich in lead but too badly punctured to hold whiskey." A California native, Dr. Goodfellow, who ultimately left Tombstone for a flourishing San Francisco practice, gained national recognition as a surgeon. Henry P. Walker, "Retire Peaceably to Your Homes: Arizona Faces Martial Law, 1882," *Journal of Arizona History*, X (Spring 1969), p. 7. Dr. George E. Goodfellow clipping file, Arizona Historical Society, Tucson. Odie B. Faulk, *Tombstone: Myth and Reality* (New York, 1972), p. 95.

*Dr. George E. Goodfellow, a Tombstone resident
and one of the best surgeons in the West.*

Courtesy Arizona Historical Society Library

who had stopped with him. Grounds was buried in the Boot Hill Graveyard, where Peel was also buried. Today Peel's grave is the only one marked with a headstone. There is nothing to show what other bodies are lying there.

I shall always believe that, if the office had let me go alone to arrest the men, I could have done it and no one would have been killed.[4]

Hunt was placed in the hospital and his brother Hugh came out from Texas. Within a couple of weeks his brother drove up to the hospital one midnight. Hunt wrapped a blanket around himself and got into the buggy, and they drove off to a hiding place in the mountains. In the fresh air from the pines he recovered so that he was able to start back toward Texas. Sheriff Behan had sent a deputy to try to find them. He received word from the deputy that he had them located, but that it would take a posse to take them, because they were surrounded by friends, and the outlaws kept them posted as to what was being done. He advised sending the posse out in the night over different routes so that the outlaws would know nothing about it.

Behan did as the deputy requested, but before the posse got there Hunt and his friends had started

[4]This could well have been true, for, as *Helldorado* shows, Breakenridge had remarkable success in enforcing the law in situations involving such notable outlaws as John Ringo and Curly Bill Brocius. On such occasions his mastery of the psychology of the Western outlaw was used to carry out the law while avoiding violence.

to leave the country. Hunt was still very weak, and the first night out they camped in what was known as Rustler Canyon, now called Hunt's Canyon. Early next morning while they were cooking breakfast they were attacked by a band of Apaches and Zwing Hunt was killed. Before he died he managed to get his gun and kill one of the Indians. His brother escaped on a hobbled horse, and ran through the timber for about a mile. Then he pulled up and removed the hobbles and rode six miles to Camp Price, where there were soldiers and scouts. They went back with him and buried Zwing under the tree where he was killed and carved his name on it.[5] In a short time the posse that had been sent after him came up following his trail. They dug up the body for the purpose of identifying it, as some of them knew him, and found that the wound in his lung was still not healed.

The morning after Zwing Hunt escaped, I had volunteered to take up his trail and try to recapture him, but the sheriff told me he had other work he wished me to do. Hugh Hunt returned to Tombstone and told about the fight in which his brother Zwing was killed. He claimed the property—a horse

[5]Carved on the tree were the words, "Z. Hunt, May 31, 1882." Rustler Canyon where Zwing Hunt died is in the Chiricahua Mountains of far eastern Cochise County not far from the ghost town of Galeyville. Douglas D. Martin, *Tombstone's Epitaph* (Albuquerque, 1951), pp. 160-62. Writers' Program of the Work Projects Administration, *Arizona: A State Guide* (New York, 1940), pp. 374-375.

and guns—that belonged to Zwing at the time of his arrest, but made no claim for any money, as both Hunt and Grounds were nearly penniless when they were captured.

As I was returning from Sulphur Spring Valley, shortly after Sheriff Behan returned from his unsuccessful trip after the Earp crowd, I met John Ringo in the South Pass of the Dragoon Mountains. It was shortly after noon. Ringo was very drunk, reeling in the saddle, and said he was going to Galeyville. It was in the summer and a very hot day. He offered me a drink out of a bottle half-full of whiskey, and he had another full bottle. I tasted it and it was too hot to drink. It burned my lips. Knowing that he would have to ride nearly all night before he could reach Galeyville, I tried to get him to go back with me to the Goodrich Ranch and wait until after sundown, but he was stubborn and went on his way. I think this was the last time he was seen alive.

A family by the name of Smith was living near the mouth of Morse Canyon, and about noon the day after I met Ringo, Will Smith took his rifle and went out to hunt for a deer. About two o'clock in the afternoon Mrs. Smith heard a shot and remarked, 'I hope Will got the deer,' but Will came in very soon after and said it was not he that had fired the shot. A little later a teamster who had been hauling lumber from the sawmill up the canyon came to the house and told them that John Ringo was dead just down the canyon.

On the opposite side of the creek from Smith's house were five large blackjack oaks growing in a semicircle from one root, and in the center of them was a large flat rock which made a comfortable seat. Ringo was found sitting there with a bullet hole in his head.

His watch was still running, and his revolver was caught in his watch chain with only one shot discharged from it. The report that came to the sheriff's office at the time was that one of his cartridge belts was on bottom side up and nearly all of the cartridges had dropped out of it, while in the other belt were several cartridges the lead of which had been chewed up showing that he had tried to get moisture in his mouth. His boots were gone and he had taken off his undershirt and torn it in two, and wrapped it around his feet, and when he was found the shirt had worn through, showing that he had walked for some distance.

All the evidence went to show that sometime during the night he had been overcome by the whiskey he had drunk and had gotten off his horse, taken off his boots and hung them over his saddle, and lain down and gone to sleep. His horse became thirsty and got away from him and started for water. It came to the Chiricahua Cattle Company's ranch with the boots on the saddle. When Ringo awoke, he must have been crazed for water and started out afoot. He was within sound of running water when he became crazed with thirst and killed himself.

At the present time, there are several different stories regarding his death, but the one that was told at the time of his death is the one I believe is the true statement. It is borne out by the statement made by fourteen citizens, residents of the Turkey or Morse Mill Creek neighborhood for the information of the coroner and sheriff of Cochise County, July 14, 1882.[6]

Ringo's grave is located behind the trees under which he was found. It is piled high with rocks.

Frank Leslie tried to curry favor with the Earp sympathizers by claiming it was he who killed Ringo in self-defense, but the evidence proved this to be a lie. We all knew that Leslie would not care to tackle him even when he was drunk.

[6]Still another of the unresolved mysteries of the violent history of Tombstone and Cochise County is the death of John Ringo, last seen by Breakenridge on July 11 or 12 and whose dead body was found on July 14, 1882. Did he die a suicide or was he killed by Wyatt Earp (who claimed to have returned surreptitiously to Cochise County for this purpose), or Johnny (behind-the-Deuce) O'Rourke, or Buckskin Frank Leslie? Jack Burrows, "John Ringo: The Story of a Western Myth," *Montana: The Magazine of Western History*, XXX (October 1980), pp. 12–15, does not bother to discuss the weak case for Leslie and persuasively refutes the claims for O'Rourke and Wyatt Earp. Burrows concludes that Ringo committed suicide but not because he was "crazed with thirst" (he was found in a tree directly above Turkey Creek), but because, Burrows suggests, the moody Ringo was suffering from depression, stemming, perhaps, from his sisters' rejection and, with most of his outlaw friends dead or running from the law, there was "no escape from himself."

The general election to elect county officers and legislators was held in November, 1882. At that time a man could swear-in his vote in any precinct he happened to be in on election day, but he had to swear that he had been a resident of the Territory for the preceding six months.

I was sent out with the blank ballots to the different precincts, and wound up at the Cienaga Ranch in the San Simon Valley. A Texas cattle company had bought this ranch early in the spring of 1882, and moved in there with a big bunch of cattle. There were quite a number of men working for them, and the election was held right at the home ranch.

I arrived there the night before election, and Jess Henley, the manager of the ranch, told me that they were all strangers in the country and knew none of the persons running for office. They had received a lot of ballots from Norton and Stewart, merchants in Willcox where they did their trading. Both of these merchants were Republicans, and they had sent Henley a lot of Republican ballots. There were several Democrats on the ticket that I expected to scratch, but when they told me they were going to vote the tickets that the merchants in Willcox had prepared for them I quickly changed my mind, and told them I had always heard that Texas cowboys were Democrats, and I was going to stay around and see how Texas Democrats voted so that I could tell them in Tombstone about it.

William M. Breakenridge,
while he was deputy sheriff of Cochise County.

Next morning I said to them, 'This is the way Arizona Democrats vote,' and I took a straight Democratic ticket and voted first. Then I talked the whole bunch of them into voting the same way. The precinct was right on the line of Arizona and New Mexico, and a rancher living just over the line, about twenty feet in New Mexico, said, 'Well, there will be one good Republican vote cast, anyway.' But I immediately challenged his right to vote in Arizona, and I carried seventeen votes home from this precinct, and every one of them was a straight Democratic vote.

At that election in the fall of 1882 a Republican by the name of Ward was elected sheriff. He took over the office January 1, 1883. At the city election Dave Nagle was elected the city marshal. I remained with Sheriff Ward as deputy that spring and summer. About the time we got through assessing the county, the mines closed down on account of the low price of silver.

Tombstone had always been a four-dollar-a-day camp, and the mine owners offered to continue work providing the miners would work for three and a half dollars a day. They refused and, of course, the mines had to shut down. At the same time the Hudson Bank closed its doors, and it looked as if the bank would be mobbed. Sheriff Ward assigned about twenty deputies inside the bank, all heavily armed. I was one of them. But through the intervention of the Federal Judge and other influential citizens the miners were induced to disperse.[7]

This ended the prosperous times in Tombstone.[8] When the mines closed down there were between sixty-five hundred and seven thousand people living there, but within six weeks not even two thousand remained. The gamblers left for new fields, saloons closed up, and, with the exception of a few miners who took a lease on some of the mines and worked them for themselves, everybody that could get away did so. Soon such rustlers and stage robbers as had not been killed had left the country, and Cochise County was as quiet from that time as it is today.

[7]The miners' strike began on May 1, 1884, and, in the course of the walkout, the eminent mine manager, E. B. Gage, was almost lynched by the overwrought strikers who were ultimately cowed by soldiers brought over from Fort Huachuca. Followed by its Tombstone branch, the Safford Hudson Bank of Tucson failed on May 10, 1884. John Myers Myers, *The Last Chance: Tombstone's Early Years* (New York, 1950), pp. 232–33.

[8]Unmentioned by Breakenridge is the chief cause of the end of the Tombstone boom: the invasion of the mines with underground water. Pumps did control the water level from 1881 to 1886 but on May 12th in the latter year a fire destroyed the Grand Central Mine pumping system. A quarrel between the owners of the Contention and Grand Central mines about sharing the cost of further pumping was left unresolved, and the encroaching waters ended deep mining in Tombstone until a new pumping system revived it, temporarily, from 1902 to 1909. The latter renaissance of deep mining brought no restoration, however, of the boom which had ended in 1886. Faulk, *Tombstone*, pp. 171–73, 180–85. Martin, *Tombstone's Epitaph*, chapter 13.

XV

Life after Tombstone

I WENT into partnership, with a man named Mason, in a ranch situated in the lower end of the Sulphur Spring Valley, and adjoining the road from Bisbee to the Horseshoe Pass in the Swisshelm Mountains. Right after the mines closed down in Tombstone I moved out there. It was possible to cut hay almost any place in the valley that season. We had a hay camp about five miles from our ranch and put up quite a lot of it. Our ranch was on the route taken by Mexican smugglers to and from Mexico. They always passed during the night and stopped at our pump to water their animals, but never molested anything.

When I was prospecting in the Dragoon Mountains in the winter of 1879, I had become well acquainted with Al Bennett and his wife, and also with Ben Scott. There were a number of prospectors in the camp and Mrs. Bennett was an angel to all of them. No matter how deep the snow or how severe the cold, if anyone got sick she would nurse him and see that he did not suffer for good things to eat. We all swore by Mrs. Bennett. That summer of 1883, while Mason and I were on our ranch, Bennett and Scott started with a load of freight for the mines at Nacosari, Mexico. After leaving Fronteras, they stopped for lunch and just after they started on their way, they were ambushed by Apaches. Bennett was shot twice in the groin and Scott through the right arm. After first grabbing their canteens, they managed to crawl into the brush for about a quarter of a mile and waited until dark. The Indians were afraid to follow them up, as they were both well armed, but the redskins did go to the wagon and ransack it, and broke open the boxes. There were about six hundred pounds of Hercules powder in the load and when the Indians set fire to the wagon, the explosion scattered pieces of it all around them. The Indians made off with their horses, and after dark Scott started for Fronteras afoot to get aid. Some men driving from Nacosari came along the next morning, and Bennett, hearing them, fired his pistol. They found him and took him to Fronteras. Scott arrived there at about daylight. A Mexican courier immediately started out for Tombstone with the news of the affair, and I happened to be in town when he arrived. Mrs. Bennett asked me if I would go to Fronteras and do what I could toward getting her husband brought to Tombstone. Dr. Willis also started with an ambulance, but he had to go by way of the custom house on the San Pedro River, fifty miles farther than across country. I started that evening by way of the Sulphur Spring Valley, stopped that night at my ranch, and the next day crossed the line at Agua Prieta where

Douglass now stands, and reached Fronteras about one o'clock that afternoon, twenty-four hours ahead of Dr. Willis. Bennett died soon after the courier left and was buried during the morning of the day I got there.

The Mexicans living in Fronteras were a poverty-stricken lot, but they did everything in their power to alleviate the sufferings of both Bennett and Scott. After the ambulance arrived, we endeavored to get permission to bring Bennett's body to Tombstone, but could not do so, as a permit would have to come from the Governor at Hermosillo. We did get a permit to bring Scott out the way I came, provided we would return to the custom house from Tombstone so as to release the ambulance that had been bonded through there.

The Doctor brought some canned stuff with him, however it took me two hours the next morning to find enough in Fronteras to make a square meal. I bought one egg in one place, two at another, and so on until I got about a dozen, and some corn bread at another place, coffee at still another, and, with what the Doctor brought, we managed to get a rather good breakfast.

We brought Scott out and he recovered from his wound without having to lose his arm. Soon afterward Mrs. Bennett got permission to bring Bennett's body from Mexico, and Scott went after it. On the way back he was sitting on the seat of the wagon with his rifle between his feet resting on the footboard. A jar of the wagon dislodged the rifle and it struck the bottom of the wagon and was discharged. The shot killed Scott.

On our way out from Fronteras with the ambulance, we stopped at my ranch overnight, and early next morning a sheriff's posse came by trailing some robbers that had held up Bisbee the night before and killed several persons.

A number of the outlaws who had left Cochise County went up into the hills in the vicinity of the mining camp of Clifton, where there were better opportunities to get away, as the place was rather isolated, and, like all mining camps at that time, full of gambling saloons and dance houses. Some of the outlaws got very bold, and hold-ups both day and night were frequent. One gang, consisting of Frank Heath,[1] Dan Dowd, alias Big Dan, C. W. Sample, alias Red,[2] Tex Howard,[3] William Delaney, and York Kelly,[4] had got so bad that they were notified to leave town. They got out in the night and went down into Sulphur Spring Valley and made a camp near the ranch of Frank Buckles. Heath went ahead into Bisbee to spy out the land there with a view to robbing the mining company's payroll. The rest of the gang followed him there a day or two later. They arrived after dark.

[1] Here Breakenridge was referring to the leader of the gang, John Heith (sometimes given as Heath).
[2] This was Owen W. (Red) Sample.
[3] That is, James (Tex) Howard.
[4] This was Daniel (York) Kelly (or Kelley).

Heath met them just outside of Bisbee, posted them as to where they would find the money, and then returned to town. The gang came in about seven-thirty and at once held up the company store which was run by Castenada and Goldwater, and made Goldwater open the safe.[5] They took all the valuables from it, then went into the back room where Castenada was lying sick in bed, and took about seven hundred dollars in gold from under his pillow. Tex Howard and Red Sample went inside the store and posted the other three outside to guard them, and those outside began shooting up and down the narrow street.

They killed the assayer, J. C. Tappinier,[6] as he entered the store. Deputy Sheriff D. T. Smith,[7] who was in a restaurant eating supper, heard the shooting. He came running out and told them that he was an officer and to stop shooting, and they shot and killed him. Mrs. Roberts[8] was killed by a bullet which was fired through the boardinghouse window

[5]Michael Goldwater (1821–1903) and Joseph Goldwater (1830–1884) were two ambitious brothers who came to Arizona from Russian Poland by way of England and California. Michael (Big Mike) was the grandfather of Senator Barry M. Goldwater. It was Joseph Goldwater who was in the store in Bisbee when it was robbed by the Heith gang. Goldwater biographical file, Arizona Historical Society, Tucson. Barry M. Goldwater, *With No Apologies: The Personal and Political Memoirs of United States Senator Barry M. Goldwater* (New York, 1979), pp. 17–20.

[6]That is, John C. Tappinier (or Tappiner).

[7]That is, D. Tom Smith.

[8]That is, Mrs. R. H. (Annie) Roberts.

where she was standing looking out, and then they shot J. A. Nolly through the body and Indian Joe through the leg.

They took about twenty-five hundred dollars, then mounted their horses, and departed with leisure. Heath did not assist in the murder and robbery, and did not leave with them, but met them just outside of town and got his share of the spoils. He remained behind and next morning joined the posse that was trailing the men when they came to my ranch, but he soon left them and went to Tombstone. Sheriff Ward started with a posse from Tombstone, and Deputy Sheriff William Daniels was in charge of the posse from Bisbee.

The outlaws returned the way they came, and about half of them were at Frank Buckles's ranch the next morning. There they scattered and went into the Chiricahua Mountains. Daniels and his posse identified them as soon as they reached Buckles's ranch, and Daniels returned to Tombstone and arrested Heath. Howard and Sample returned to near Clifton and went into hiding in the hills, but had separate hiding places.

The crime was committed on December 8, 1883. Deputy Sheriff John H. Hoover and A. G. Hill, with a posse of eleven others, captured Sample and Howard near Clifton on December 16th. Howard was suffering from a bullet wound in his back. Special Officer Tucker captured York Kelly at Deming, New Mexico. He wired Sheriff Ward at Tombstone to come after him, which he did, and Kelly was soon landed in jail with Heath, Howard, and Sample. Deputy Sheriff Daniels followed William Delaney down into Mexico, and captured him at the Minas Prietas Mine in Sonora. Soon after, he caught Dan Dowd at a mining camp in the Sierra Madre Mountains in Mexico.

All six were indicted by the grand jury, and Heath was the first one who was brought to trial. The other five were then tried together. In the case of Heath the jury brought in a verdict of murder in the second degree.[9] The next morning a mob of about thirty men who lived in Bisbee and Tombstone came to the jail, took Heath out, and hanged him from a telegraph pole, and then threatened to hang the entire jury if they brought in any more such verdicts.

While the other five outlaws were in jail awaiting their trial, Kelly and Howard were taking their exercise in the corridor when they became involved in a dispute which led to blows. Tex Howard was getting the best of it when the officers separated them; as they were led away Tex said to Kelly, 'I hope they'll hang you first, you s—— of a b——; I want to see you kick.'

[9]In Tombstone on February 19, 1884, Sample, Howard, Kelly, Dowd, and Delaney were found guilty of murder in the first degree and sentenced to hang. On February 21, 1884, Heith was found guilty of second-degree murder and sentenced to life in prison but, as Breakenridge shows, died before serving his sentence.

They were all found guilty of murder and sentenced to be hanged on March 28, 1884. The sheriff was set to execute them according to the law.[10] He sent out a few invitations to witness the hanging. I received one of them, but I did not care to attend. I believe this was the first legal hanging that happened in Tombstone.

I have seen several men hanged by Vigilance Committees, five in all, but I never attended a legal hanging.

In the spring of 1884 I sold my ranch and went to H. C. Hooker's Bonita Ranch to make a survey and map of his holdings for him. William Whelan, his foreman, was laid up for nearly two years with rheumatism, and I took his place while he was not able to attend to his work, and at the same time made a map of the ranch and surrounding country. There was considerable difference between the freight rates from San Simon and Willcox east, although they were only fifty miles apart, and Mr. Hooker decided it would be better to drive his cattle to San Simon for shipment. He asked me to ride over the route and see what the facilities were for water for them on the trip.

I went by way of Bowie, and then from there to Apache Pass. Just as I arrived at the creek where

[10]The hanging of as many as five persons at one time has been quite rare in the history of capital punishment in America, and to this day it remains one of the most notable events in Tombstone's remarkable history.

The lynching of John Heith, February 22, 1884.
Courtesy Arizona Historical Society Library

there was running water, I saw a moccasin track in the sand. I at once thought it was an Indian, so, tying my horse in a thick bunch of willows, I took my rifle and started to trail him up. I had gone only about a mile when I ran across General Crook, who was up there hunting and he was wearing moccasins.[11] I told him I thought sure I was going to find an Indian, and at that time it was open season on Indians. He had left his horse a short distance from where I had left mine, and we returned together and rode to Fort Apache.

I found there was plenty of water in the pass to water our cattle, and we drove them to San Simon for shipment. It took four days to make the trip, as compared with two days to Willcox. After Hooker made this shipment, the railroad changed their freight rates and gave him the same rate from Willcox as they did from San Simon.

[11]Historians of our own era echo General William T. Sherman's view that General George Crook (1828-1890) was the greatest Indian fighter in American history. Some of Crook's most impressive successes were scored against the Apaches in Arizona during the 1870s and 1880s. Crook's unostentatious encounter with Breakenridge was typical of this general who could be scathing in criticism of his peers but whose modesty and consideration won him the affection of the rank and file. Howard R. Lamar, ed., *The Reader's Encyclopedia of the American West* (New York, 1977), pp. 277-78. Robert M. Utley, *Frontier Regulars: The United States Army and the Indian, 1866-1891* (New York, 1973), pp. 392-93 and *passim*. George Crook, *General George Crook: His Autobiography*, ed. Martin F. Schmitt (Norman, 1946).

The Hooker Hot Springs, that lay nearly twenty miles from the ranch, was quite a health resort at that time, and in the summer a good many of the officers at Fort Grant used to take their families and go there for a few weeks' outing. They generally took the band with them and had plenty of music, so I tried to spend the weekends there. Colonel Shafter was commander of the post at Fort Grant, and a charming entertainer. He was a great lover of good horses and kept a handsome span of roadsters for his own personal use.

Mr. Hooker had a middle-aged Mexican working for him as a cowboy, named Marijildo Grejildo. He had been captured by the Chiricahua Apaches in Sonora in 1850, when he was only ten years old, and lived with them until he made his escape in 1858. For a long time he was employed by the Government as a scout and interpreter. He had worked for Mr. Hooker for a number of years, and was a top hand in handling stock. He was an expert with the lasso, and was Hooker's leading man at roundups when it came to branding cattle. He was married, and his family lived on the Gila River, above Safford. He left Mr. Hooker's employ and moved back to his ranch and died there.

While I was at the Hooker Ranch, W. K. Meade was appointed United States Marshal for Arizona. This was in 1886. He wrote and offered me a position as deputy at Phoenix. I accepted, and as it was a fee office, I was allowed to do surveying whenever

*W. K. Meade, U.S. marshal for Arizona,
who appointed Breakenridge to be
deputy marshal at Phoenix.*

I was not engaged doing work for the marshal.[12]

At the next general election in Maricopa County I was elected county surveyor, and in 1889 a committee from the Senate at Washington was appointed to investigate various sites for reservoirs in the Western Territories. The board of supervisors of Maricopa County, upon the urgent solicitation of the Phoenix Chamber of Commerce, instituted measures looking to a thorough examination of our water storage necessities and facilities, in view of the impending visit of the special Senate committee. I was instructed by the board to make a thorough examination of the Salt and Verde Rivers, with a special view to the availability of points on these streams for water catchment purposes.

The Chamber of Commerce requested James H. McClintock, as scribe, to write up the expedition. John R. Norton, canal superintendent for W. J. Murphy, contributed his services, and also furnished the pack animals. I hired a cook and horse wrangler, and we started out early in August. We followed along the base of Superstition Mountain,

[12]Virginia-born William Kidder Meade went West, settled in Arizona, got into mining, and as an early Tombstonian was both a legislator and a rising power in the Democratic Party. During his terms of office (1885–89 and 1893–97), President Grover Cleveland appointed Meade to be the United States Marshal for Arizona. Meade, like Bob Paul, used the marshalship to carry on an aggressive campaign against outlaws. Larry D. Ball, *The United States Marshals of New Mexico and Arizona Territories, 1846–1912* (Albuquerque, 1978), pp. 165–66, 243, and *passim*.

over the same old trail that had been used by the Apaches for ages, and is now known as Apache Trail Highway. We found a number of sites suitable to use for dams, but the water storage basins were too small until we came in sight of the wide valleys of the Tonto Creek and Salt River, above the head of the narrow canyon where the Roosevelt Dam now stands; and we saw that we had found an ideal spot for a dam and reservoir.[13]

Our surveying equipment was very limited. We measured the distances either by stepping them or by counting the steps of McClintock's blue mare. The elevations we got with an aneroid, the directions with a small open sight compass, and the levels with a hand level. We were careful in making our survey with our limited means, and were gratified in later years to find that it was substantially correct.

After satisfying ourselves about the depth to bedrock and the character of the rock in that vicinity, we went to the upper end of Tonto Creek, the east Verde, the main Verde, and the site of the Horseshoe Dam; and then to old Fort McDowell, where we swung back up the river toward the location we

[13]Located about fifty miles east of Phoenix and built from 1906 to 1911, the spectacular 284-foot high masonry dam named after Theodore Roosevelt was the first large barrier of its kind to be built by the federal government for irrigation. Apache workers who built the access road through precipitous mountain country were so dependable that they worked in squads without white supervisors. Writers' Program of the Work Projects Administration, *Arizona: A State Guide* (New York, 1940), pp. 366–67.

The Roosevelt Dam completed in 1911.
The original site, located and surveyed
by William M. Breakenridge, was the junction
of Tonto Creek and the Salt River.

had made at the head of the canyon on Salt River. This location was so much larger and better for a reservoir site that we put in most of our time there in trying to get a fair measurement of it. The dam was built some twenty years afterwards.

On our return, as the water in Salt River was low, we journeyed down through the narrow canyon and had to cross and recross the river every few hundred yards, as the water would hit first one side of the canyon and then be deflected back to the other side. But it was much better traveling than over the rough Apache trail.

In my report to the board of supervisors I estimated that the cost of building the proposed dam and reservoir would not exceed two million dollars, and that a dam two hundred feet high built at the head of the box canyon at the junction of the two streams, where it was only two hundred feet wide and the walls of the canyon were perpendicular for one hundred feet, would back the water up Salt River sixteen miles and up Tonto Creek ten miles, making a V-shaped lake twenty-six miles in length, averaging two miles in width, and with an average depth of eighty feet. Senator Stewart, of Nevada, one of the Senate committee having the matter under investigation, was rather skeptical, and seemed to think that I was exaggerating. I told him that if the committee would take a three-day ride with me on horseback, I would show it to them, but they declined.

The Government had several surveying parties camped on the river for years getting the daily and yearly flow of the water by actual measurement, and the annual rainfall, before they built the Roosevelt Reservoir.

XVI

Capture of Geronimo

From the time Geronimo, one of the chiefs of the San Carlos Apaches, escaped from the San Carlos Reservation in Arizona after he had surrendered to General Crook, until he again surrendered to General Miles[1] in September, 1886, at Skeleton Canyon, he committed a great many murders and robberies of isolated ranchers. In the summer of 1886, after General Miles had succeeded General Crook, he ordered Captain Lawton[2] to take his troop and certain Indian scouts and follow Geronimo

[1] An outstanding Civil War record prefaced a postwar career that saw Nelson Appleton Miles (1839-1925) score notable victories over Indians in the West and rise to become commander-in-chief of the Army. Vain and pompous, he was, however, an able commander and a great hero in Arizona, because it was he who obtained Geronimo's final surrender and was, contrary to General Crook, the strongest defender of the federal government's policy of the permanent exile of Geronimo and other hostile Apaches from Arizona. Virginia W. Johnson, *The Unregimented General: A Biography of Nelson A. Miles* (Boston, 1962).

[2] Tall and soldierly, Henry Ware Lawton (born 1843) was a tough veteran of the Indian wars of the West who received and met his greatest challenge in the pursuit of Geronimo deep into Mexico in 1886. In the Spanish-American War he attained the rank of major-general and in 1899 was killed in service against Filipino insurgents. *Dictionary of American Biography*, XI (New York, 1933), pp. 62-63.

wherever he went; to never give him time to rest and recuperate, and to capture or kill all of his band.

By an agreement between the United States and Mexico armed United States troops were allowed to enter Mexico and follow the Apaches wherever they went. Captain Lawton kept after them so closely that they had no time to rest, no time to hunt for wild game, or to gather in any provisions. However, Geronimo had taken fresh horses at every ranch they came to, and in this way he managed to keep out of the way of Lawton and his troops. At this time Geronimo had about thirty-five followers.

At Albuquerque, New Mexico, on July 13, 1886, General Miles ordered Lieutenant Gatewood[3] to take two friendly Indian scouts named Kateah and Martine, with a message to Geronimo and Natchez demanding that they and the rest of those with them surrender. Gatewood and the two Indians arrived at Fort Bowie, Arizona, July 15, and outfitted there for their trip into Mexico. Then they proceeded to a town called Carretas in Mexico, where they joined Lieutenant Perkins's command and traveled with him as an escort. On August 7th, after a march of over one hundred and fifty miles, they met and joined Captain Lawton and his command on the Arros

[3]Lieutenant Charles B. Gatewood played a key role in gaining Geronimo's surrender. Yet, Gatewood never received adequate recognition (in contrast to Lawton) from the army and was still only a first lieutenant when he died in 1896. Robert M. Utley, *Frontier Regulars: The United States Army and the Indian, 1866–1891* (New York, 1973), pp. 388–92.

Brigadier General Nelson A. Miles and his staff.
Miles is fifth from the left.
Captain H. W. Lawton is fourth from left.

River in the Sierra Madre Mountains. The troops had kept Geronimo moving over a rough, circuitous route, and they stayed together until they reached Fronteras, in Mexico, and but a short distance below the international line. Here Gatewood struck the first trail of the Indians he was after. He borrowed Tom Horn, a packer who was with Lieutenant Parker, and who spoke the Apache language,[4] to ride with him as an interpreter, and with his two scouts they went ahead of Lawton's command and on August 24th, reached the hostile camp which was located in the rough mountains near the great bend of the Bavispe River.

[4]General George Crook greatly enhanced the mobility and success of the Army in fighting Apaches and other Indians by replacing cumbersome wagon trains of supplies with the much more flexible trains of pack mules that were able to follow the troops directly to the scene of the action. Packing a mule so as to obtain proper distribution of the maximum load on the animal's back was a highly developed skill, and Crook spent hours personally inspecting the packs on the mules. Tom Horn (1860–1903) was one of Crook's best packers as well as being a scout. With the Apache wars concluded, Horn went north to Wyoming where he ended his career ignobly as a murder-for-hire employee of big cattlemen against stock thieves. In this connection, he was convicted and hanged for the ambush murder of a fourteen-year-old son of a sheepman. Utley, *Frontier Regulars*, pp. 48–49, 196, 378. Dan L. Thrapp, *The Conquest of Apacheria* (Norman, 1967). Donald E. Worcester, *The Apaches: Eagles of the Southwest* (Norman, 1979). Howard R. Lamar, ed., *The Reader's Encyclopedia of the American West* (New York, 1977), pp. 513–14. Tom Horn, *Life of Tom Horn . . .*, ed. Dean Krakel (1904; reprinted, Norman, 1964). Lauran Paine, *Tom Horn: Man of the West* (Barre, Mass., 1963).

The two Indian scouts went ahead and entered Geronimo's camp. One of them, Martine, returned before sunset; the other remained in the hostile camp all night. At first they were afraid to enter the hostile stronghold, but they were assured by Geronimo that they would not be injured, so they went in and delivered the message they were charged with. Martine came back to state that Geronimo and Natchez desired to 'talk peace,' and asked Gatewood to meet with them the next morning on the river about three miles from where he was camped. Gatewood bravely went alone with his interpreter to the appointed place, where he met Geronimo, Natchez, Geronimo's brother, and one other, and told them that General Miles demanded that they come with Captain Lawton and Lieutenant Gatewood to Skeleton Canyon and surrender unconditionally. At first they refused, but asked for another day to talk it over.

In the meantime Captain Lawton and his command came to where Gatewood was camped. The next morning Geronimo sent word that he wanted to talk to Gatewood again, and asked that Lawton remain in his camp until after the conference. Geronimo agreed to go with them to Skeleton Canyon to meet General Miles, provided they would allow him and his followers to travel by themselves and retain their arms until after they had their peace talk with the General.

One of the first acts of General Miles when he

took command of the Geronimo campaign was to round up all of Geronimo's tribe and their relations and families that were still on the reservation, and deport them to Fort Marion, Florida. Gatewood told the Indians about this; the first they knew about it.

Captain Lawton agreed to the terms asked for by Geronimo, and they started for Skeleton Canyon, but the Indians got several scares on the way and started to bolt several times. At one time they did bolt and scatter into the mountains, but Gatewood went after them and assured them they were in no danger and persuaded them to return. They again got uneasy when they got to the canyon and General Miles failed to meet them when they expected him to; but at last he reached there, and Geronimo—the wily old scoundrel—before he would surrender made the general promise he would not turn them over to the civil authorities for trial for the murders committed by them while they were on the warpath.

W. K. Meade was United States Marshal at that time and I was a deputy under him, and when General Miles arrived at the railroad station at Bowie with his prisoners to deport them to Florida, I was sent there with a warrant for Geronimo, Natchez, Dutchy, and Chatto, charging them with murder. True to his agreement the general refused to let me have them, and they were deported. There was plenty of proof against them and no doubt they would have been hanged if they could have been brought to trial. This was in September, 1886.

From Bowie they were first taken to the military post at San Antonio, Texas, and held there about three weeks. Then the Secretary of War ordered General Sheridan to send Geronimo, Natchez, Fun, Percio, Abnandres, Nahi, Yahneza, Touze, Bishi, Sophonne, Fishnolth, Chatto, La Zaiyah, Molzos, Kilthdigis, and Lonah to a fort in Florida, there to be kept in close custody until further orders. The remainder of the band captured at the same time, consisting of eleven women, six children, and two enlisted scouts (Dutchy was one of them), were sent to Fort Marion, Florida, and included with the Apache Indians already deported to that place.

On October 18th, Captain Charles L. Cooper, of the Tenth Cavalry, started from Fort Apache after Chief Mangus, and captured him. With Mangus were two bucks, three squaws, two boys, and one girl. They were also deported to Florida and placed with Geronimo and Natchez.

The rest of the Apaches who were left on the San Carlos Reservation were peaceable and were farming and stock-raising, and did not venture off the reservation, as at that time it was open season on Apaches if they were found away from the reservation. They lived in small villages of eight or ten tepees with a captain over each village. They were not molesting any of the white race at this time, but they had a good many quarrels among themselves,

Presentation ceremonies, Levin's Park, Tucson,
November 8, 1887, at which time General Nelson A. Miles
was given a gold sword by the people of Arizona
in recognition of his capture of the hostile Indians
under Geronimo.

and a number of them were killed. Along about 1889 there had been nine of them arrested on the reservation, by the Indian police, for murder among themselves, and they had been turned over to the United States marshal. When they were tried in the Federal Court there were thirty or more witnesses brought from San Carlos to appear against them.

They were all found guilty of murder or of assault with intent to murder and sentenced to from ten to thirty years in the penitentiary at Columbus, Ohio. One of them was a middle-aged Indian named Has-tin-de-to-da, who was sentenced to thirty years. He burst out laughing when told his sentence, and began talking to the interpreter. The judge asked what he was saying, and was told that he said it was a good joke on the judge, for he was not going to live that long. Five of them were tried in the Federal Court at Tucson, Arizona, and four of them in Phoenix, and the same witnesses were used against all of them. The Indians made good witnesses, for, although they were testifying against their own blood relatives, they told the truth, and claimed that, according to Indian laws, they were justified in what they had done. Marshal Meade was anxious to have the witnesses get back to the reservation with what little money they got for their mileage and per diem fees. As it was about three hundred and fifty miles by rail from San Carlos to Phoenix, and only about a hundred miles across country by trail, he conceived the idea of sending them to the Silver King Mine by wagons and from there letting them walk over the trail to the San Carlos Reservation. He told me to go with them and deliver them back to the agency. It surely was not a desirable trip as they were a sulky lot of brutes, and resented having their near relatives sent away.

We started from Phoenix with two four-horse teams to haul the Indians to the Silver King Mine. I led a good saddle horse and rode on one of the wagons until we reached there. It took us two days. The next morning at daybreak we started over the trail for the reservation. The Indians led the way over the trail and I followed behind them. They were on foot while I was on horseback, and I was well armed, but it was a lonely ride. When we stopped for them to rest and cook their lunch, I sat down a short distance from them and ate the lunch that I had brought with me. After a short rest they told me they were ready to go on and we started. When we had gone about two thirds of the way, at a place called Bloody Run, there were two ranchmen plowing in the field. As soon as the Indians came in sight the ranchmen ran for the house. The Indians stopped and I rode ahead to the ranch. When I got there I saw the two men and three women come to the door, all holding rifles. I rode up and explained the situation to them, but they stood there until I had got the Indians past them and out of sight. This was the reason that I had to go with them, for the few settlers in the country looked on them as they did on rattlesnakes and would not hesitate to shoot them as soon as they saw them.

We arrived at the reservation about dark, and I was certainly glad to get rid of my charge. It took me three days to return to Phoenix.

On my return I was told to take the nine Indian prisoners to Columbus, Ohio, and so with Elliott Walker, clerk of the court, Jack Halbert, sheriff of Maricopa County, and William Zent, a ranchman, as guards, we started with the four Indians that were being held in Phoenix, and at Tucson picked up the other five. They were the best prisoners to handle I ever had anything to do with. They looked on me as their friend and 'meal ticket.' I had riveted shackles on their ankles, but did not handcuff them. When we went through the Raton Tunnel, the car in which we were riding was not lighted, and they were not expecting the sudden darkness. You could not hear them breathe while we were in the tunnel, but as we came out into the light again, they gave a regular war whoop. It was a great surprise to them; also the immense corn and grain fields we passed through filled them with amazement.

One of the prisoners was called Captain Jack, and he was the head of one of the villages. One day I asked him why he had killed the other Indian. He could talk a little English, and told me that some two years before an Indian in another village had killed one of his men, and it was necessary for him to get even. He said, 'I could not sleep, I could not eat, my heart swelled, and I had to kill an Indian in that village to get even.' It was not necessary for him to kill the Indian that had killed his follower, just so he got an Indian out of that village. It was Indian law and justice.

By the time we got to St. Louis it had been wired ahead that we were on the train, and at all the stations where the train stopped there was a crowd to see the Apaches. It was a regular Wild West Show.

One of the Indians named Bronco Jim was something of a wit. At one of the stations in Illinois where we stopped for dinner, two ladies came into the car to see the show. One of them asked him what he had done to have to wear those shackles. He held up three fingers and replied, 'I kill um three white woman one day.' It is needless to say they got out of there as soon as possible.

We reached Columbus about midnight, and there were several newspaper reporters there to meet us. I told the guards to go to the hotel and engage rooms, and I would take the Indians to the penitentiary and come back as soon as possible. There was a large bus there to carry us to the prison, and I invited the reporters to ride with us. They did not care, however, to trust themselves in the bus with the Indians with only me to guard them, so I went alone and delivered them to the officer in charge. He told me they were the first prisoners he had ever received with riveted shackles. He had to get the blacksmith out of bed to remove them.

*Five of the nine Apache Indians taken to the penitentiary
in Columbus, Ohio by William M. Breakenridge.
Note the riveted shackles on their ankles.*

After getting the Indians into the penitentiary, I went to the hotel. As it was rather late, we all retired to our room. The bellboy showed us to our room, which was a large double-bedded room, and turned on the light. When we were ready for bed, the question arose as to how we should extinguish the light, as we were all afraid of getting an electric shock if we tried it. None of us had ever noticed how it was put out. One of the party wanted to call the bellboy back and have him extinguish it, but I told him if we did so we should be the laughing stock of the city, so I told them to get into bed and I would try it. Knowing that paper was a non-conductor, I placed a newspaper on the floor under the light, and, standing off at arm's length, I reached up and turned it out expecting to get a shock. I know the rest of the gang were disappointed when they saw that I did not get what all of us expected.

The next morning we went to the jail to get our shackles, and bid the Indians goodbye. They had brought a lot of their buckskin and bead work with them, and when they learned that they could not use any of it they gave me a lot of it. I left most of it with the officers of the jail for their museum, but took a pair of long-legged moccasins and a pack of monte cards, made out of buckskin scraped very thin like parchment, and with the different figures painted on them by the Indians. I then went on to Washington to visit our delegate to Congress, Mark Smith, as this was the first time I had ever been East, and I presented him with the moccasins and Mrs. Grover Cleveland with the monte cards.

One of the Indians was sick when we started from Arizona. He grew worse on the trip. This man and one other of the prisoners died in the penitentiary in the spring of 1889. Indian sympathizers at once got busy at Washington, and claimed the 'poor Indian' could not live in that climate. And they had enough influence to have all of the Indians sent back to Arizona, to have a new trial for their crimes in the Territorial Courts instead of in the Federal Court which had already sentenced them to the penitentiary at Columbus. They were tried in the Territorial Court, and most of them were sentenced to imprisonment at Yuma.

Some years later, while I was at the World's Fair at St. Louis, I saw Geronimo there selling his photographs, and was told that he was a superintendent of the Indian Sunday School. But there were no more depredations committed by the Indians after Geronimo and his band were deported.

When I went to Washington, I stayed seeing the sights about ten days, and enjoyed my visit very much. As it was summer, travel was not heavy, and on my return there were but few in the sleeping car. After breakfast I passed into the smoking car, where one man was sitting alone, with a newspaper. I was looking out of the window when on passing a station I saw Barnum's circus advertised, and it was coming East. Without thinking I spoke out loud, 'If we meet that circus before we get to St. Louis, I am going to camp.'

The man looked up and asked me if I was from the West. I told him yes. He said that if I would go with him to St. Louis he would show me the biggest circus in the world. He was rather flashily dressed with plenty of jewelry, and I sized him up as a confidence man. I had heard of them, but had never met one. So I told him I would be delighted to go with him. At the dinner station we met the circus, and he went to the telegraph office to send a message while I was watching the show.

Just before we reached St. Louis, I asked him what hotel I had better stop at, and he replied that he had wired his wife to meet the train and we would go direct to his home. Then I was sure I had met a confidence man. Sure enough, upon arriving at the station, there was a lady there to meet him whom he introduced as his wife. We went direct to their home, where we had supper, and then he said it was too late to see the big circus that night, but we went to an open air opera.

The next morning he called for his team and took me downtown and showed me through the city, and then down to the wharf where we went aboard a steamer called the *Hudson*. Everybody touched his hat to my host and greeted him cordially, and I began to think I had made a mistake in regard to him. Then I found out that it was his steamer, and that he was the captain of it.

I spent a very pleasant day with him and he did everything he could to show me the sights in St. Louis. That night after supper he took us out to Kensington Garden to see the Fall of Pompeii, and it was a splendid show. We got back to their home about two o'clock in the morning, and I bade them goodbye, as I was going to catch a train for the West early that morning.

I told Mrs. Allison that I owed her an apology for coming to their home a total stranger, but I had been fooled. When I met her husband I took him for a confidence man, and as I had heard about them I wanted to see how they worked. She replied, 'He is, that is the way he got me.' Frank Allison had a hearty laugh, and said he had me guessing, so he kept it up. I corresponded with them for several years after this.

A great deal has been said about the summer heat in Arizona, but St. Louis in that August was much warmer than Arizona ever was. On reaching the hotel I found that the heat in my room was such that I could not sleep, so I went to the office about four o'clock in the morning, and asked the night clerk what time the first train went West. He asked me where I wanted to go, and I told him to Yuma to get cool. Yuma never was as hot as it was in St. Louis at that time!

XVII

Tracking Outlaws

SENATOR TABOR, of Colorado,[1] owned the Vulture Mine nearby Wickenburg, Arizona. He had a Scotchman named Gribble as superintendent. One morning Gribble drove up to the assay office and brought out forty pounds of gold bullion, and with one mounted guard and a driver started for Phoenix. Three Mexicans waylaid him when he was about halfway, killed him and his two men, shot one horse, and took away with them the other two horses and the gold. As soon as the news reached Phoenix the sheriff sent a posse after them, but the

---

[1] Horace A. W. Tabor (born 1830) on the basis of ownership of Leadville silver mines became Colorado's greatest "bonanza king." He gained the honor of a thirty-day appointment (1883) in the United States Senate. He spent his millions lavishly and in Denver built the spectacular Tabor Grand Opera House, 1881. Giddily, he threw over his first wife, Augusta, and married a beautiful young divorcee, Elizabeth McCourt Doe (known as Baby Doe), to whom he had been attracted in Leadville. By his death, in 1899, however, Tabor was bankrupt, and thirty-six years later his widow, Baby Doe, died in destitution in a shack next to the played-out Matchless Mine which had been Tabor's best producer. Duane A. Smith, *Horace Tabor: His Life and the Legend* (Boulder, 1973). Writers' Program of the Work Projects Administration, *Colorado: A Guide to the Highest State* (New York, 1941), pp. 137-40, 180-81.

robbers had a long start. I was then in Tucson and some citizens in Phoenix asked me to come there as soon as possible and take the trail. On my arrival I found that the sheriff's posse was two days ahead of me, but I went after them with three or four men that I knew I could depend on.

It was no trouble to follow the trail, as the sheriff's band had good trailers, and we soon got to know the robbers' tracks from those of the sheriff's party. When we reached the pass in the Hacquehala Mountains, nearly due west of the Vulture Mine, we saw by their tracks that the murderers had doubled back on their trail. They had gone through the pass toward the Colorado River, and then, making a big circuit, had come back through the pass toward Vulture, and the sheriff was still following their tracks. This put us ahead of the sheriff. We found where the fugitives had evidently buried something at the foot of a tree and afterward dug it up again. The only tracks we saw leading away from there were the tracks of the three Mexicans. We followed them down the wash from this pass, and some distance down the wash we found two horses that had given out and been turned loose. From that point there was only one horse track.

We had to go to Vulture to get something to eat for ourselves and for our horses. It was only a short distance away. On arriving there we learned that one of the men we were following, named Valenzuella, had got breakfast from a Mexican family the morning before and gone back toward the pass. We took up his trail, which was fresh, and when we got to the pass that night we found the sheriff's party had just arrived, having tracked the murderers around the circuit for over sixty miles after they entered the pass.

The facts were that when the three Mexicans came back through the pass they buried the gold bullion, as it was very heavy to carry on horseback, and then started toward the Vulture Mine to get supplies and perhaps fresh horses from some of their Mexican friends, intending to return and get the gold bar. The two men whose horses gave out must have dismounted at some place where it was so rocky that they left no trail, and had taken their saddles and bridles off; then the other drove the loose horses down the draw for a way and turned them loose. They were completely played out when we saw them. Then the last remaining rider, who proved to be Valenzuella, deserted his comrades and went back and dug up the bar of bullion and was trying to get away with it. Here we saw that Valenzuella, after digging up the buried gold, had gone down the Hassayampa River toward the Gila, and was evidently trying to get into Old Mexico.

Next morning we took up his trail, and about noon at the mouth of the river we found his horse dead. He had been caught in the quicksand when his rider had tried to go across the Gila River. We found where the Mexican had cached his saddle, bridle, and rifle, and, as it had rained slightly before we got there, his footprints were plainly to be seen in the road leading down the river toward the Gila Bend Dam that was being constructed.

Our horses were very tired, but we hurried on. Just before we got to the dam, Will Smith, a railroad detective, Mike Curtion, Frank Prethero, and myself were together in the lead. The rest of the posse was some distance behind. As we rode into the camp we saw a man picketing a mule and asked him where the man was that just came into camp afoot. He seemed flustered and did not answer at first. Just then a Mexican came out of the foothills afoot, and made for the brush where the cook house was. It was supper time and he was going for his supper. The three men with me, thinking he was the man we were following, ran after him. I noticed a Mexican standing near the rear of a wagon, and when I again put my question to the man with the mule, he pointed toward the Mexican and said, 'There he is.' At the same time the Mexican ran for the hills, which were only about twenty feet from him. I was about twice that distance from them. I holloed for him to stop and throw up his hands, and started my horse as fast as I could after him.

He reached the rocks ahead of me. They were very steep, but he began to climb, and had got some fifteen feet up when he turned and shot at me with his pistol. I then fired at him with my rifle, and the rest of the men, hearing me call to him to throw up his hands, came back on a run and fired at him over my head. I shot only once, but some of us hit him and I saw him fall. I did not go up to him, but ran back to where he had been standing, picked up his blanket, and found the gold bullion wrapped in it. Then I knew we had the right party. He was shot in the head with a rifle bullet, and had Gribble's watch on him when he was killed.

The next day the whole party except myself returned to the Vulture Mine, taking the corpse with them in a wagon they hired at the dam. They hoped they would catch the other two murderers. I had to be back in Tucson on the United States Marshal's service, so I left them and went to Phoenix.

The sheriff's party did not reach the dam until after the short fight with the murderer was over and the bar of bullion recovered. I never knew for sure whether they found the two men they went back after or not. I think they did not find them.

During my forty years as an officer, I never shot at a man until after he had first shot at me.

A United States surveyor, George Roskruge, was sent out to survey a township close to the lines of Old Mexico. A man named Ortez, who had a cattle ranch near there, came out with armed men and ran him off, saying that they were in Mexico and not in the United States. Ortez was indicted in the Federal Court, and I was sent after him. I took one of Roskruge's men, called Bronco Steve, with me to show me the way. Before we started I was told Ortez was a bad Mexican, so I stayed all night at a ranch a few miles from where he lived and the next morning early drove to his ranch. I saw him come out of his house and go to his pump house. I followed him up, went in, and told him I had a warrant for him. He first said he did not understand, but I had been told that he spoke good English, so I told him that I knew that he did understand, and that he would have to go with me. He went to the door and said something to one of his men, who immediately started toward the line where the Mexican soldiers were camped some three miles away. He asked permission to go to his house to change his clothes and I told him he could, provided he did it in a hurry, as I did not intend to wait until the soldiers came.

We were soon on our way, and his wife hitched up a team and followed us. When we arrived back at the ranch where we had stayed all night, we stopped for breakfast. While we were eating, we saw three soldiers coming. I told Steve to guard the prisoner, and if they attempted to molest me to shoot him rather than let him get away. I then went out and met them at the gate. The officer in charge had his son, a young man I knew in Tombstone, with him as interpreter. He said I was kidnapping a Mexican citizen and would have to give him up. I showed him my United States warrant and told him that Ortez was living in the United States, had his stock there, and had been arrested there, and that if the officer and his men did not return to Mexico at once I would arrest them for being an armed force in the United States and take them to Tucson with me. He apologized, and said that he had been told that I was there unlawfully. Then they returned to their camp and we started for Tucson.

We stopped that night at the Hemmy Ranch, and next day drove into Tucson. It was Sunday and Ortez was afraid that he would have to go to jail, as he could not have his bail fixed that day. When we got to the Palace Hotel I saw Mr. Saminago and the hotel owner Mr. Marsh. They both said they were friends of Ortez, and would go on his bond whenever it was fixed by the court. I told them I would turn him over to them if they would be responsible for his appearance in court the next day. Ortez thanked me and was on hand the next morning. After the court fixed the amount of bail required, his friends went bail for him.

He told me on the way up that the United States made him pay taxes, and the Mexican Government made him pay duty on what supplies he brought in from Tucson, and while he would have preferred to find that his ranch was in Mexico, he was glad to have it settled either way.

Major Wham, paymaster for the army, while on one of his monthly trips paying the troops at the different posts, had finished the paying off at Fort Grant and was on his way to Fort Thomas, on the Gila River. While going through the Cedar Spring Canyon, at the north end of the Graham Mountains, he found the road obstructed by a large stone in the center of the road, and no room to pass it with a wagon on either side. His escort of colored troops were infantrymen, and were riding in two army wagons, while Major Wham and his secretary were in a light road wagon bringing up the rear.

The soldiers all got out of their wagons and, leaving their guns, gathered around the rock preparing to remove it, and Wham and his secretary walked up to where they were to learn what the trouble was. A volley was fired at them from among the rocks at the side of the canyon and several of the soldiers were wounded. It was too late to go back for their guns, and all they could do was to retreat down the canyon. They were soon out of sight, with Major Wham and his secretary leading. The robbers broke open the strongbox and got about twenty thousand dollars in gold and some silver. The gold was mostly in twenty dollar pieces.[2]

As soon as the news reached Fort Thomas, troops were sent out to trail the robbers, but a large drove

[2]On May 11, 1889, Major Joseph W. Wham was robbed of over $28,000 by thirteen men who ambushed the pay wagon from nine miniature rock forts above the road. One of the most audacious crimes in Western history, it was an immediate sensation in Arizona. Larry D. Ball, *The United States Marshals of New Mexico and Arizona Territories, 1846–1912* (Albuquerque, 1978), pp. 176–80. Otto Miller Marshall, *The Wham Paymaster Robbery* (Pima, Ariz., 1967). Jay J. Wagner, *Arizona Territory, 1863–1912: A Political History* (Tucson, 1970), pp. 266, 283–84, 315. Ball, Marshall, and Wagner are the sources for notes 3–6, following.

Fort Thomas, Arizona Territory about 1885.
Courtesy Arizona Historical Society Library

of cattle had been driven over their trail and it was completely obliterated.

There was a Mormon settlement a few miles from the scene of the robbery, and some of the men there were suspected of the robbery. Marshal Meade sent me to Fort Thomas on the first train, and I went from there to the canyon where the crime was committed and was convinced that the robbers had gone toward the Gila River where the Mormon settlement was. While in Fort Thomas I found a colored woman who used to cook for Mrs. Hooker when I was at the ranch in 1885–86.[3] She was a camp follower now and left Fort Grant just ahead of the paymaster's escort. She told me that she came through the canyon just as the robbers were placing the rock in the road. They were masked, and told her to hurry around the bend in the road ahead and not to look back, and to forget that she had seen anything or they would get her. She said she would not appear as a witness, as she was afraid of them, and would deny that she had told me anything if she was subpoenaed, but said she recognized several of them, and some of them were Mormons. She told me that she knew Cunningham, Webb, and Follett, and was sure they were in the gang. She described one of them as being lame, and Webb answered the description.

After consulting with the officers at the fort, one of them swore out a warrant against Cunningham,

[3]The woman was Frankie Campbell.

who was a saloonkeeper and gambler. I arrested him
and turned him over to the commanding officer.

A noted character, known as Cyclone Bill, was at
Solomonville drinking, and he insinuated that he
was one of the robbers; he was very lame and answered the description of one of them. He was arrested and I went to Solomonville to bring him in.[4]

The two prisoners were heavily ironed and taken
to Willcox on a dead-axle wagon, with an escort of
some twenty soldiers. There they were turned over
to me to take to Tucson. When we left Willcox on
a passenger train, I took their handcuffs off them so
that they would not be too conspicuous, but left the
shackles on their feet. Cunningham thanked me for
relieving him of his handcuffs, but Cyclone Bill
asked me to take his leg irons off also.

I told him, 'No, I will leave them on you for your
own protection.' He replied, 'You must be afraid of
us, and what do you mean by my needing them for
my own protection?'

I told him that if I took them off he would be
damn fool enough to try to get away, and I should
have to kill him, and I did not want to do it. Cunningham got a good laugh out of it.

I landed them in jail that night in Tucson, and
soon after, Webb and one of his sons, and Lem
Follett and several other Mormons were arrested
and brought to Tucson for trial. The Government

[4]William Ellison (Cyclone Bill) was eventually released
on the basis of an alibi.

had a good case against them, but they had too many friends who were willing to swear to an alibi, and there were too many on the jury who believed it no harm to rob the Government. Major Wham, when on the witness stand, swore that he recognized some of the twenty dollar gold pieces that were found hidden in a haystack at Follett's farm. The attorney for the defense[5] took some marked gold pieces from his pocket and asked the judge to mix them up with the ones in evidence. He then asked Wham to pick them out, and, of course, he could not do it. The jury evidently did not pay much attention to a witness who could swear to twenty dollar gold pieces. All of the prisoners were acquitted,[6] and soon after, Cunningham was hired by the Government to take charge of the teams on the boundary

[5]This was Mark Smith. See note 5 in chapter X.

[6]The trial, November 11–December 14, 1889, was as sensational and controversial as the robbery itself. The prosecution was hampered by strong public opinion in favor of the defendants who were looked upon as inoffensive Gila Valley farmers persecuted by an overbearing federal government while there was scant sympathy for the black soldiers who were the targets of the robbers' bullets. To these handicaps of the prosecution was added the unimpressive testimony of the key witness, Major Wham. As Breakenridge drily commented, "the jury did not pay much heed to a witness," Wham, "who could swear to twenty-dollar gold pieces." Yet, no credible alternative to the trial defendants has been produced as perpetrators of the robbery, and Marshal Meade and the prosecution team felt that anti-government community sentiment had deprived them of victory in the case. Four of the triumphant defendants later received prison terms for other, unrelated offenses.

survey. Soon after, he died while working with the engineers.

The Mormons soon left the country and moved to Mexico. Owen Wister was visiting some of the officers at Fort Thomas at the time, and wrote the story in a book called 'The Pilgrim of the Gila.'[7]

The United States marshal was kept busy with mail robberies and train and stage hold-ups. A band of train robbers held up the eastbound mail train near Pantano, and killed the engineer. Marshal Meade took a posse and followed them into Mexico, but he neglected to get a permit to enter with an armed force. The posse was arrested by the customs officers, their guns and horses taken from them, and they had to walk out of there.[8]

Bob Paul, who was a Wells, Fargo detective and railroad special officer, received permission to go after the robbers, however they were quickly arrested by the Mexican authorities who received the reward for them. While they were in custody of the Mexicans

[7]Owen Wister (1860–1938) was a Pennsylvania aristocrat and a good friend of Theodore Roosevelt. Best known as the author of *The Virginian* (1902), the prototypical formula-Western novel, Wister's story of the Wham robbery, "A Pilgrim on the Gila," was first published in *Harper's Magazine* and later in a collection of Wister's short fiction in *Red Men and White* (1896). Howard R. Lamar, ed., *The Reader's Encyclopedia of the American West* (New York, 1977), pp. 1280–81. Marshall, *Wham Paymaster Robbery*, p. 82.

[8]It was the outlaw gang of Larry Sheehan which Meade pursued into Mexico, resulting in the detention of Meade and his posse in the town of Janos for two weeks in March 1888. Ball, *United States Marshals*, pp. 174–75.

they were shot. The Mexicans claimed they were attempting to escape.[9]

After Marshal Meade's term had expired, I continued to work at surveying in Maricopa County. One day I got a wire from Judge Barnes, an attorney in Tucson, to come there and make a survey for an English company, known as the Santa Cruz Water Storage Company, for a reservoir on the Santa Cruz River. On my arrival I was instructed to get a party and try to find a storage basin for water somewhere between Tucson and the Mexican line, and to run a line for a canal from there to Tucson.

I found within a very short time that there was no good site for a dam to store water in on the Santa Cruz, and so reported.

But the English company had sent an agent with eighty thousand dollars to spend, and he did not want to stop work until he had spent some of it. So I was instructed to run a canal line down the valley following a two-foot grade along the foot of the mountains, and try to find some storage for water in the dry gulches that ran from the mountains to the river that could be filled by flood waters, before he decided on a head for the canal or where he would take it out from the river. He also told me to lay out a canal, forty feet wide at the bottom and five feet deep, out on the mesa where the head of the canal,

[9] According to Ball, *United States Marshals*, p. 175, it was a "combined force" of Mexicans and Paul and his men which wiped out the Sheehan band.

whenever it was located, could be connected up with it. As the fall of the river was twenty feet to the mile, this was not difficult. He let a contract to build a dry canal before he knew whether he could get enough water to fill it.

The contractors built two miles of this canal out on the mesa before the company sent a representative out from England to see what their agent was doing. I had made a report every month condemning the scheme, but the agent suppressed my reports. Fortunately I had kept a copy of my reports and was able to produce them, and to show their representative that I was not a party to the canal plan. The representative of the company stopped all work, paid all bills, and I gave him a copy of my reports showing it was a huge swindle.

XVIII

Named Special Officer

AT THE change of the Administration in 1889, Bob
Paul was appointed a United States marshal,
and I made an application for the position of special officer for the Southern Pacific Company. Vic
Wilson was also an applicant for the position. He
was an old Texas Ranger, and a very brave and
good man, and had worked for the company in
Texas as a conductor. He got the appointment.

Two or three years later he was killed by Evans
and Sontag, who were train robbers in California.
They robbed a train near Visalia and were diligently hunted, but they kept out of the way. The
chief special officer in San Francisco asked Wilson
to go there and help run them down. Frank Burns,
a deputy from Yuma, was up there with several
Yuma Indians as trailers, and they were joined by
Vic Wilson, Dan Overhall, a sheriff of that county,
and Will Smith from Los Angeles, who was special
officer for that division. There were several others
in the party.

They were coming upon a farmhouse in the
mountains one day when the Indians said they saw
tracks going in there. When the posse got to the
gate leading into the house, Overhall and Wilson

got off their horses and started toward the house, the rest of the party remaining on their horses. A man came out of the house and started for the well after a bucket of water, and they asked him if he had seen anything of the men wanted. He shook his head, and they continued toward the house. Just as they got there, Evans and Sontag opened the door and killed them both.[1]

Then the robbers escaped into a cornfield that was within twenty feet of the door, and the posse stampeded and left their dead comrades lying there. The Indians came back first, but they refused to go into the cornfield. The posse was then sent home, and I received a wire from Mr. Fabins, chief special officer, asking me to meet him in Los Angeles.

I met him there and he offered me the appointment of special officer of the Tucson division between Yuma and El Paso. He asked me to travel to Visalia and see if I could be of any assistance in tracking and running down the robbers.

When I arrived, there must have been a hundred men in the hills; the woods were full of them. There

[1]After a series of five train robberies in the San Joaquin Valley, 1889–1892, Chris Evans and John Sontag fought two gun battles with law officers at Evans' house in Visalia in August and September, 1892. They then were trailed to Sampson's Flats in the Sierra Nevada foothills where Vic Wilson and Deputy Sheriff Andy McGinnis were killed in a shootout on September 13, 1892. Eugene B. Block, *Great Train Robberies of the West* (New York, 1959), chapter 5. C. B. Glasscock, *Bandits and the Southern Pacific* (New York, 1929), chapters 3–9.

Early Southern Pacific express train about 1890.
Courtesy Arizona Historical Society Library

was a large reward offered for the bandits; men were getting lost from their camp or companions, and firing off guns to try to find them, and it was useless to try to do anything while such a mob was there. I stayed ten days, then one morning I told the boys goodbye and returned to Visalia, and took the train for Los Angeles. I told Fabins that I was no good up there as I was not acquainted with the country, and knew nobody. I might even meet the robbers and not know it, because there was no one that I dared ask questions. After the big mob got tired and left, there might be something to do, and I would go back then, if still desired. Several months later, George Gard, United States marshal for California, went to Visalia with a large posse. Through some ranchers who were his friends, he succeeded in catching the bandits in an open field. Sontag was shot and killed, and Evans was wounded. Sontag's brother was also arrested, and he and Evans were found guilty and sent to the penitentiary for life.[2]

I now took up my home in Tucson, in the performance of my new duties. There was a lot of petty boxcar stealing going on, and I was kept busy hunting the thieves and goods. At one time I captured two Mexicans who had stolen two cases of rifles

[2]On June 11, 1893, Evans and Sontag were cornered by Gard's posse in the mountains where at the "Stone Corral" Sontag was killed and Evans was wounded and captured. After a long stretch in prison, Evans was pardoned in 1911. He died in 1917. Glasscock, *Bandits.*

from a boxcar en route to San Francisco and had buried them on the river bank near Benson. At another, I recovered nearly a wagonload of goods that had been thrown out of a car by a white man. He jumped from the train after throwing off the goods, and carried them into the brush about a hundred yards from the track, then took the back track into Tucson. He walked at least twenty-five miles after he had carried the heavy goods into the brush to conceal it, so that he put in the whole night at hard work.

The next morning, as the section gang was going to work on the track, they saw the broken boxes where he had dumped them from the train. The news was wired to the superintendent and I was notified at once. As there was no train for several hours, I took a hand car and ran down there, and found all the goods hid in the brush. The section men gathered them all up, and, placing them on two hand cars and a push car, I started for Red Rock, the nearest station.

Just as we were leaving, I saw a wagon come up to where we had found the goods. A Chinaman and a white man were in the wagon; they drove slowly until we were about a mile away from them, when they turned around and went rapidly back toward Tucson. As Red Rock was but a few miles away, I went there and sent a message to the sheriff describing the men. As they entered the town he arrested them. The Chinaman said that the other man had come to him and told him that he had the goods hid out there and got him to agree to buy them.

The thief got a very light sentence of a year. This was because while in jail awaiting trial, he stopped a train robber from escaping. He served his time and came back to Tucson. As soon as he got to town, he laid his plans for another robbery. Another convict had been discharged the day before this Kelly was. He came to me and said Kelly wanted him to go along and throw off a lot of sugar from a car. I told him to go ahead and I would protect him, and for him to come to me as soon as he could leave Kelly and report what they had done. They got a car that night, but by mistake got one loaded with beans instead of sugar. They threw off one sack of beans and carried it off the right-of-way. I found their tracks and, on arresting Kelly, found that his shoes fitted the tracks. The young man with him turned State's evidence and Kelly was convicted, getting ten years for this, his second offense. He said he would get me as soon as his term was up, but I heard nothing more from him.

While he was lying in jail the first time waiting for his trial, three train robbers held up an east-bound train at Maricopa, and robbed the Wells, Fargo Express car. The robbery occurred about eleven o'clock at night, and I left Tucson with a special engine and a boxcar to carry my saddle horse. I wired to Casa Grande for Billy Stiles and Felix Mayhew to be at the train with their saddle horses, and we were on the ground at Maricopa before daylight. We soon learned who the men were, as they had been hanging around the town all day. At their camp I found a poll tax receipt belonging to Oscar Rogers, whose true name was Oscar Touraine. The other two were Frank Armour and Ed Donovan. We found their horse tracks leading toward the Gila River below Phoenix, and followed them to the river. Someone of their gang gave them away to the sheriff in Phoenix.

The officers learned that they had a place of rendezvous about eight miles west of town on the river. On receipt of a despatch telling him about the train robbery, Sheriff Murphy and Deputy Widmer immediately started for this rendezvous, and arrived just after the outlaws got there. Their horses were tied to some trees and the men were at a haystack getting hay for them. Armour came back first with his arms full of hay, and, on being told to throw up his hands, dropped the hay and drew his pistol, but before he could use it he was shot in the arm by one of the posse. The other two, hearing the shooting, lit out afoot through the brush and got away. I wired to all stations to look out for them, and two or three days later Rogers was arrested within a short distance of Yuma while he was getting breakfast at a ranch.

Rogers and Armour were taken to Florence, the county seat of Pinal County, where the robbery took place, and had their examination and were held for the grand jury. We kept Armour in the Florence jail, and I took Rogers to the Tucson jail so as to keep them apart. Rogers was an athlete and took his exercise in the jail yard turning handsprings with his shackles on. While he was in jail in Tucson, he got hold of a piece of wire, managed to pick the plaster from between the bricks in the wall, got several of the bricks out, and no doubt would have escaped if the boxcar thief Kelly had not given him away to the jailer. We never could get any trace of Donovan. He was never seen or heard of after leaving the camp where Armour was captured.

When the time for their trial was set, I took Rogers back to Casa Grande on the train, and from there to Florence in a two-horse buggy. When the team came up to the depot for me to drive to Florence, I took my pistol off and handed it to the station agent. I told him I should not need it on the trip. Rogers was very strong, and I did not intend that he should take it away from me on the trip. He smiled when I told him to get into the buggy with me, as he thought I was going to take him to Florence alone, the same as I had brought him from Tucson. Then Mr. Mayhew came up on horseback and I told him to get my shotgun from the agent and follow us over and to use the gun if necessary. We got through nicely. Both robbers were found guilty and sentenced to the penitentiary. At that time there was a law that the penalty for train robbing was death. Rogers was sentenced to hang, and

Armour to life imprisonment. Governor Hughes reduced Roger's sentence to life imprisonment and
the next Governor reduced it to ten years. Armour
was pardoned on account of his health after he had
served five or six years, and Rogers served his ten.

The superintendent's office received a report that
the section house at Sweetwater had been robbed,
and I was sent down there to investigate it. Sweetwater is about fifteen miles west of Casa Grande. At
Casa Grande I got Billy Stiles, who was an expert
trailer, and who had been with me on several trips
after criminals,[3] and we went down on a handcar.
We found that Mrs. Vincent, the section foreman's
wife, while alone at the section house, had been
held up by two Mexicans, who came in and tied her
up in a chair and gagged her. Then they ransacked
the house and took her gold watch and other jewelry, together with a small sum of money.

She managed to get untied from the chair, but
had to wait until her husband arrived from work
before she could give the alarm. We got there about
twenty-four hours after the robbery. We quickly
took up the trail and followed it afoot about a mile
north of the railroad, where the men had stopped

[3]William Larkin (Billy) Stiles was, as Breakenridge notes,
an effective law officer, but he went bad as did another able
lawman, Burt Alvord, whose rampaging gang of train robbers Stiles joined. Stiles escaped the law in Arizona but was
killed in Nevada in 1908 while serving as a deputy sheriff
under an alias. Bill O'Neal, *Encyclopedia of Western Gunfighters* (Norman, 1979), pp. 298–99.

and exchanged their heavy shoes for rubber-soled tennis shoes.

This made tracking them much more difficult, but we followed them until they struck the road from Sacaton leading toward Tucson through Picacho Pass. After satisfying ourselves that they were headed in that direction, we returned to Sweetwater, and the handcar took us to Casa Grande. It was getting late, but we got a conveyance and drove north to the road where we last saw the tracks and saw that they were still following it. We remained in Casa Grande that night, and early next morning caught a train going east; and at Picacho, where the road crosses to the south side of the railroad track, we again found their tracks, and we continued on the train to Red Rock. Here we heard of them passing, and again found their trail, and just before our train reached Rillito, at Wakefield's ranch, we saw them entering a cornfield.

The train stopped to let us off, and we surprised them in the field and arrested them. Just as we came on them and told them to throw up their hands, one of them threw something away. We disarmed them—they had two large knives and a pistol—and I held them while Stiles hunted up the object that we saw them throw away; it was Mrs. Vincent's watch. We walked them to Rillito, and held them there until the first train bound west came along, and took them to Casa Grande and placed them in jail. The robbery occurred on Monday morning about eight o'clock, and we caught them on Wednesday afternoon about three, sixty miles from the place where they committed the crime.

Nearly all the stolen property was recovered, and the Mexicans were sentenced to several years in the penitentiary.

In December, 1893, the northbound express train on the Southern Pacific Railroad was held up at Roscoe, a small station about twelve miles from Los Angeles, and the express car robbed by two masked men. Detectives were busy for some time, but could not get any clue as to who the robbers were. On February 16, 1894, the train was again held up at the same place. This time the robbers signaled the engineer to stop, but he pulled his throttle farther out, and with increased speed ran into a blind siding, where they had thrown the switch, and ditched the train, killing the fireman and a boy who was stealing a ride on the front end of the engine. The express car was then blown open by the use of giant powder and the safe rifled. And again the robbers got away without leaving any clue or trail. There were several arrests made, but the officers could get no evidence as to who committed the crime. The money taken was mostly in Mexican silver dollars, amounting to about twelve hundred.

The next fall John, alias Kid, Thompson and Charles Etzler came to Phoenix, Arizona. From there they went to Tempe, and had a camp near town on the river. Etzler hired out to a man named

*John "Kid" Thompson, train robber, who was
finally apprehended after a long chase.*

Courtesy Arizona Historical Society Library

Baker who lived on Tonto Creek, where the Roosevelt Dam is now, and told him the story of how he came to be with Kid Thompson. Baker sent word to me and brought Etzler to me at Phoenix.

Thompson had told him that he and a man named Johnson had held up both trains, had taken the Mexican money to Johnson's ranch in the little Tejunga Canyon, and had buried it until the excitement was over. Kid Thompson went to Dakota to visit his people until it was safe to divide the spoils. On his way back he took up with Etzler, and the two were beating their way to Los Angeles. He told Etzler all about the two robberies, and said that if Etzler would go with him to Johnson's ranch, he— the Kid—would get his share of the buried money, and then they would go to Arizona and rob a train near Maricopa. Etzler agreed, but when they got to the ranch, Johnson refused to dig up the money, as he was afraid the Kid would sell it to the Chinese in Los Angeles, and the detectives would find it out. But he told them to go to Tempe and he would send them the Kid's half by Wells, Fargo Express in a box marked surveyors' instruments.

They beat their way to Tempe, and in a few days Johnson sent them the money. Thompson took a little at a time into Phoenix and sold it to the Chinamen there, and had disposed of nearly all of it when Etzler got scared of the train robbing proposition, and one day, while the Kid was in a barber shop getting a haircut, Etzler told the city marshal that he could get the Kid easy, and that he had a pocket full of Mexican money with him. The marshal evidently did not believe him and said he was going to supper, but would see him when he came back downtown.

Then Etzler got afraid that the Kid would find out that he was giving him away, so he hired out to help drive some stock to Tonto Creek and told Baker all about it.

I took Etzler that night on the train to Los Angeles and turned him over to the officers there. They went at once to Johnson's ranch and dug up the rest of the Mexican silver where Etzler told them it was.

Will Smith, the Southern Pacific detective in Los Angeles, returned with me to Phoenix on the first train. I learned that Thompson was stopping on a ranch near Phoenix, and we went out there to arrest him, but he was in town at the time we got there. Much to my surprise Smith said to the ranchman, 'Tell the Kid that Will Smith, the Southern Pacific detective, wants to see him to get some information, and for him to call at the Commercial Hotel.'

As soon as we got away from the ranch, I told Smith that it was all off and the Kid would get away, unless we hid close by until he returned from town and arrested him. But Smith claimed that he knew Thompson well, had talked to him several times in regard to the robbery, and paid him for information and help, and that Thompson would be glad to come and see him.

The next day we went out to the ranch and the ranchman told us that when the Kid received Smith's message, he got on his horse, saying he would go to town to see Smith, but actually left for parts unknown. I knew that, before he went to California, he had worked on a ranch near Aguas Calientes, on the Gila River, and had a lot of friends in that vicinity. I got John Slankard, a deputy United States marshal, to go down there and try to locate him. Slankard found his camp, but the Kid evidently saw him first, as he had left it in a hurry and taken nothing with him. Slankard tracked him up the river to near Phoenix, where his tracks showed that he had circled the city and gone on east.

Billy Moore, deputy sheriff of Maricopa County, was on his way to his ranch up the Salt River, and I asked him to look out for Thompson. At the Crabtree Ranch, about thirty miles from Phoenix, he learned that Thompson had passed the day before, and that there was a young man with him. Moore made up a posse consisting of I. E. Crabtree, John Kemp, E. E. Watkins, E. G. Keith, and himself and went after them, overtook them about dark in the Four Peak Range, and called on them to surrender. They refused, took shelter under an overhanging cliff, and began shooting. The posse returned their fire, and, as it was very cold up there, the outlaws were froze-out before morning and surrendered. The young man with Thompson gave his name as Colonel Tupper.

Moore brought the men to Phoenix, with one of Thompson's wrists tied to the horn of the saddle, and his feet tied together under the cinch. He turned the men over to me. Thompson waived extradition papers, and I took them to Los Angeles that night. In the meantime the officers there had arrested Johnson and he confessed to both robberies. The men were both convicted and sentenced to long terms in prison. They had both been arrested before, but the officers could obtain no evidence against them.

I don't remember what happened to Tupper. He was only a boy and evidently wanted to become a Western desperado. There was a fight over the reward, and it was taken into court, but Billy Moore and his posse won out and received the full amount. I made affidavit that I made no claim to the reward, and that I believed Moore and the posse were the only ones entitled to it.

XIX

Chasing Train Robbers

IN THE latter part of January, 1895, a Southern Pacific express train was held up about five miles west of Willcox by Grant Wheeler and Joe George, two cowboys working in the Sulphur Spring Valley near Camp Rucker. Mounted on good horses they trotted into Willcox, where they were both well known, and purchased a lot of giant powder, fuse and caps, and rifle and pistol ammunition, saying they were going to do some mining near Dos Cabezos. Leaving town they went to where they expected to rob the train and staked their horses. They walked back to Willcox, and arrived at the depot just as the train arrived.

Climbing on the train between the engine and the first car, they went up on the engine and covered the engineer and fireman with their pistols, ordering them to stop the train out about three miles from town. They made the fireman get down and cut off the mail and express car from the rest of the train, and then had the engineer move the cars ahead about two miles to where they had left their horses and the giant powder. The express messenger, realizing it was a hold-up, took what valuables he could, and, as the train slowed up the second time, jumped out of the side door and ran back to the passenger cars that had been left on the main line.

The outlaws made the engineer break open the express car door and were surprised to find the messenger gone. They made several attempts to blow open the safe. There were eight sacks of Mexican silver dollars in the car with a thousand dollars in each sack. The men laid giant powder on top of the safe and then placed sacks of the Mexican money on top of it for tamping, and set it off. They had to make several attempts before they blew the safe open, and the explosions scattered Mexican dollars all over the ground for some two or three hundred feet. Wheeler and George gathered up what money and jewelry they found and left on their horses, going south toward the Chiricahua Mountains.

Sheriff Fly[1] was in Willcox that night, and at daylight took the trail with a posse, and followed the robbers to where they entered the mountains. They had lots of friends in there who would protect them, and here the trail was lost. I was in Tucson at the time, but got to the scene of the hold-up about sunrise next morning. I found a pair of spurs at the bridge where the car was robbed, and at the place where the men left their horses I found a quirt.

A couple of the clerks from the office in Willcox

[1]Before becoming sheriff, C. S. Fly was a well-known Tombstone photographer. It was adjacent to his lodging house and photography shop that the gunfight between the Earps and Holliday and Billy Clanton and the McLaurys took place on October 26, 1881.

Grant Wheeler, train robber,
who killed himself when confronted
by Billy Breakenridge and a posse.
Courtesy Arizona Historical Society Library

came out and I put them at work gathering up what Mexican silver they could find, but a lot of the Mexican section hands were there also and they kept what they found. The Mexican women and children belonging to that section house were busy for the next couple of weeks raking the ground with garden rakes, looking for the dollars.

In Willcox some cowboys that I knew quite well told me that the spurs belonged to Joe George and the quirt to Grant Wheeler.

John Thacker, a Wells, Fargo detective,[2] came from San Francisco and met me in Tombstone. We had different ideas as to the best thing to do to find the robbers, but we could get no information as to whether they were in the mountains or had passed through them into Old Mexico. As I was well acquainted all through the mountains, I proposed to go in by myself and try to learn if the men were still in there, and ordered a team to be ready for me about two o'clock that afternoon. Thacker objected, and wired San Francisco that I was interfering with his plans, and I received a telegram telling me to let Thacker handle the case and to assist him if he wanted me to. I showed him the wire, and he said he had the case well in hand and would call on me if he needed me.

[2] John N. Thacker, a leading Wells, Fargo detective was noteworthy for arresting Black Bart (Charles E. Bolton) who had robbed twenty-seven California stagecoaches from 1875 to 1883. Edward Hungerford, *Wells Fargo: Advancing the American Frontier* (New York, 1949), pp. 146–48.

I left him and returned to Tucson, where I had plenty to do. He stayed in the Tombstone vicinity for about a month and accomplished nothing, and then went back to San Francisco. One of his plans was to get one of the outlaws' friends to bring them a bottle of drugged whiskey, and, after they fell asleep, to hog-tie them and bring them to him in Tombstone. The friend told the bandits about it and they laughed about his trying to catch birds by putting salt on their tails.

At that time the Southern Pacific and the Wells, Fargo Companies were rather unpopular with the people. It was claimed that their freight and express charges were exorbitant, and whenever a train was held up a great many sympathized with the robbers. As long as Wheeler and George remained in hiding in the mountains among their friends, it was almost impossible to catch them.

One of my cowboy friends told me that there was a young lady living in the Chiricahuas who had a photograph of Wheeler in her album, and I gave him twenty dollars to get it for me. He brought it to me within a few days and I had a lot of copies of it made.

On February 26, 1895, the men came out of their hiding place in the mountains, and again held up the same express train, this time at Stein's Pass, New Mexico. They recognized the engineer and fireman, and greeted them with, 'Well, here we are again.' They made a blunder in their hurry and only cut off the mail car, leaving the express car attached to the train. When they got to the place where their horses were, they discovered their mistake. They did not molest the mail car, but told the engineer to go back to his train, and soon after he had left them he heard a loud explosion. The men had evidently exploded their giant powder and given up as a bad job. Getting on their horses, they left the country.

This happened about ten o'clock at night, a hundred and fifty miles east of Tucson. I got a posse together, we loaded our horses into a boxcar, and were at Stein's Pass before daylight. Unfortunately, it had snowed in the pass all night long, and in the morning the country was covered with snow and the trail covered up. So after circling around nearly all day we had to give it up and return home.

About three weeks later I got a clue that led me to Durango, Colorado. I reached Durango about supper time, and after getting my supper went to see the sheriff, and asked him to send a man with me down to the San Juan River. Joe Smith, well-known in that country, and a splendid officer, left with me that night about eight o'clock for Farmington. We drove about seventy miles, arriving about noon. Here we rested our team until nearly night, and from the photograph, which was recognized by a lot of people there, we learned that Wheeler was stopping with a ranchman named Short, about twenty-five miles down the river. It was rumored that Short was a fugitive from Texas.

Late in the afternoon we drove down the river until we knew we were in the vicinity of Short's place. Smith knew a ranchman there, and he put us up for the night. The family had not gone to bed, and after putting up our team we showed them the photograph. They recognized it at once, and the wife said, 'Why, that is the man the children call the bad man.'

When he first arrived there, not knowing where the gate was that led to the river, he let down a rail fence to take his horse to water. When he got to the water, his horse would not drink, and he got mad and shot the horse. They told us that he had been stopping about a quarter of a mile from there, but had left two days before we arrived. He had taken a trail that led by a hidden spring in the mountains, which was a great place for outlaws, and a fine place to hide stolen horses, and the trail to Cortez, the county seat.

The Navajo Indian Agency at Ship Rock, was only a few miles from there. We could not follow the trail in the buggy, so next morning we got two Indians to take Wheeler's trail and learn if he stopped at the spring. They returned in a few hours and reported that there was no one there, and that he had continued along the trail toward Cortez.

Next morning we started and, after passing the place where the trail came into the road to Cortez, we had no trouble in following him by his photograph, until we got near Cortez. There we lost all trace of him. The local sheriff sent out two deputies, but they could not find the trail. Cortez is close to the Blue Mountains in Utah, which is a great resort for outlaws in hiding, and Smith knew the country well. He proposed that he should go in there, while I should take the team back to Durango, and meet him at Grand Junction on the railroad.

I started that afternoon for Mancos on my way to Durango. I had gone only about ten miles when I came to a farmhouse. The ranchman's wife recognized Wheeler's picture and told me he had passed there the day before, and inquired the way to Mancos. On reaching Mancos after dark, I showed the liveryman the photograph. He at once said, 'This man is camped out in a pasture about a quarter of a mile from here.'

I hired the liveryman to ride back to Cortez after Smith that night. He met Smith on the road, as he too had learned that Wheeler was in Mancos. There were two cowboy deputy sheriffs in town that Smith knew, and we consulted with them. One of them had gone through the pasture hunting for a stray horse, and saw Wheeler on top of a haystack where he had been sleeping. They passed the time of day and Wheeler said he would be downtown directly, and, as he had to get his horses up, he would bring the stray horse with him if he found it.

We could see the haystack where he had camped plainly from my room in the hotel, and we decided that the two deputies at Mancos should meet him when he came in and ask him to have a drink. While at the bar they would grab him and disarm him, so that no one would get hurt.

We saw him bring up his two horses, put a light pack on one and saddle the other. But instead of coming to town, he went into a gulch that ran down toward an irrigating ditch close to town. It looked as if he were alarmed and was getting away, so we saddled up and went after him. As we neared the gulch, he came up the bank. One of the officers told him to throw up his hands. Wheeler replied that he had not done anything and would not do it, and started to step back into the gulch. When one of the officers fired at him, he disappeared and none of us were anxious to go to the rim of the gulch to see what had happened to him. Just as he went down the bank he fired a shot, but we did not know what he had shot at. Going back across the ditch where we had left our horses, one of the men mounted his horse and ran past the mouth of the gulch. As he did so he saw Wheeler lying with his head almost in a small fire that he had built to cook his breakfast. We went to him and found that when he stepped back into the gulch, he had placed his pistol in his mouth and shot himself through the head. He was broke and had gone down the gulch to cook his breakfast, as he had no money to buy it in town.

At the coroner's inquest it was brought out that he had got acquainted with a cowboy the day before and told him that the officers were after him, but he thought he had got so far away that they had lost his trail, and that he did not want to kill anyone, but he would kill himself before he would surrender. He had on the same pair of trousers he had on at the time his photograph was taken. He told the cowboy that his name was Wheeler, and wanted him to go in with him and rob the Mancos bank; he said it could be done very easily.

I then took Wheeler's back track and went to see Dan Short where he had been stopping. He had told Short all about their robbing the train; said he and George agreed to separate while they were on the Blue River; he was going to his brother-in-law's at Salida, Colorado, and George toward Socora, New Mexico. Before he came to Short's place he stopped for a short time with Mr. Sanderson, who lived a few miles above Farmington on the San Juan River. Here he left a few things saying he would call for them later. Mr. Sanderson at one time owned the ranch at Soldier Holes, Arizona, and I had a very pleasant visit with him, but found nothing of any value in the things Wheeler had left there.

I returned to Durango intending to take the train for Tucson. Here I learned that a man who resembled Donovan, one of the men who had robbed the express train at Maricopa, the first of October, 1894, was at work near Pagosa Springs, Colorado. I lost no time in reaching that place. But I soon discovered that the man I had come after was not Donovan. His name was Ben Mitchel, and he was wanted

by the sheriff of Brown County, Texas. I arrested
him and wired the sheriff, who sent for him at once.
Donovan never was found.

Before Wheeler and George made their first robbery near Willcox, George was sick in the hospital
in Tombstone, and shortly after he left, a letter
came for him; the nurse told me about it and gave it
to me. It was from his sister in Beebe, Arkansas. I
wrote to the postmaster there. He wrote me that
George was in the Panhandle, in Texas, and was
writing to his sister from a small town called Liv-
ingston, under an assumed name. As soon as I returned from running Wheeler down, I wrote Gard
and asked him to let me go after George. But I was
told to wait, and he never was caught.

Wells, Fargo Company was paying half the expense of the Southern Pacific special officer, and
John Thacker, chief detective for Wells, Fargo, was
sore because I had caught Wheeler. So he reported
to his company that he had met some men who
knew Wheeler; they had told him that Wheeler was
alive; that I had collected the reward and paid it to
the men that were with me, but that we had got the
wrong man. Mr. Fillmore, general manager of the
Southern Pacific Company, told Wells, Fargo to
handle this kind of case themselves, and he would
abolish the office of special officer, and I went to
work as claim agent for the company.

I was kept busy looking after the claims against
the railroad, and near year-end Mr. Randolph,

superintendent of the Southern Pacific Company, Tucson division asked me if I thought Thacker would try to get the Wells, Fargo Company to object to my being reappointed as special officer. I told him I was sure he would, but Mr. Randolph said he was going to ask for it anyway. Shortly after the first of the year I said to Mr. Randolph that I guessed Thacker had blocked my getting the old job. He said he had overlooked asking for it, but would do so at once, and calling in his stenographer dictated a letter to Mr. Fillmore asking to have me reappointed.[3] It was done at once; my appointment dating from the first of January, 1896.

But from this time on I did not pay much attention to train robbers; that work was in the hands of Wells, Fargo detectives.

Brave Jeff Milton, a typical Southerner of the old

[3]Epes Randolph (1856–1921) was a top engineer who built a thousand miles of Southern Pacific line in Mexico and in 1905–07 saved the lush Imperial Valley of southeast California from inundation by Colorado River flood waters. Descended from the aristocratic Randolph family of colonial Virginia that produced the mother of Thomas Jefferson and the first president of the Continental Congress, Epes Randolph (who concluded his career as president of the Southern Pacific of Mexico and the Arizona and Eastern Railroads) "looked like a Methodist minister, but . . . could play poker for $1,000 a chip" and explode into a sulphurous vocabulary belying his appearance of gentility. *Dictionary of American Biography*, XV (New York, 1935), 357–60. Neill C. Wilson and Frank J. Taylor, *Southern Pacific: The Roaring Story of a Fighting Railroad* (New York, 1952), pp. 124, 144–46.

school, was born in Florida. I am not going to give the date of his birth, for these middle-aged men don't like to have their age told until they get as old as I am. Then they don't mind.[4]

As a boy, he was anxious for adventure, and struck out for Texas before he was twenty years old. He joined the Texas Rangers, of which he is still an honorary member. After a few years of that service he resigned, and went on to New Mexico where he held the positions of deputy United States marshal and also deputy sheriff.

From there he drifted into Arizona, and at the time I first met him, over forty years ago, he was customs inspector at Tucson, Arizona. Tucson at that time was a port of entry. The exports and imports were not very heavy, and he had a lot of idle time on his hands. Tucson was rather a gay town, and the few families living there were great entertainers. Fort Lowell, about eight miles east, on the Rillito Creek, was also a lively place, and the officers and their wives vied with the good people in Tucson in entertaining, so that there was something doing all the time.

[4]A son of Florida's Confederate governor, Jeff Davis Milton was born on November 7, 1861. He became one of the premier lawmen of the Southwest, and, as Breakenridge states later, became best known for his service as El Paso police chief in the 1890s. Milton spent his last years in retirement on a ranch outside of Tombstone; he died in 1947. J. Evetts Haley, *Jeff Milton: A Good Man with a Gun* (Norman, 1948). Bill O'Neal, *Encyclopedia of Western Gunfighters* (Norman, 1979), pp. 233–36.

Milton was a great favorite at both the post and at Tucson, and was a welcome guest at both places at their festivities. But he soon tired of doing the society act, there was not enough excitement about it, and he longed to get back to where there was some real danger and sport, so he resigned his position in Tucson and started back to Texas. Later he accepted a service with the Pullman Company. He was put on a run down in Old Mexico, and one day one of the high officials in the Mexican Government service, while drunk, undertook to run the train as he thought it ought to be run, and attempted to take charge of the Pullman. Milton objected, and in the melee that occurred he shot the Mexican officer, and had to get away from there pronto.

On returning to El Paso he was made chief of police there. This was at the time that El Paso was overrun with desperate men. John Wesley Hardin, John Sellman, Bass Outlaw (Sam Bass?),[5] and many others were having their own way down there. George Scarborough, who was a brave officer, was there at this time. John Sellman shot and killed John Wesley Hardin in a gunfight they had, and later killed Bass Outlaw; then George Scarborough had to kill Sellman, and it was very lively in the town. After Milton took charge, he soon cleaned it up without having to kill anyone, and it was quite peaceful for a time.

[5]Bass Outlaw was in El Paso. Sam Bass had been killed in Round Rock, Texas, in 1878.

When his term as chief of police expired, he took on service with the Wells, Fargo Express Company and was messenger on their train between Nogales and Benson, Arizona. On one evening in February, 1900, while he was in his car exchanging packages with the agent at Fairbank, he heard someone say, 'Throw up your hands and come out of the car,' and on looking up he saw a cowboy using a row of citizens as breastworks and pointing his gun at him. There were five of the bandits.

Milton replied, 'If there is anything in this car you want, you will have to come after it.'

With that they began shooting. At the first shot a bullet struck Milton in the arm and shattered the bone. Although badly wounded, he reached for his shotgun. With one hand he returned the fire, and one of the robbers fell, mortally wounded. Milton then threw the door shut, but did not lock it, and, as he was fainting away from the pain that his wound gave him, he threw the safe keys into the corner of the car behind some sacks.

When he came to, the engineer was in the car with him. The robbers had forced the engineer to enter the car ahead of them. They could not find the keys to the safe, and, seeing Milton lying there, as they supposed dead, they got frightened and fled, taking their wounded companion with them, and got nothing from the car.

Milton was rushed into Tucson and given first aid, and from there was sent on to San Francisco.

(I went along with him.) Here the physicians operated on his arm, and had to take about two inches of
bone out of it. His arm has been crippled ever since.
While he was in the employ of the Wells, Fargo
Express Company he was sent out with a posse several times on the trail of train robbers and captured
several of them. He also had to shoot some of them,
which could not be helped. For the past fifteen
years or more he has been immigrant inspector, and
is now living at Fairbank. He is the same brave officer he always was, and, while he is not seeking trouble, he has never been known to dodge it.

In the meantime the robbers that wounded him
had left, their trail pointing toward the Chiricahua
Mountains. The next morning Sheriff Scott White
took up their trail and with his posse found Three-
Fingered Jack—or Jack Dunlap, which was his right
name—on the trail where he had been abandoned
by his companions. From him they soon learned
who the rest of the robbers were. Their names were
Bob Brown, George and Lewis Owens, and Bravo
Juan.[6] They were all captured within a few days,
with the exception of Bob Brown, and placed in the
Tombstone jail. About two months later Brown was
captured in Texas and brought to Tombstone.

Captain Bucky O'Neil, who was killed at San
Juan Hill while with the Rough Riders, was at one
time sheriff at Prescott, and ran down some train

[6]Bravo Juan Yoas and the others were members of Burt
Alvord's gang of train robbers.

robbers who had held up the Santa Fe train near
Flagstaff. One of them was named Smith. While
serving his time, he was taken sick, and was not
expected to live. Governor Hughes pardoned him
out of the penitentiary with the proviso that he was
to leave the country. He then went to Nogales and
crossed the line into Mexico.

Mr. Farragut, the paymaster for the Southern Pacific de Mexico, heard Smith was down there with
two or three renegade Mexicans, and as the railroad
company at that time paid off in cash from their pay
car, instead of with checks, Farragut was afraid that
they might hold him up. So I was sent down to try
to locate him. I went as far as Guaymas, where the
annual fiesta or carnival was going on, but could
hear nothing of him. On my return I stopped in
Hermosillo, Sonora, called on one of the head officials there, and told him my troubles. He could
speak good English, and he said to me, 'We have
more renegades among our own people than we
care for, and do not want to harbor any foreign
ones. You find your man and I will have him killed
before he does any mischief.' There are some laws
in Mexico that I have great respect for!

I left there next morning on an early train for
Nogales, and at the summit just south of there, we
had to take a side track for another train. I walked
up toward the front end of the train where the train
crew were, and saw my man Smith sitting on the
engine. They were burning wood in their engines,

and the fireman, whenever he could, picked up a man to pass the wood to him. Smith was getting a ride for passing wood. He had done nothing that he could be arrested for, and he got off the train in Nogales on the Mexican side of the line. I asked the chief of police on each side of the line to let me know when Smith left, and the next thing I heard was that he had gone to New Mexico.

Shortly after, I heard of him working on a ranch above Clifton, in the mountains. There was a gang of train robbers hiding in that vicinity, led by Jack Ketchum, alias Black Jack.[7] One day Smith was sent into Clifton after supplies. These outlaws met him and told him if he mentioned their being in there, they would kill him. At that moment, Smith had no intention of giving them away, but when they threatened him it made him mad, and as soon as he got to town he informed the sheriff of their place of hiding, and told him that they got their breakfast at a ranch which was situated on a trail leading down from their stronghold. There was a place on the trail where it led through a large pile of rocks, and he told the officers that he would place them on the

[7] Here, Breakenridge confuses William (Black Jack) Christian with Tom (Black Jack) Ketchum. The episode related by Breakenridge involved Black Jack Christian who had become leader of an outlaw gang in present Oklahoma before coming to Arizona. In Arizona, he headed the shifting High Fives gang which eventually hid out in Black Jack Canyon, twelve miles southeast of Clifton. O'Neal, *Encyclopedia*, pp. 56–57, 175–76. Donald N. Bentz, "Alias Black Jack Christian." *Old West*, VI (Spring 1970), pp. 52–54, 79–80.

trail where they could capture every one of the outlaws, with no danger to themselves, if they would
come there after dark and wait on the trail, where
he would hide them, until sunup when the outlaws
come down the trail for breakfast.

The officers came out and took position as he
told them, until they saw smoke coming from the
ranch about daylight. By this time it was very cold
up there. The officers got cold feet and decided
they would go to the house and get warm, and make
the arrest when the men came in. They had not
gone over fifty yards from their hiding place behind
the rocks when the outlaws came around a turn in
the trail. The posse opened fire. Black Jack was
killed, and George Musgrave, one of the band, mortally wounded. The rest escaped among the rocks.
None of the sheriff's posse was injured.[8]

By 1903, the work of a special officer and a claim

[8]On April 27, 1897, Deputy Sheriff Ben Clark led a five-
man posse to the outlaw refuge, resulting in the gun battle
and Black Jack Christian's death. Tom Ketchum, an outlaw
cowboy out of Texas, headed a gang of bank and train robbers in New Mexico and Arizona known as the Snaky Four.
When Ketchum heard of William Christian's death, he took
the latter's nickname of Black Jack because of their tall,
dark resemblance to each other and because Ketchum as-
pired to be Christian's successor in bold outlaw conduct.
Eventually, Black Jack Ketchum was captured and sentenced to death. He died gamely, ascending the steps to the
gallows on April 25, 1901, in Clayton, New Mexico, and
calling out to the witnessing crowd, "I'll be in hell before
you start breakfast, boys!" O'Neal, *Encyclopedia*, pp. 56–57,
175–76. Bentz, "Alias Black Jack Christian."

agent was getting too heavy for one man, and I was offered my choice. I chose the post as claim agent under Mr. Sessions, who was chief claims attorney in San Francisco. The hobos were very thick along the line of the railroad, and the Superintendent wanted an officer who would ride the freight trains at night and look out for them. I did not mind hunting train robbers, but I did not care to ride freight trains during the winter nights looking for tramps. As I was getting along in years, I chose the easier job and remained in the claim department hunting evidence in personal injury cases.

Shortly after I was appointed claim agent there were a number of passenger train wrecks, and quite a lot of passengers were killed or injured. The Esmond wreck was a head-end smash of two passenger trains. There were four killed, seven sent to the hospital badly injured, and twenty slightly injured but able to continue on their journey.[9] We settled with most of them and got their releases.

[9]The train wreck just west of Esmond, Arizona, took place on January 28, 1903, when the telegraph operator at Vail failed to deliver a crucial train order to the westbound *Sunset Limited* with the result that a head-on collision occurred between it and the eastbound *Crescent City Limited*. Eight died in the Esmond wreck. An oddity was that the rear sleeping car of the *Crescent City Limited* became detached during the wreck and rolled back fifteen miles downgrade to Tucson where, undamaged, it came to a stop without mishap. Robert B. Shaw, *Down Brakes: A History of Railroad Accidents . . . in the United States of America* (London, 1961), pp. 181–82, 480.

There were a lot of legitimate claims, but just as many that were fraudulent. Mr. Sessions came down from San Francisco, and we did not have trouble in making settlement of all legitimate claims, but it took hard work to get proof of the ones that were fakes. There was one gambler who was not injured, but claimed his baggage contained in a trunk was burned up and worth twenty-five hundred dollars. It consisted of some very valuable clothing and a faro box so made that he could draw almost any card he wanted to from it. It was so valuable that, in order to keep the mechanism of it a secret, he had to have the parts made in different places. He also claimed a large chunk of onyx from which he made loaded dice. One of the gamblers told him he was a sure-thing gambler, and could not collect for his gambling devices. He replied he was not a gambler, he was a speculator. 'Yes,' replied his friend, 'you are a separator, not a speculator.' He finally settled for a hundred dollars.

The accidents came rather fast for a time, but I was successful in getting most of them settled reasonably, and we had very few lawsuits. The investigation of claims kept me on the road a large portion of my time, and I traveled over a good portion of the United States as well as Canada and Mexico. I made one trip over the Mexican Central lines to the City of Mexico. I was down there two weeks and managed to see a great deal of that beautiful city, but I liked Guadalajara much better.

The Esmond train wreck.
A head-on crash of two passenger trains.
Courtesy Arizona Historical Society Library

XX

Passing of an Era

O<small>F ALL</small> the officers, rustlers, and outlaws that were on hand during the early days of Tombstone, there are only two alive today, as far as I know. These two are Wyatt Earp and myself.

John H. Behan, the first sheriff of Cochise County, died some twelve or fifteen years ago in Tucson, Arizona. Virgil Earp never returned to Tombstone after he took the body of his brother Morgan to their home in Colton, California, for burial. Some ten or twelve years later I met him in Prescott. He left there and I was told that he went to Texas, and a few years later I was told that he was dead. Warren Earp was employed to drive the mail stage between Willcox and Fort Grant. He was shot down in a quarrel in a saloon in Willcox, and killed. Doc Holliday, Sherman McMasters, Mysterious Johnson, and all the rest of the crowd that left Tombstone and Arizona with Wyatt Earp, are all dead. Frank Leslie is reported dead in Alaska. Dave Nagle, who was a deputy sheriff under Behan, and was elected city marshal of Tombstone, died at his home in Oakland, California, about a year ago.

In 1925 I was employed to hunt up all the old-timers that I could find who were in Tombstone from 1879 to 1881, to learn if they could give any information regarding an event that occurred there during that time, and for which an important lawsuit had been brought in the courts. Nearly all of the old-timers had left Arizona and settled in California and other western States. I found a number of them that I had not heard from for over forty years, but a large number of the early pioneers of Tombstone had died.

I learned that Wyatt Earp was living in a small mining camp just north of Blythe, on the Colorado River, named Vidal. There was a copper mine close by there and he lived at Vidal during the winter months, but on account of the desert heat during the summer, he made his residence in Oakland, California. I spent one whole day with him, and we had a very pleasant visit. It was the first time I had seen him in forty-three years, and on making inquiries regarding old friends and acquaintances, we soon learned that they were nearly all dead, and we soon had a large graveyard built.

During the summer of 1926, I took an automobile trip through Cochise County looking for the old camps and towns that have been abandoned. At Tombstone, we found that a large number of the houses built of lumber had been removed to other mining camps. Fires had destroyed many other buildings, and three-fourths of the business houses were empty and boarded up. It looked much like a deserted village. From a city of eight thousand it has dwindled to one of about five hundred, but the mines are still being worked on a small scale by leasers, and it is still the county seat of Cochise County. Both Richmond and Waterville had disappeared. Of Contention and Grand Central, where the two mills were located, with the exception of the tumble-down walls of the mills and the tailing dumps, there was nothing left to show that there ever had been prosperous towns there.

We found it was impossible to get to Charleston with a car because the bridge had been washed away, and there were deep washes on each side of it, so we walked in. There was nothing left but the adobe walls of the old buildings, partially fallen down. All the woodwork was gone, and mesquite trees six inches through were growing up inside the walls and in the streets. Just below the townsite is a deep canyon. A survey has been made there for a dam to be built for water storage. After the dam is completed, the old town of Charleston will be many feet under water.

From there we went to the towns of Naco, Douglass, and Agua Prieta, and found them flourishing border towns. From there we started out to find Galeyville, which was the resort for the rustlers and outlaws in 1879 and the early eighties. This town had been built on a high mesa between the forks of the north and south branches of Turkey Creek, on the eastern slope of the Chiricahua Mountains, but nothing was left to mark where it had once stood

except the slag dump of the old smelter. The buildings here had been built of rough lumber, and they
had all disappeared. After the place was abandoned
the Apaches burned everything down, and it was
hard to find a foundation stone of any of the houses
that were left.

About a mile above, on the south fork of Turkey
Creek, was a mining camp called Paradise. This at
one time was quite a prosperous mining town, and a
little mining is still being done there.

Then we went down into San Simon Valley and
around the north end of the mountain where we
struck the old Butterfield Overland stage road,
which had been abandoned for years. We found
great difficulty in getting over it toward Fort Bowie,
and had to leave our car when within a half-mile of
the fort and walk the rest of the way. The fort was
just a tumbled-down mass of ruins. At the spring
where the post used to get its drinking water, we
found a ranchman. He had settled on the spring,
and had about three or four acres of fine peach trees
growing. He found a ready market for his fruit at
the railroad stations from ten to thirty miles from
there. He told us that he saw ten times as many
aeroplanes as he did automobiles, as it was the air
route between El Paso and San Diego. It was very
difficult to get through Apache Pass, as the road had
been abandoned for years, and all the soil had been
washed out of the road, leaving deep ruts and sharp
rocks standing up. This road, we were told, was

only used once in a while, and then by bootleggers.

This part of the country looked more abandoned and primitive than it did forty-five years ago.

At the breaking-out of the World War, I went to Washington and tried, through our Senator, Mark Smith, to get sent overseas. I claimed that as I was a railroad man I could be useful in getting supplies to the front, for I knew that if I could only get sent over there I should soon get to the front. But they said I was too old, and they would not have me. So I returned and continued to work for the railroad company until after the Armistice was signed and the war was over.

The Southern Pacific Company demands that when any of its men reach the age of seventy years, they be retired. At this time I had reached the age of seventy-two, and I was retired on a pension. As I look back, if I could live my life over again, I think I should like to live the same kind of life.

Index

INDEX